THE POWER OF PRACTICE MANAGEMENT

Since 1996, Bloomberg Press has published books for financial professionals on investing, economics, and policy affecting investors. Titles are written by leading practitioners and authorities, and have been translated into more than 20 languages.

The Bloomberg Financial Series provides both core reference knowledge and actionable information for financial professionals. The books are written by experts familiar with the work flows, challenges, and demands of investment professionals who trade the markets, manage money, and analyze investments in their capacity of growing and protecting wealth, hedging risk, and generating revenue.

For a list of available titles, please visit our website at www.wiley.com /go/bloombergpress.

THE POWER
OF PRACTICE
MANAGEMENT

Best Practices for Building a Better Advisory Business

Matt Matrisian

BLOOMBERG PRESS

An Imprint of

WILEY

Published by John Wiley & Sons, Inc., Hoboken, New Jersey.
Published simultaneously in Canada.

Library of Congress Cataloging-in-Publication Data:
Matrisian, Matt.
  The power of practice management : best practices for building a better advisory business
/ Matt Matrisian.
       p. cm. – (Bloomberg financial series)
  Includes index.
  ISBN 978-1-118-12117-7 (cloth); ISBN 978-1-118-50745-2 (ebk);
ISBN 978-1-118-50746-9 (ebk); ISBN 978-1-118-50769-8 (ebk)
  1. Business consultants.   2. Consulting firms–Management.   3. Small business–Management.
I. Title.
  HD69.C6M38 2012
  001–dc23
                                    2012001525

Contents

PART III: HARNESSING HUMAN CAPITAL

Foreword

Think about why you became a financial advisor. What is the purpose of your practice?

If you are like most of the successful advisors we work with, you didn't choose this route so you could develop operational processes or plan the smallest details of your next client appreciation event.

My guess is that you chose this route to make a difference in the lives of your clients and to enjoy your own financial and professional success as well. You can devote more time to your purpose if you spend less time running your business. Inefficient systems, undefined marketing plans, and ineffective strategies affect your bottom line and take away from the time you spend with your clients. Engaging and integrating practice management solutions—such as those offered in the pages to come—can help you spend more time meeting with the right clients, generating referrals, and creating your vision of success.

You want to build a practice and offer value-added services. And you want those services to offer profound value that translates into fact and feeling you can project and your clients can embrace.

And by profound I mean simple and clear. Everybody appreciates being treated well. Everybody admires honesty. Everybody wants excellence and value. Everybody wants to feel a part of something bigger than they are.

These values shape my view of the financial advisory business. They are universal and they are powerful. I strive to live this concept in my work life on a daily basis, and I think the key to making a business successful is alignment—alignment with people like you and your clients. Ultimately, we both want to make a difference in investors' lives and grow the business in the process.

We believe our purpose is serving those who make a positive difference in the lives of their clients and in their businesses. We wrote this book with that very purpose in mind.

Gurinder S. Ahluwalia
CEO, Genworth Wealth Management
July 2012

Introduction

Genworth Financial Wealth Management, Inc. serves independent advisors like you—people who want to make a difference in the lives of their clients and in their own practices. With the strong heritage and legacy of expertise created by AssetMark Investment Services, Inc. and Quantuvis Consulting, we have been helping advisors with business questions and needs for nearly 20 years. We provide practice-building tools and resources and work through consulting engagements on specific business issues—all aimed at growing advisory businesses into successful top-performing firms.

Over the years, we've talked with advisors about what makes a top performer, and we discovered that the differentiators between top firms and those who follow are not just simple assumptions:

- *Practice Model*—In our experience, each type of practice model experiences both success and failure.
- *Expertise*—Technical expertise is not a stable predictor of success.
- *Experience*—There are many successful advisors with limited experience, generating millions in revenue.

Building a successful practice is about more than just an advisor's ability to generate revenue and manage the business. It goes beyond client care, professional competence, understanding asset allocation, and running retirement planning projections.

It's about running a business better in order to achieve your goals.

Success that meets established business goals seems to be highly influenced by the discipline that advisors bring to building, growing, and managing the business.

These lessons hold true whether you're a small, solo advisor who simply wants to run a more profitable business, an emerging firm trying to drive and manage growth, or an established firm working to transform a successful business into an enterprise with offices in multiple locations.

As we consult and coach advisors, we analyze how things *are* versus how advisors *want* them to be. Areas of improvement or obstacles to overcome are noted, and we create a list of potential opportunities. Then comes the discipline discussion, consisting of three simple, but very difficult, questions:

- Are you willing to be uncomfortable?
- Can you approach the business with an "owner" mind set?
- Will you make the changes that make a difference?

While most answer "yes" to the above, there is a distinct difference between discussion and implementation.

A two-partner firm approached us with a goal of doubling revenue while improving the partners' quality of life. They had reached maximum capacity and could not break through their assets under management (AUM) plateau. We assessed the situation and defined several areas for improvement, including fee structure changes, hiring of qualified staff, and formalizing operations.

By incorporating business discipline, they were able to overcome the difficulties hampering success. They raised fees to be more commensurate with services, increased their minimums, upgraded their brand, reorganized staffing, and developed a systematized service model. They now are preparing their business for transition during the next five years so that they can realize the greatest possible value and enjoy a smooth, seamless, and successful transition.

This firm did not grow due to our ability to dispense advice. They grew because the partners understood the practices they needed to employ, developed a plan, deployed it with discipline, and aligned their behavior—and business decisions—with their goals.

We created this book with one purpose: to share the principles and practices that have helped some of the country's best advisory firms become even better. Throughout these pages, we share with you our experiences and our findings and data from our Genworth Wealth Management/Quantuvis Best Practices Series Studies 2010 so that you may develop a solid roadmap and "how to" manual toward building a better business. Where noted, we cite research from other parties within the industry, but we also feel our studies of advisors and their businesses provides a comprehensive, thorough examination of the issues facing professionals such as yourself.

It's our dedication to helping you build a better business.

PART I

Business Strategy and Planning

CHAPTER 1

A Look at the Landscape

To say the last decade was tumultuous is to understate the painful technology bust at the beginning of the twenty-first century, the subsequent housing boom, and the subprime crisis, which spurred one of the worst recessionary environments since the Great Depression.

Where We Stand Today

Today, markets around the world are far more interdependent and interlinked than they were in the past. Financial strains span the globe, keeping markets locked in a state of unprecedented volatility. And advisors have to struggle to drive growth and profitability, while serving clients well and building long-term value.

One of the nonfinancial by-products of this tumultuous time is a sharp decline in the trusted part of the trusted advisor relationship. In the wake of the financial crisis, consumers struggle to discern the difference between the next Bernie Madoff and an advisor with the best of intentions.

While banks and wirehouse brokerages still significantly outpace independent advisors in assets and number of advisors, there has been a steady migration of captive advisors to independent status. There are two key reasons for this transition to the independent channel. The first, less publicized driver is that brokerage firms are pushing lower-performing advisors out of the system. The second, widely known reason for the transition is that advisors are looking for freedom from proprietary products, so they can act in what they feel is the best interest of their clients, build their own businesses with distinct brands, and, ultimately, realize business value—not for some large Wall Street enterprise, but for themselves.

In the process, advisors face mounting challenges. The cost of doing business continues to rise, driven largely by increases in labor and health care costs and

3

the ever more demanding and complex requirements of regulatory compliance. Moreover, the days are gone when advisors could simply service clients well and wait for the phone to ring. The next generation of growth will not be driven so easily by the same happy trifecta as the last. Advisors can no longer rely solely on passive growth to fuel their future growth; they now recognize the need to warm up and exercise their atrophied marketing muscles.

Consumers, too, have been unintended passengers on this roller-coaster ride. Baby Boomers are hitting key transitions in their working lives, with the first Boomers having turned 65 in 2011. An estimated 76 million Baby Boomers need to plan for critical turning points that lie ahead. With the decline starting in 2007 of their home and 401(k) values, many Boomers' needs—and the resulting demand—for financial advice is likely to rise as quickly as the numbers applying for Social Security.

No one knows exactly what the future holds; however, many lessons have emerged from the recent past. Chief among them is that managing investments and clients is only a part of what advisors need to do to be successful.

A Peek into the Future

Advisors now realize that market returns alone aren't sufficient to drive the growth of their firms. Given worldwide financial problems, ongoing market volatility, and weak economic growth, it isn't surprising that advisors we've surveyed viewed stock market performance as their top challenge in the next three years. Other nonbusiness challenges cited were managing client expectations and industry regulation, which has become a moving target since the meltdown.

Almost all other challenges that advisors foresee fall squarely into the practice-management box. Most advisors struggle to manage their time, and often, their profitability. They lack coherent brand and marketing strategies to assure a steady flow of appropriate and higher-paying prospects, and they struggle with finding and managing qualified staff. They need to master their work lives by creating business systems: developing specific goals and road maps to reach them, managing their own financial growth, and creating more effective operations and more efficient ways to use staff and technology. In addition, by mastering these issues to build the value of their businesses, they can sell or transition out of the practice with something to show for all of the hard work. All of these issues can be addressed by implementing best-practice management strategies.

More than ever, the advisory business is about client service. More than market returns, selling products, or designing financial plans, firms that provide predictable, high-quality service, and do so profitably, will see greater growth and value premiums. Most advisors rank client service as the number one business opportunity during the next three years (see Figure 1.1).

FIGURE 1.1 Opportunities for Advisors during the Next Three Years

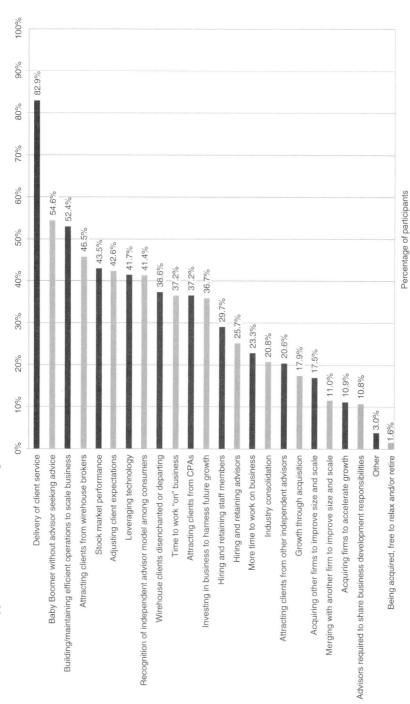

Advisors frequently rank tapping into the Baby Boomer market as the number two opportunity in the near future. As mentioned earlier, the first Baby Boomers hit 65 in 2011; today, almost one-quarter of the population is between 45 and 63 years old, the primary age range for asset accumulation. Although we've all heard that client referrals drop when the markets do, if some 76 million Baby Boomers needed financial advice before the financial crisis, they're more likely to need it afterward.

Interestingly, "building/maintaining efficient operations to scale business" is a third opportunity many advisors wish to realize. Yet many firms still are reluctant to invest in human capital. Businesses willing to invest in staffing now to develop capacity down the road, while investing in business development, will be well positioned to take advantage of the growth opportunities ahead.

Let's take a look at the broader industry trends that studies, demographics, and experience suggest advisors will face going forward:

- Clearly, the Baby Boomers will represent a big opportunity in the decade ahead. Being a huge and vocal cohort, their search for financial advisors may create greater consumer awareness for the industry, increasing the demand for financial advisory services.
- Client bases are aging along with the population, driving a transition from accumulation to distribution. A study of a major institutional client firm found that the size of client accounts within that firm peaked when account holders reached age 64 and began to decline steadily thereafter. Our work with advisory firms supports this assertion. An increase in attrition related to client deaths is also on the rise. Add to this the fact that fewer clients are coming on board to offset these aging trends, and new client acquisition is becoming increasingly important.
- Advisors will focus more on building and realizing value for their firms so they can expand or contract. Some advisors will want to ease out of the business; others will be looking to grow larger, whether organically by hiring more advisors and staff, scaling up their processes, or through mergers or acquisitions.
- In order to realize the value in their businesses, advisors will need some kind of workable succession plan, whether that means finding and hiring a successor advisor in a solo practice, creating appropriate partnership and ownership agreements in an ensemble firm, or selling outright to another company. This will likely lead to increasing competition for qualified next-generation advisors, those who can successfully help transition the founders out, while leading the firm into the future.

Key Trends in the Advisory Business

We've seen a growth in these trends during the past few years and expect them to continue as advisory firms increasingly shift their focus from pure sales and service to driving improved business performance. Here are some of the issues that firms are facing and the solutions we will focus on throughout this book:

- *Focus on growth.* The financial fallout since 2008 has left many firms realizing that while good client service is a client acquisition strategy, it's a passive one and cannot be the only source of new business if firms want to control their growth.

  Client referrals will undoubtedly continue to drive the acquisition of new clients, but that won't be enough. We will explore in the business development section the options for advisors to take proactive action to create a prospect-and-client pipeline. This may include hiring a business development officer or reengineering the firm's brand to create a culture of client referrals as part of a disciplined marketing plan.

  To survive and thrive, regardless of market circumstances, firms will need to evolve from a founder-reliant culture dominated by personal brand to more formalized, firm-driven strategies for driving growth. Findings from a Genworth Wealth Management/Quantuvis Best Practices study highlight that top-performing firms are more focused and more disciplined in their business development efforts. The firms that best manage their business development strategies will have their choice of the most satisfying, most profitable client relationships in the future.

- *Creating a compelling value proposition.* When we ask advisors what they do, more often than not, they say financial planning, investment management, or wealth management. Given these answers, it's not hard to imagine why the average consumer doesn't claw his or her way to an advisory firm's doorsteps. The reality is that advisory services are needed by many but sought by few.

  To create a compelling value proposition for new clients, advisory firms need to take a hard look at how they brand and position their services in the marketplace. Firms have an overwhelming tendency to sell features, benefits, and attributes, such as being objective, knowledgeable, expert, caring, and service driven. Consumers expect and deserve these behaviors from any advisor, which means they are not differentiators.

  Advisors are realizing that it is the outcomes they deliver to clients and, more particularly, how they package and present these outcomes that position and differentiate them in the marketplace.

- *Managing financial performance.* Advisory firms have disciplined processes for reporting and managing the performance of their clients' financial health, yet few but the largest and most sophisticated firms proactively manage their own financial performance.

  Financial reporting and performance benchmarking help advisors objectively gauge the health, performance, and value of their firms. A disciplined process for gathering and using financial reports and benchmarking data can also help firms identify where their challenges and opportunities lie.

Advisors need to establish effective financial reporting processes and define the type of reports to review, decide on a schedule for uncovering problems, and make changes that will get them closer to their financial goals. For example, firms that identify below-target revenue and/or profitability in their financial reports can look at benchmarking reports to find out which metrics, such as average client size and average fees, are driving this result. Armed with this information, advisors can evaluate their account minimums and conduct a competitive pricing scan to determine where they can make changes to increase revenue and profitability.

Top-performing firms also tend to rely on performance benchmarking to gauge their financial progress at the bottom line, rather than using less meaningful top-line measures of revenue and assets under management. This empowers firms to better understand what's happening to their profitability and why. Advisors will have a distinct advantage if they can grasp how their business behavior drives their business outcomes and what specific elements of their business can be improved to drive better overall performance.

- *Optimizing operational performance.* As firms become more relationship focused, delivering predictable high-quality client services is a greater priority. To offer consistent, reliable, and superior service, advisory firms will need to standardize their processes and manage their people, technology, and outsourcing relationships so the firm can function more efficiently and effectively. This will allow for a dramatic increase in scalability as well, which is critical in growth companies.

  In other words, firms must develop their operational infrastructures to maximize advisors' client-facing time. Yet our experience with firms of every size and type suggests that the average firm grows faster than its investment in infrastructure. As a result, the back office that services clients struggles to keep pace.

  Our findings indicate that top-performing firms invest, on average, two times more in operational infrastructure than their peers and yield profits that are five times greater. To improve operational performance, firms need to assess their business strategy and goals, then reengineer every aspect of their business to ensure complete alignment between the two. This entails developing and adopting a plan to capitalize on strategic uses of processes, people, technology, and outsourcing.

- *Institutionalizing the business.* Founders/owners are realizing that they can't take care of everything personally and, at the same time, provide more and better client service while turning a healthy profit. Institutionalizing the business starts with defining all of the key business systems in the organization, evaluating those systems, and then identifying and making improvements. Next comes documenting the steps in the system with a level of detail that ensures they can be independently repeated by a new owner(s) and staff with the same results on a consistent basis.

Institutionalization is the holy grail of business performance, elusive to all but a select few advisory firms. This isn't because the club is members only, but rather because it requires a great deal of work. Yet in order to offer regularly superior service, ensure scalability, and create lasting business value that lives beyond the founder/owner, firms need to systematize and scale business practices.

- *Harnessing human capital.* While operational infrastructure, technology, and outsourcing can support a firm's goals for driving growth and institutionalizing operations, the delivery of financial advice remains a people business built on service and relationships. Although solo practitioners with no staff, or small firms with only a few staff members, may believe themselves exempt from this discussion, our experience and our research suggest otherwise. These firms have just as much to gain from better harnessing their human capital as do their midsize, large, and fast-growing counterparts.

For one, advisory firms are likely to find that acquiring and retaining talent will be increasingly challenging and costly in the future. And the younger-generation advisors who will presumably carry on these firms are few and far between. Firms would do well to develop new advisors and capable staff internally through effective employee management.

Moreover, advisors often struggle to hire and maintain productive team members. They need to learn how to manage their people effectively, so they can spend more of their own time with clients.

- *Developing a systematic service model.* Advisory firms tend to do one thing with remarkable consistency: take on any and all clients who come their way, regardless of size, situation, or fit. This happens for two historical reasons. First, many small-business owners take the view that the best way to grow revenue to ensure their firm's existence is to gather as many clients as possible. Second, our profession has its roots in the sales culture of the 1970s and the 1980s, when the goal of financial advisors was selling products and meeting quotas. Since then, the advisory profession has become far more focused on relationships than on sales, yet the mind-set of attracting and accepting any and all comers has changed little. The result is that the average advisor has a mosaic of clients, ranging from those with less than $100,000 to those with millions, and many in between. This is not a recipe for client profitability. Servicing such a disparate group of clients with so many diverse issues and needs is exceedingly difficult to do well and nearly impossible to do profitably.

Advisors often claim they must treat every client differently. In chapters that follow, we suggest that advisors are confusing experience with process. As a result, they dilute both client service and profitability. In our view, the goal is to develop a standardized way to deliver specialized, systematized services based on specific client segments. There needs to be a clear process to determine which clients receive which services from whom, when, and how. This is a total game changer that dramatically increases the quality of client services, advisor and staff productivity, and ultimately the bottom line.

- *Increased reliance on outsourcing.* Outsourcing parts of their businesses allows advisors to scale up their operations, spend more time with clients, and give their staffs more time to support client service. A growing trend is the outsourcing of asset management services. Back in a 2009 study, 31 percent of advisory firms were already reporting outsourcing asset management and another 21 percent were considering doing so. Today, outsourcing of this once-sacred function continues to be on the rise.[1]

The rising popularity of outsourcing may be partly due to the burden of balancing money management with client management, especially during a downturn when an advisor's time may be better spent deepening client relationships and developing new ones. Advisors also view investment management services, unlike the delivery of financial advice, to be more easily commoditized, sensitive to pricing competition, and not requiring a relationship to be effectively performed. Outsourcing investment management and other business functions can appreciably increase a firm's capacity and revenue, especially for smaller to midsize practices.

- *Better and/or professional management.* Advisory firms are realizing that better business management is as important to ongoing success as rainmaking and client service. For many advisors, with competition for their time increasing and their capacity constrained, the demands of working "in" the business are constantly competing with the need to work "on" the business. The multiple facets of running a business, which include business strategy and planning, sales and marketing, human capital, financial management, operations, client services, financial planning, investment management, compliance, and more, are simply overwhelming.

In addition, most advisors prefer managing client relationships to managing the business, so firm owners often find themselves at a crossroads: they either choose to spend more time on business management, at the expense of advising and acquiring clients, or they turn to professional managers to take over these functions so they can focus on revenue-producing activities.

The conclusions of "Mission Impossible II," a 2009 white paper released by Pershing Advisory Solutions, still ring true. It shows that as firms increase in size, so does their reliance on dedicated management roles. The Pershing white paper noted that 14 percent of advisory firms with more than $1 million in annual revenue added dedicated management; 76 percent of firms with $3 million to $5 million in revenue did so; and 86 percent of firms with $5 million in revenue had such positions.[2]

Do dedicated managers drive firm growth, or does firm growth produce the need for dedicated managers? The answer is likely both. Our experience consulting with growing firms to develop professional management roles suggests two things. First, that the previous findings are true, and second, that even firms with as little as $1 million in revenue can realize significant benefits from hiring a professional business manager.

Sharing control with a nonowner who is not, in most cases, an advisor can be difficult. Nevertheless, for advisory firms that are committed to growth, improved productivity, and increased profitability and value, as well as operational excellence and sustainability, the benefits of professional management can far outweigh the challenges. Regardless of size, advisory firms are recognizing that the mom-and-pop shop mind-set that got them into business is insufficient to tap into their full potential.

- *Building business value.* Advisors need to recognize the difference between selling a book of business and selling a business. Many advisors sell their book of business for a decent return, but this model hardly maximizes the value that advisors can receive for years of hard work.

Beyond fancy formulas, value is ultimately defined by the predictability of future cash flows, proven profitability, scalable operations and service models, and a systematic approach to generating new business. As advisors realize the importance of monetizing what may well be their greatest asset, building business value is of growing importance.

Too often, advisors don't plan ahead for selling their firms. As a result, those who make the decision on short notice look to multiples of revenue as an easy way to estimate and establish firm value. Yet this approach represents an aggregate average of sales reported and doesn't account for the underlying fundamentals of the firms. It also fails to account for the many private transactions that never make the radar.

Such an informal method for establishing value often leads to disconnects between motivated sellers and knowledgeable buyers. If two firms both have $1 million in annual revenues, but one has a profit margin of 25 percent, and the other a profit margin of 5 percent, they are hardly worth the same multiple of revenue. Or if two firms have the same revenues and profit margins, but one firm has an average client age of 50, with clients well in the accumulation phase, and another firm has an average client age of 65, with clients transitioning into the distribution phase, are the future cash flow and value of these businesses the same? Advisors need first to understand how to create firms with value, and then determine what is involved in realizing that value.

CHAPTER 2

A View into Top-Performing Firms

How do advisors enter this brave new world and build more profitable businesses? One way is to look to the firms that have done it best. The Genworth/Quantuvis Best Practices Study Series has conducted surveys on more than 3,000 advisors during the past several years to explore the difference between top-performing firms and the balance of the advisor population.

A View of Top-Performing Firms

We wanted to identify trends and best practices of top-performing firms so they could be emulated by advisors looking to improve their own performance (Figure 2.1).

The study examined the financial performance of top-quartile advisors measured by total owner income, including all job compensation plus all ownership returns. The remainder of the advisor population consists of the approximately 75 percent of advisors that do not deliver top performance.

Given the methods of analysis, top performers obviously outperform their peers. What is surprising is that they do so by such wide margins. Significantly, top performers outperform their peers by 5.1 times total annual revenue, 5.1 times more operating profit, and 4.8 times greater total owner income.[1]

Findings from the Genworth/Quantuvis Best Practices Study Series show that top performers:

- Harness human capital better than do their counterparts. For example, they employ and make more efficient use of nonprofessional staff so advisors can spend more time on revenue-producing activities.
- Invest more in operational infrastructure to achieve higher productivity. Not only are top performers larger, they more effectively optimize the

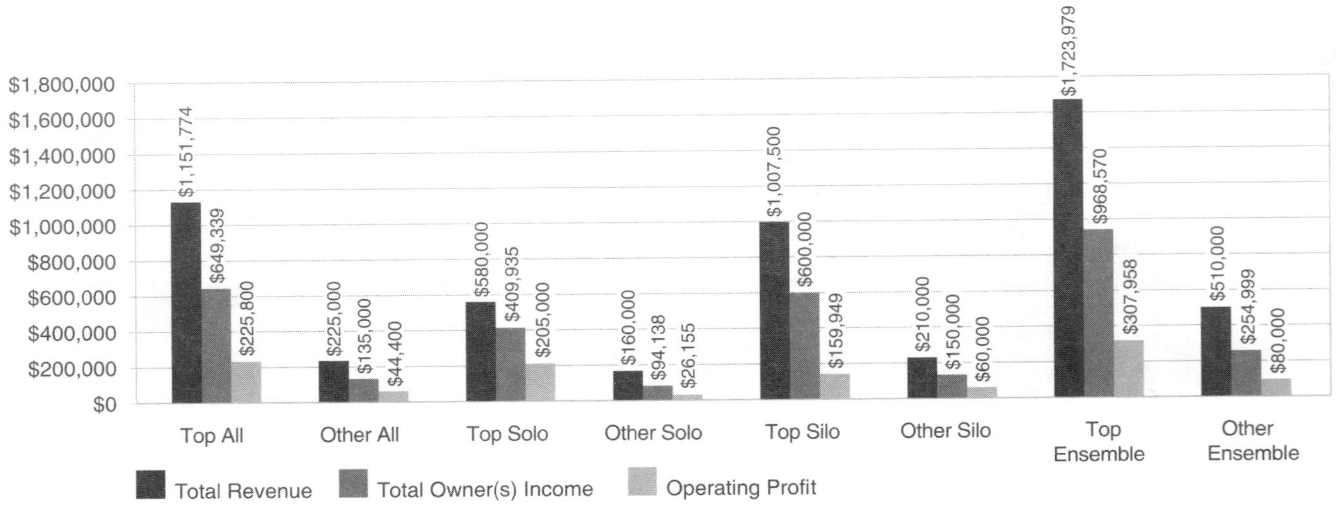

FIGURE 2.1 Top Performers versus Peer Performance across All Participants and Practice Models

operational side of their businesses by using technology and outsourcing more frequently.

- Generate three times more fee-based revenue than all of their other revenue sources combined.
- Are more likely to be financial planners and wealth managers (52 percent of top performers versus 30 percent of total advisor population).[2]

Combined, these business practices enable top performers to manage significantly more clients, assets, and revenue per advisor, generating a higher profit per client, as depicted in Figure 2.2.

Top-performing firms have greater revenue and better performance metrics, but again this raises the question of which came first? Do these firms generate revenue that allows them to build better infrastructure, hire more staff, and attract larger clients, or is putting those systems in place what leads to greater revenue?

Our study findings and consulting work indicate that both are happening. Many large firms have little profit to speak of, and many early and emerging firms invest in building out their businesses, which results in accelerated growth. Each firm goes through its own unique development process.

Top Performer Best Practices

On average, top-performing firms tend to outpace other firms in terms of client acquisition, client retention, productivity, and revenue. They are able to do so by focusing on several key areas within their business.

Harnessing Human Capital

Top firms generate and sustain higher revenue partly because they make a bigger investment in human capital resources. The typical top performer has a total firm head count of seven, compared with three for their advisory firm peers. This increases the firm's capacity to source and support clients, which in turn yields higher revenue.

Note that top performers have twice as many advisors as well. Because advisors source and manage client relationships, having more than one is critical in driving top performance. In addition, top-performing firms have four times as many staff members in comparison to their peers, which allows advisors to use their time more efficiently and focus on revenue-producing activities.

What's more, as depicted in Table 2.1, firms with higher head counts show greater specialization of roles, demonstrate improved focus on business development for advisors, and often allow for the addition of a business development position.

Operational Leverage

We found that top-performing firms also use technology and outsourcing more frequently than their peers, with 66 percent of them using client relationship

FIGURE 2.2 2008 Median Business Performance Metrics of Top-Performing and Other Advisory Firms

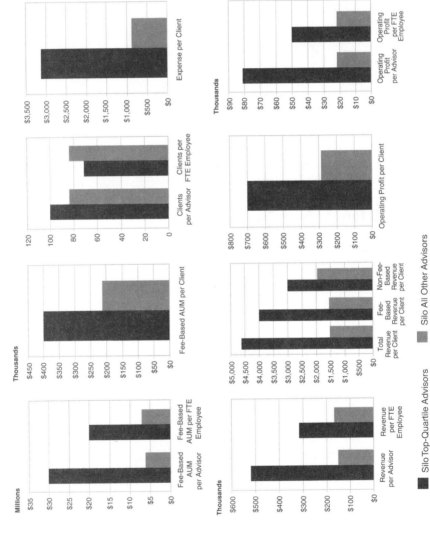

TABLE 2.1 2008 Median Business Performance of Top-Performing Firms

2011 MEDIAN BUSINESS PERFORMANCE	TOP—187 FIRMS	OTHER—561 FIRMS
Total Owner(s) Income	$ 649,339	$ 135,000
Income per Owner	$ 417,341	$ 113,000
Fee-Based AUM	$ 66,600,000	$ 8,000,000
Total Revenue (Annual)	$ 1,151,774	$ 225,000
Total Expenses	$ 914,553	$ 138,000
Operating Profit	$ 225,800	$ 44,400
All Clients	247	130
Fee-Based Recurring Revenue Clients	145	40
Fee for Fee-Based Clients (bps)	92	81
Owners	2.00	1.00
Advisors	2.00	1.00
Staff	4.00	1.00

management (CRM) software, compared with 49 percent of other advisory firms. Firms that fully leverage CRM software can maintain more information more efficiently and productively to enhance client service.

In addition, these top performers outsource their operational processes more than their lower-performing peers do. As outsource providers demonstrate their ability to perform work more effectively, while maintaining or reducing costs, advisors are realizing that they can improve productivity and performance by focusing their valuable human capital on functions that can't be easily commoditized.

Although they have higher assets under management (AUM) per client and revenue per client, top performers also have more clients per advisor and fewer clients per full-time employee. Thus, their performance is not driven solely by more and larger clients, but also by their ability to service those clients more efficiently and profitably.

Business Development

It's important to note that top-performing firms do not appear to attract more clients than their counterparts do; instead, they appear to attract larger clients, focus more consistently on their target client group, and ultimately see a much higher return on their investment of time and money in marketing. As a result, they may generate more than four times more revenue per client than their peers. Looking at overall business performance and marketing, we can begin to see the correlation between greater targeting and larger clients.

The top performers indicated that 60 percent of their new business came from client referrals, compared with 50 percent for their peers, as depicted in Figure 2.3. This is due in part to a more systematic approach to getting referrals and a greater focus on specific targeted clients.

FIGURE 2.3 Primary New Business Sources

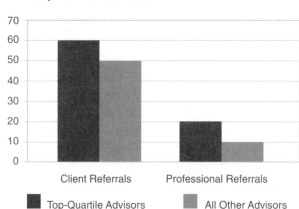

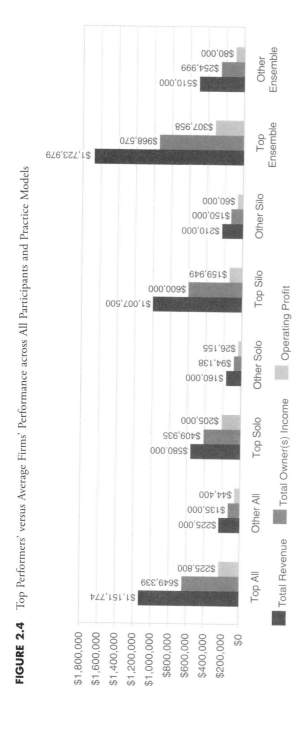

FIGURE 2.4 Top Performers' versus Average Firms' Performance across All Participants and Practice Models

Total Revenue ■   Total Owner(s) Income ■   Operating Profit ▨

Top All
Total Revenue: $1,151,774
Total Owner(s) Income: $649,339
Operating Profit: $225,800

Other All
Total Revenue: $225,000
Total Owner(s) Income: $135,000
Operating Profit: $44,400

Top Solo
Total Revenue: $580,000
Total Owner(s) Income: $409,935
Operating Profit: $205,000

Other Solo
Total Revenue: $160,000
Total Owner(s) Income: $94,138
Operating Profit: $26,155

Top Silo
Total Revenue: $1,007,500
Total Owner(s) Income: $600,000
Operating Profit: $159,949

Other Silo
Total Revenue: $210,000
Total Owner(s) Income: $150,000
Operating Profit: $60,000

Top Ensemble
Total Revenue: $1,723,979
Total Owner(s) Income: $968,570
Operating Profit: $307,958

Other Ensemble
Total Revenue: $510,000
Total Owner(s) Income: $254,999
Operating Profit: $80,000

FIGURE 2.5 Median Business Performance by Top-Performing and Average Advisory Firms

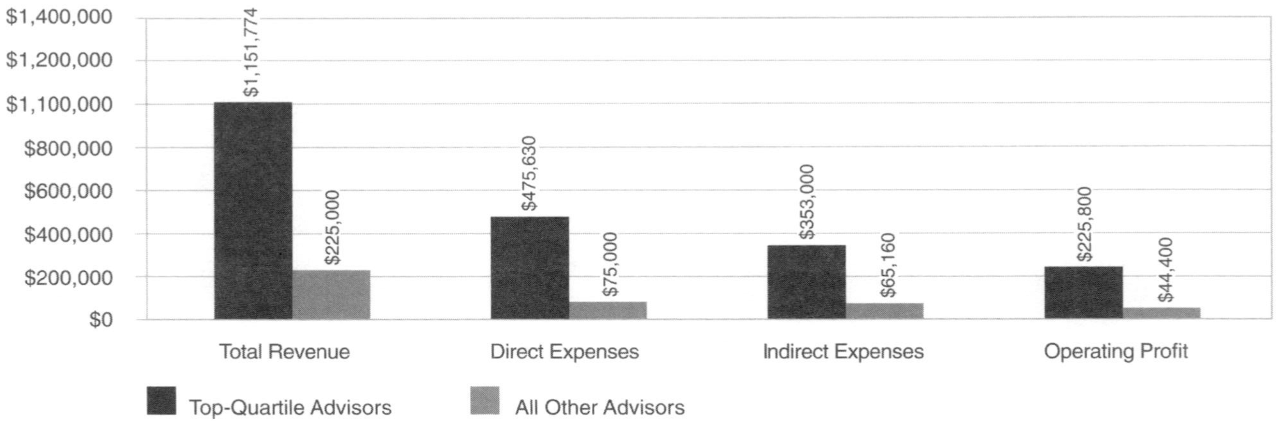

Top-performing firms appear to spend more on marketing but may get more and larger clients as a result. Though they spend almost four times as much in total marketing dollars as other firms do, top performers make a return on marketing of $1.63 per marketing dollar spent, as compared with only $1 per marketing dollar spent for all other firms.[3]

Financial Performance

Managing larger clients comes at a price but with a reward. Top performers spend three times more per client, but they also generate four times as much operating profit per client.

Although lower-performing firms have a larger operating profit margin, 21 percent compared to 18 percent for top performers, they have vastly larger operating profits in absolute dollars. While the cost of maintaining a top-performing business is higher and results in slightly lower profit margins as a percentage of revenue, the overall financial performance, including profits, increases significantly for those firms. They reap nearly four times the income per owner of other firms. It should also be noted that data were reported on the median financial performance of top performers, and 50 percent of them performed better than the median. By practice model, these firms spend more on marketing and have a higher acquisition cost per client, which may well explain why they see faster growth, greater AUM and revenue, and larger client size.[4]

Interestingly, top-performing advisory firms significantly outpaced their counterparts across all business models—solo, silo, and ensemble (Figure 2.4)—so, clearly, best practices are agnostic when it comes to type of practice. In addition, top performers surpassed other firms in median total revenue, direct expenses, indirect expenses, and operating profits (Figure 2.5). A comparison of key performance metrics (Table 2.1) shows a significant performance gap between top performers and other firms across numerous performance metrics, including total owner income (5×), income per owner (4×), fee-based AUM (8×), total annual revenue (5.1×), operating profit (5×), clients (2×), fee-based revenue (3+×), owners (2×), advisors (2×), and staff (4×).

CHAPTER 3

New Thinking for New Results

It takes a new way of thinking for an advisory firm to evolve from a personal, entrepreneurial practice into a sustainable business. Replace instinct and intuition, the common drivers of decisions, with information and facts based on an objective view of business performance, which translates into the desire to align business behavior (how advisors act) with business goals (what advisors want) to build a better firm. Achieving this alignment is easier said than done, and we will explore the best practices for doing so throughout this book.

Advisors need to look more closely at what their expenses are, how their teams work together, how they build operational efficiencies, and how they systematize their business processes. They must establish goals, analyze options, make decisions, develop plans, continuously review performance, and make ongoing adjustments to their plans. If this sounds familiar, it's exactly what they do for their clients. Surprisingly, only a minority of advisors plan and manage their businesses the way they plan and manage their clients' financial lives.

That is starting to change, for many advisors realize they can't do it all themselves. Business performance is a more effective criterion for creating a satisfying and successful firm than is following the personal desires and whims of founder/owners from day to day. Technical prowess and ability to sell services will impact future success less than the ability to build, manage, and grow the business. To build a business with transferrable value requires advisors to face the future with the same disciplined approach they espouse to clients: They must plan, measure, and manage their own performance just as rigorously.

Despite the challenges facing the advisory profession, the demographics suggest there is opportunity ahead for those advisors who can effectively build their businesses to capitalize on the opportunity. This starts with thinking about the firm in a new way: by focusing on the business side of the practice and making a commitment to change for better business performance.

This kind of thinking applies whether the advisors are solo practitioners or ensembles; commission only or fee based; wealth managers, asset managers, bank trust companies, or family offices; independent broker-dealers (IBDs), registered investment advisors (RIAs), or investment advisor representatives (IARs); and whether they have ambitions simply to create a nice lifestyle income or to build a nationally dominant enterprise.

It requires advisors to transform their behavior from what is easy and instinctive to what is effective. Often, the reality is that no matter what we might want otherwise, our behavior tends to enforce the status quo. However frustrating or difficult the circumstances, it may be easier to keep things the same than to develop the discipline needed to change behavior and, with it, circumstances.

The most successful advisors we encounter have made the leap from personal behavior to business behavior. In one client firm, the advisors noted they were dissatisfied with their small clients, difficult staff, and low revenues and profits. Yet they continued to take on the small clients, ignore the staff issues, and keep financial performance stagnant. Instead of stepping outside the box and operating from a business perspective, they continuously rationalized and justified their decisions. By contrast, advisors at another client firm in a similar situation spent two years reengineering their business by increasing minimums and fees, proactively addressing staff issues, and managing their business with a healthy bottom line in mind. It was by no means easy, as it required them to step well outside their comfort zone. It was, however, well worth the effort, as it yielded a doubling of firm profits.

Einstein once said, "No problem can be solved with the same consciousness that created it." If advisors want something new and better but bring the same thinking and behavior with them to work each day, they can largely expect the same result. Obtaining a different result requires a different perspective and the discipline to design, develop, and deploy the solutions that will enable change.

CHAPTER 4

The Four Essential Disciplines

Working closely with advisors of nearly every size and type has led us to develop essential disciplines that collectively define strategies for how advisors can better build, manage, and grow their businesses: business strategy and planning, business development, human capital, and operations optimization.

These four elements combine to form the four Genworth Business Disciplines, a comprehensive, integrated approach to helping advisory firms build more satisfying, successful, scalable, sustainable, and salable businesses.

Advisors can work to master the best practices within each of these four disciplines to maximize their firms' performance.

Business Strategy and Planning

Some advisors have a solid vision of what they want but aren't sure how to attain it, while others work furiously with no true vision or strategy. Business success comes from defining a clear vision, developing a deliberate strategy, and designing the performance management infrastructure needed to establish a solid growth opportunity. Equally important is a firm's ability to align its strategy, plans, clients, staff, and operational systems into a congruent whole that is greater than the sum of its parts. The discipline includes:

- Strategic planning
- Business planning
- Target client profile
- Financial reporting and management
- Performance benchmarking
- Creating and realizing value

Business Development

Whether gaining new contributions from current clients, developing strategic alliances, prospecting in the marketplace, or fostering referrals to acquire new clients, all advisors engage at some point in the sales and marketing activities that collectively make up business development. Increasing demand for financial advice creates an environment of unlimited potential for firms that understand the strategies, structures, and systems that support effective marketing and in turn drive steady, sustainable growth. The business development discipline encompasses:

- Brand building
- Developing a sales approach
- Marketing materials
- Marketing plan
- Creating and managing referrals
- Developing the rainmaker role
- Prospect process
- Sales and new client process
- Tracking and reporting

Human Capital

For many advisors, adding staff and other advisors promotes growth and continuity, but it also brings added challenges and complexity. Knowing how to harness the talents of managers, advisors, and staff for greatest productivity is crucial to building a sustainable, scalable business. Designing strategies and standards for hiring, training, managing, compensating, and advancing employees is more effective when firms have access to proven best practices and processes. The human capital discipline includes:

- Hiring and on-boarding
- Training and development
- Performance management
- Organizational structure
- Job descriptions
- Career advancement paths
- Compensation planning
- Adding professional management
- Culture and team building

Operations Optimization

At the end of the day, it's not how many clients a firm can handle or how many dollars it has under management that represent ultimate success; the broader barometers are how well the firm serves its clients, how satisfied the owners and the team are, how financially successful and sustainable the firm is, and how much value is retained and ultimately realized. All success is achieved through a winning combination of strategy and execution. Many advisory firms struggle to develop a clear and compelling strategy, and many more struggle with how to align their operating model with their strategy to create a disciplined plan for executing it. Optimizing operations is the process of defining, documenting, systematizing, and institutionalizing a business so that it transforms from a people-driven practice into an organized business enterprise. The operations optimization discipline includes:

- Time management
- Firm communication model
- Key business systems
- Client segmentation
- Client profitability analysis
- Client service plans
- Technology tools

Although every advisor/owner has his or her own unique situation, needs, and goals, the Genworth Disciplines and the best practices that support them all play an instrumental role in helping advisors build more purposeful, productive, and profitable businesses.

The Genworth Consultative Process

We use a basic business improvement system that can be implemented by any advisor without a consultant and is particularly useful when advisors are interested in putting professional management systems in place (Figure 4.1).

The Genworth Business Audit and Business Optimization Plan process encourages the advisor to engage in the following activities:

FIGURE 4.1 The Genworth Consultative Process

Discover — Diagnose — Develop — Design — Deploy — Deep Breath

1. *Perform due diligence.* Assess the condition of the firm, define goals, and establish priorities with the greatest opportunity for impact. The idea is to "look under the hood" to understand the relationship between behavior and outcomes and to define the business vision and goals.

2. *Diagnose the problems and the opportunities.* We examine strength, weakness, opportunity, and threat (SWOT) areas that have a significant impact on the firm, including behavioral, business management, and performance issues that fall short of best practices and can be improved to drive better business performance.

3. *Develop a plan based on clearly established priorities.* We focus on a disciplined approach to business optimization and formalize it in a deliberate plan of action for greatest firm impact and benefit. We then develop a process for implementing these improvements and a practical timeline in which to achieve them.

4. *Design customized solutions based on best practices.* Reengineer specific areas of business to optimize performance and maximize results. The aim is to draw on best practices while respecting the fact that they need to be customized to each individual situation.

5. *Deploy the solution.* Once each solution is designed, we develop a meaningful plan for introducing, teaching, and launching it so it can be integrated effectively into the firm's operating model and rhythm. We continue to monitor and manage performance in that area by developing quarterly benchmarks, annual business reviews, owner/manager ongoing review schedules, and team check-ins.

6. *Take a deep breath.* At the end of each phase, advisors pause, take a deep breath, reflect on the work completed, review the business optimization plan priorities, and assess their ongoing appropriateness. Advisors can adjust the priorities to meet business needs and move on to create the next customized solution.

The Four-Phase Business Life Cycle of an Advisory Firm

Advisory firms follow an evolutionary path as they grow, develop, and mature. Various consulting firms have characterized advisory firms and their phases of maturity based on factors such as revenue, assets under management (AUM), and rate of growth. These characterizations and related comparisons can be useful in exploring a specific study subject or population of advisors. However, we find that a broader, simpler view of how advisory firms grow and mature is more helpful to firms grappling with how to build better businesses.

To this end, we have characterized four general stages of a business life cycle: the early stage, growth, maturity, and transition depicted in Figure 4.2.

FIGURE 4.2 Four-Phase Business Life Cycle

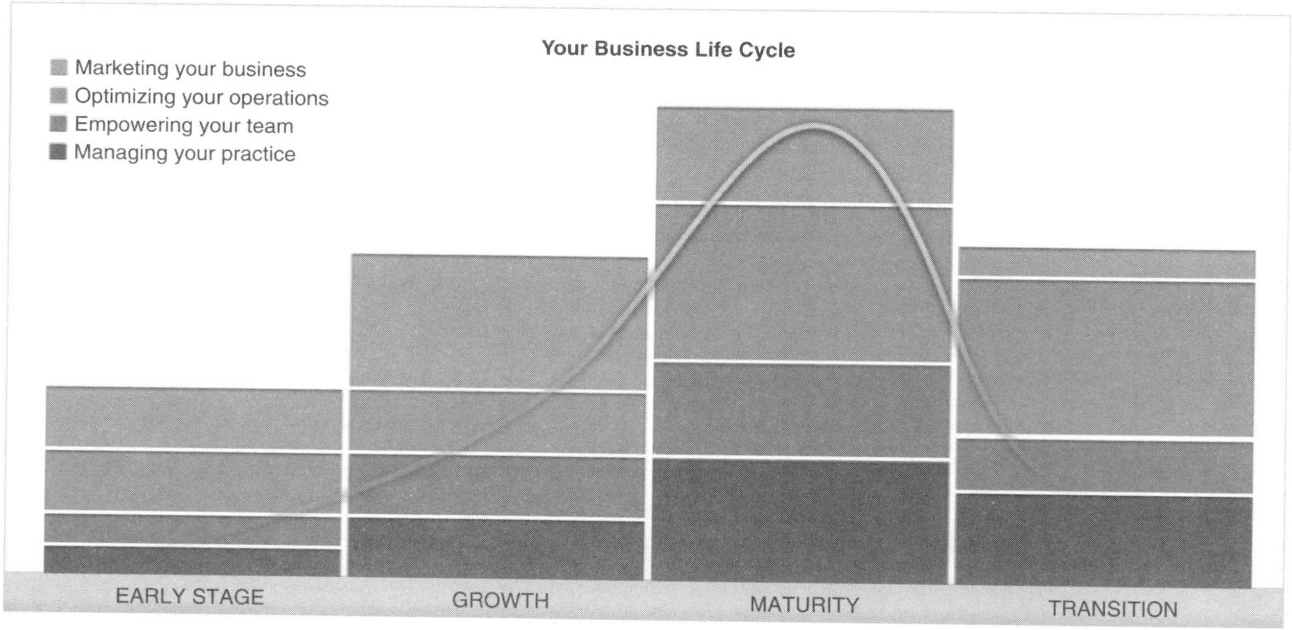

Your Business Life Cycle

Marketing your business
Optimizing your operations
Empowering your team
Managing your practice

EARLY STAGE   GROWTH   MATURITY   TRANSITION

Although the time horizon for maturity and transition through the phases is different for every firm, the process seems to flow as a relatively consistent experience. Understanding the key stages of advisory firm development and their accompanying strengths and struggles can help advisors better understand where their firms are in the context of overall development. This in turn helps prepare advisors to make key decisions about what steps to take going forward. When applied through the lens of the four Genworth disciplines, it provides a meaningful foundation and context for how advisors may best advance their growth and development, either within their current stage or into the next one.

We will discuss three of the four stages—early business, growth, and maturity—in detail in this chapter. The fourth stage—transition—is discussed in Chapters 31 through 33, focusing on succession planning.

Early Stage

The early stage of the business life cycle (or "early practice") is typically a newer practice, whether a solo run by one advisor, a silo of cooperative advisors, or a newly formed ensemble firm. Practices in this stage are largely run by advisor instinct and intuition, without any disciplined approach to managing and growing the firm. There is little or no operational structure, strategy, staff, or the systems typically developed in the later stages. Operations are motivated by the advisor's demands and work style, and the practice is completely dependent on the advisor(s) for direction, propelled primarily by entrepreneurial desire and vigor.

The business style of these firms can be characterized as "go and grow," with the urge for growth eclipsing all other business priorities.

- *Primary business driver.* Early practices are almost exclusively focused on the need to generate revenue and income.
- *Strengths.* In early practices, the advisor lifestyles and income needs drive the business behavior, which tends to be focused on fueling growth. Advisors tend to have more freedom, flexibility, and control because their personal style determines how the practice is managed. Early practices typically have no or minimal staff and few if any operational processes. While there's no efficient way to leverage the advisor's time and build business value, life can certainly be simpler.
- *Struggles.* The early practice is dependent on the advisor and lacks clear business strategy and plans, people management, and process development. It can't behave as anything more than a professional practice. Advisors often perform all tasks within the business, even when they have staff, as there are no training and processes for staff to follow. They feel pressed by constant demands on time that distracts them from essential business development activities. These

advisory firm owners typically lack the time and the capital to invest in the firm's growth and development.

- *Key business priorities.* The early practice advisor has to attract new clients and fill a pipeline with new business to keep revenue flowing and growing. The priority for these practices is to build revenue into a reliable base so that advisors can turn their attention to transforming the early practice into an emerging firm.

Early practice advisors often note, "I need to grow my revenue and service my client base, but I just don't have the time to do it all myself, and I can't yet afford the help I need."

The Growth Stage

In the growth stage, advisors almost always realize that there aren't enough hours in the day to do what's required to move ahead and that the practice requires others to grow. They are better able to capitalize on advisor time to grow the client roster and count on their revenue as a reliable financial base.

The growth-stage firm aspires to achieve significant growth and begins to set its sights on more effective business planning and management. Such efforts define the typical emerging firm, with many firms meandering through this stage for the entirety of the business life cycle. Some firms can be personally, professionally, and financially successful at this stage; however, the majority struggle to build out and benefit from the best practices within each of the four disciplines and never fully manage and grow the organization in line with its potential. Many growth-stage firms will transition to other advisors and will realize some value, though more often by default than design.

In this stage, owners begin to realize the awesome potential to transform their practices into sustainable businesses. Some are driven by this potential to evolve to the next stage of development, while others are unable to move beyond this stage. This is the point at which an advisor may enjoy a satisfying and successful professional life.

- *Primary business driver.* Growth-stage firms typically provide high-quality service to a growing client base while managing time more productively to drive revenue and improve operational consistency and systems for scalable growth.
- *Strengths.* The hard work is finally paying off, with the business graduating from struggling start-up to solid revenue generator. Advisors at growth-stage firms typically are established rainmakers who can reliably fill the pipeline with new clients.

Growth-stage firms have evolved, through a combination of support staff and systems, and can now more effectively leverage the advisors' time to manage and acquire new clients. At this stage, firms typically have good client service and a satisfied client base, which grows largely due to client contributions and referrals. This level of financial success gives owners the comfort and the capital needed to invest in the business to drive more growth, systematize the business, and focus on building a scalable business that increases the firm's value.

- *Struggles.* Client meetings, phone calls, portfolio allocation, and staff management issues may have advisors falling victim to their own success. Challenges with hiring, training, managing, and paying staff seem second nature at this stage, but the stress and strains of keeping all of this going on a daily basis may take its toll. In addition, emerging firms rely heavily on clients and on the personal brand of the founder(s)/owner(s) to drive passive growth through contributions and referrals.

Although passive growth and personal brand are effective sources of client acquisition, they are not scalable business development strategies and, ultimately, may constrain growth and affect value. These challenges combine to define the hallmark of emerging firms: the competing demands of working "in" the business and making time to work "on" the business. Advisors may become so bogged down in meeting the demands of their firms' success that they lose sight of where they want to go, why, and how and when they wish to get there.

- *Key business priorities.* Emerging firms focus on delivering more and better services to a growing client base, attracting larger and more profitable clients and driving revenue growth. Though they may struggle with execution, these advisors see the need for, and value in, developing their people and designing systematic processes to support scalable growth. As revenue increases and operations expand, they may extend their focus beyond top-line revenue growth to concentrate on building healthier profit margins. Emerging firm advisors often note, "I am succeeding in spite of myself."

Maturity

The mature business operates first and foremost as a business enterprise. These firms have a well-defined strategy and effective management, no matter their size. They institutionalized their business operations to ensure quality, consistency, and scalability. In addition, they developed and followed deliberate processes for how to hire, train, pay, and promote their team members. Firms in this stage have clearly defined growth strategies and a disciplined approach to sales, marketing, and client acquisition. Mature businesses realize steady revenue growth and generate a healthy profit margin, which allows the firms to invest in growth while rewarding their owners with fair returns.

To reach this stage, advisors have moved beyond the personal and entrepreneurial styles typical of early practices and emerging firms and have improved their ability to manage daily business operations while, instead, focusing on business performance optimization. Mature businesses either develop management skills and devote time to these needs or hire professional management to do so. As they grow, these firms tend to aspire to expand their enterprise with mergers or acquisitions and/or expand to multioffice business models.

- *Primary business driver.* Mature businesses focus on scaling revenue, staffing, and client service operations to significantly increase business and financial performance and to build long-term business value.
- *Strengths.* Advisors focused on performance, productivity, and profitability hire professional managers and have defined executive, management, advisor, and staff capacities. They have evolved from a purely entrepreneurial state, and actively engage in sound business thinking and management. At the same time, they maintain a strong entrepreneurial spirit and a collaborative culture. At this stage, firms have the opportunity to differentiate among rainmakers, who focus on client acquisition; senior financial advisors, who manage the firm's largest and most complex client relationships; and service advisors, who support senior advisors and rainmakers as they grow and develop their own skills. The business is institutionalized beyond the individuals running it, with systematized staff roles, processes, and technology driving service, scalability, and profitability. Firms have formalized growth plans, operational management, and compensation strategies. The firm has the capital resources to sustain during market downturns, to invest in growth, and to further develop the business.
- *Struggles.* Mature businesses still struggle with the balance between working in and on the business and, when they hire professional managers to fill this gap, advisors often have a hard time clearly defining their roles and designing compensation and equity plans for these managers. They often have trouble recruiting and retaining dedicated business development officers and defining their roles, which would allow them to develop the staff and the systems models needed to truly systematize and scale the firm's business development efforts.

These businesses also struggle to maintain quality control and personal service during periods of aggressive growth. Advisors/owners may experience difficulty adapting to their changing roles within the firm, finding it difficult to transition from doing every task themselves to delegating daily business operations. Some businesses can become addicted to growth and may expand their offices, merge, or make acquisitions prematurely if they fail to engage a clear vision, follow their business goals, and maintain effective management during that growth.

If advisors aren't careful, this growth may outpace staff, services, and systems infrastructure, causing stress fractures and decreased efficiencies.

- *Key business priorities.* Mature businesses invest heavily in the people, the processes, and the technology needed to institutionalize and scale up their business model. At the same time, they offer more and better services to clients, with increased profitability. They actively focus on performance management and people development to recruit and retain high-quality team members who contribute to a positive firm culture. These firms prioritize business optimization to ensure that excellence in business, marketing, operations, and staff are priorities that are monitored and managed on an ongoing basis. They seek to expand their business models and financial success, while retaining the entrepreneurial spirit that helped make them successful.

Mature businesses often find, "We've achieved success; now we need to ensure and maintain quality and consistency of services while scaling growth, growing income and profitability, and building long-term business value." It is at this point that the mature business looks to the fourth phase of the business life cycle—transition.

Which Stage is Right for You?

Regardless of the stage of development they are operating in, advisors continue to struggle with working in and on their businesses at the same time. Each stage of development has its unique set of challenges and opportunities, and there is no way to avoid them.

The decision to evolve from one stage to the next typically is not a conscious one, though we propose that it should be. By understanding the four Genworth Business Disciplines and the best practices that support each area, advisors are better able to make informed and intentional decisions about how to build their firms to meet their goals and advance their futures.

Moving a firm from one stage to the next at the right time should be based on advisors' defining their goals and devising a clear path to achieve them to avoid moving into an organizational stage or model that may not be the right fit or not at the right time.

Not everyone wants to move through these stages of development. As depicted in Figure 4.3, study results indicate that 22 percent of advisors want only to build and sustain a lifestyle practice, where their lifestyle and personal income drive the business, offering little or no emphasis on scalability or value. A full 54 percent of advisors report that they want to maintain a lifestyle business that has increased value. Balancing the flexibility of the entrepreneurial practice

FIGURE 4.3   Lifestyle and Business Goals

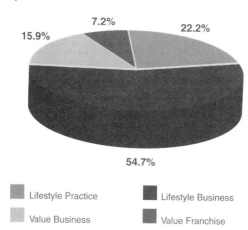

with the systems and the processes of a fully institutionalized business can be difficult but, with the right approach, do-able. Stepping-stones in between stages allow advisors to maintain the freedom and flexibility of a lifestyle business, while still employing business practices that can help them build and realize value.

In these cases, value is defined more by the client base and the assets than by actual transferable or salable value. Revenues tend to stay on the smaller side, and business value may be limited, but for many advisors this model provides some of the best of both worlds.

Nearly 16 percent of advisors report that building a firm that monetizes business value is a top priority. An additional 7 percent wish to build an enterprise with value, and then franchise this model by opening offices in multiple locations.

Having consulted with firms at every stage of development, within each of the lifestyle and business models described, and with every set of goals imaginable, we've learned that although every firm can benefit from best practices, there is no one-size-fits-all solution. A good way to make the best firms better is to understand best practices that work with the top-performing firms, learn from the experience of others, and yet have sufficient expertise to apply those lessons in a way that fits your business

Getting Started

The pages that follow set out to provide an in-depth view of best practices across each business discipline, with recommendations on how advisors can use these practices in their own firms.

CHAPTER 5

Business Strategy and Planning

Business strategy and planning are part of a defined game plan, complete with a series of decisions and activities designed to achieve specific goals. This planning, then, is really the process of figuring out what you want to achieve and deciding how to make it happen. We start with a series of questions: Where do you want to be in the future? What is the best path to pursue? What action should be taken to fill existing gaps? A strategic plan charts a clear course for where a firm is going, what it will look like when it gets there, and how and when it will get there.

A Strategy for Winning

We often find that firms lacking a business strategy and plan are driven by the "go and grow" mind-set their founders used to start the firm. These advisors hit the ground running on day one and never looked back, and their businesses may have developed in a haphazard way.

Can an advisor be successful without a strategic plan? Many are. Advisory firms with whom we've consulted over the years are successful by many measures. However, success is and should be defined differently for everyone. To some, it's working 35 hours a week, earning a healthy income, and spending more time with family. For others, it's building a dominant firm that generates tens of millions in annual revenue.

Without a plan, many advisors fail to recognize their potential and do not apply their energy to activities that will help them achieve their goals. Most advisors have ideas about what they want their businesses to be. However, they bog down in daily demands and have difficulty focusing on driving the success of the business.

The Business Strategy and Planning Process

When we talk with advisors about the benefits of having a clear strategy and plan, they often say that there's so much to do. They don't want to waste or spend time on planning. Yet when firm owners don't take the time to do something right, they often spend large amounts of time having to do it over again.

We worked with an advisory firm that wanted to hire a financial planning associate. The original request was for someone to support the firm's two principals by managing the client process, from information gathering to engagement, and then completing the necessary planning work. The firm had identified an individual with three years of planning support experience who was, by the job description, a solid candidate. This hire was a sound business decision in concept, allowing the principals time to develop a planning process.

In the last round of interviews with the leading candidate, the firm's chief investment officer (CIO) suggested that the candidate didn't have enough investment experience to deliver investment advice to clients or to serve as a strong backup to him. The CIO wanted to retire in the next few years; nowhere in the process of preparing for this hire was the need made clear that the new employee should have a depth of investment experience or the ability to deliver investment advice to clients. Nor was it ever mentioned that the CIO wished this hire would be able to fill his role with clients.

That's not to say there wasn't ample discussion around the purpose and plan for this hire; there was an abundance of it, but the firm was unable to define a strategy and stick to it. The advisors changed their minds about key decisions, often in response to how the principals were feeling on any given day. It's not surprising that this was the firm's third attempt to fill this position.

This highly successful firm needed to harness its energy around a clear strategy for executing on concrete decisions, regardless of the daily circumstances. If the staffing strategy is to free up the principals' time, that suggests one type of candidate. If the staffing strategy is to develop investment bench strength to support the CIO's transition out, that suggests another.

Follow this simple exercise to formulate a basic strategy with no more than a piece of paper and a few minutes of time:

- At the bottom of a piece of paper, write a brief description of where the business is now.
- At the top of the paper, write a brief description of where you want the business to be in five years (or some other time period).
- In the space in between, write out what you need to do to get from the bottom of the page to the top.
- For each to-do, identify when it needs to be done and who will be accountable for its completion.

FIGURE 5.1   Strategic Planning Process

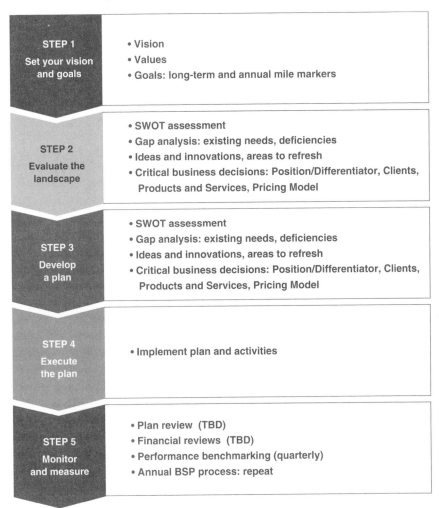

In spite of this simplified process, strategic planning is the result of thoughtful consideration regarding decision execution (when, by whom)—all with the purpose of achieving a desired goal.

As depicted in Figure 5.1, an effective strategic planning process contains the following steps, described in detail in this chapter:

1. Set your vision and goals.
2. Evaluate the landscape by conducting an analysis of where you are and the gaps to be filled.

3. Develop a plan with clear priorities, timelines, and accountability owners.
4. Execute the plan with discipline.
5. Monitor business performance and ongoing results.

Step 1: Set Your Vision and Goals

The first step is to define your vision, values, and goals for the firm. This is not your ordinary mission statement, but a rigorous conceptual framework that includes the firm's vision (where it wants to go, what it wants to be), firm values (the values and standards it will adhere to along the way), and firm goals (the key objectives the firm wants to achieve). We discuss this area in depth in the next chapter.

Step 2: Evaluate the Landscape

Getting from the bottom of the paper to the top, identify the gaps you need to bridge as you work toward your goals, whether you want to build value to sell your firm, expand to multiple offices, or double your income while working fewer hours. Assess your current condition, your competitors, the marketplace, and other areas to locate and address these gaps.

The most common exercise used is the SWOT analysis—strengths, weaknesses, opportunities, and threats. We find that many firms think SWOT is strategic planning, and that others simply think the process is a futile exercise, perhaps because they don't know how to integrate it into their planning process.

Much has been written about SWOT over the years, so we will offer only a brief review of the basics:

- Strengths are characteristics of the business that give it an advantage over others.
- Weaknesses are characteristics that place the business at a disadvantage relative to others.
- Opportunities are chances to improve performance.
- Threats are challenges that could impair or limit the business.

Examine each of the SWOT areas for both internal and external factors. For example, your firm might be the only niche service for doctors in your area, an external competitive strength. Yet if your firm has a high staff turnover, this is an internal challenge that could hamper your ability to deliver quality service and meet the needs of your growing practice.

SWOT analysis is useful because it helps you better understand the opportunities you can embrace and the challenges you may face along the path to your goals. This, in turn, helps you focus on where you need to improve.

We recommend doing a gap analysis, in addition to the SWOT analysis, to help further identify addressable deficiencies in your organization. If your goal is to double revenue during the next three years and you have only limited capacity for new clients, you will need to either substantially increase your client account size and transition away from smaller clients or add advisor capacity with a new hire.

There is a noticeable difference between a typical firm and a best-practice firm. The typical firm decides it wants to double revenue or sell in five years and will continue moving ahead. The best-practice firm decides what it wants to do and conducts a SWOT analysis to evaluate the landscape, and a gap analysis to identify what holes need to be filled if the firm is to successfully achieve its goals.

Step 3: Develop a Plan

With a clear view of where you are, where you want to go, and what the journey in between might require, you're prepared to develop a plan for achieving your goals. We find that several aspects of plan building can help you take a simple approach to a sophisticated process.

Critical Business Decisions

The first step here is to ask and answer key questions about structuring your firm to achieve its goals. Key decisions define how you will position and differentiate your firm in the marketplace, the services you will provide and to which clients, as well as how you will deliver those services and at what price.

- Why are you better than the competition?
  - *Position/Differentiator.* What makes you unique or different, and how will you position your firm in the marketplace? Are you the dominant firm, the most knowledgeable or expert, the one specifically focused on the needs of a defined niche?
- What do you provide and how?
  - *Outcomes.* What outcome will you deliver to clients? Financial planning isn't an outcome; peace of mind is.
  - *Services.* What services will you provide to deliver the outcome? Many firms say they offer comprehensive wealth management, for example, but fail to deliver a comprehensive, integrated solution to their clients.
- Who will be involved?
  - *Clients.* What clients will you serve? Anyone who says yes? Clients with a certain asset level? Clients in a specific niche?
  - *Team.* What team is required to effectively deliver services to clients at the desired level?

- How will you deliver? What process will you use to prospect and engage clients? What process will you follow to maintain the ongoing relationship?
- For what? What price or fees will you charge for your services? Will you charge planning fees, retainers, hourly rates, fees on assets, or a combination?

Build a Business Blueprint

A business blueprint is a detailed view of the strategy of the firm to achieve its goals. This blueprint will capture the critical business decisions and ensure that the relationship between decisions and goals is in alignment. For example, we asked an advisory firm what its goals for revenue, assets under management (AUM), and clients were five years down the road. The firm's advisors said they wanted to grow revenue to $3 million, reach $400 million in AUM, and add 100 clients.

When we did the math, the numbers didn't add up: Multiplying the average client size by the average fee and multiplying again by 100 clients didn't result in their revenue target, and AUM didn't match their AUM goal. When we divided the growth in AUM by the number of new clients the advisors wanted to add, it more than doubled the average client size. They claimed they were a wealth management firm, but their clients ranged from $200,000 to $3 million, with the majority under $1 million and an average account size of $500,000.

This firm had, as many firms do, made each decision in isolation without considering the relationship between them and the impact of one decision on another.

The critical business decisions and business blueprint are instrumental in developing a meaningful, viable, and effective plan, and we will discuss each in more detail throughout this book.

Organizational Development Plan

We found that advisors were more likely to adopt a simpler business plan instead of a complicated, comprehensive one. In response to this, we developed the Organizational Development Plan, defining goals, identifying business priorities for completion in order of impact, and estimating the time for completion.

Step 4: Execute the Plan

It doesn't matter whether your strategic plan is on one piece of paper or part of a 20-page document. What's crucial is your ability to execute. When we conduct our due diligence on a new advisory firm client, we hear great strategies and ideas but, in some cases, cannot identify follow-through and achievement measurements. Owners are entrepreneurs and naturally able to create a vision and come up with ideas for how to realize it, but they frequently struggle with the "chores" necessary to achieve that vision and how to track that achievement. Success in this area requires applying a systematic, disciplined approach to the crafted exercise.

Step 5: Monitor and Measure

Finally, establish how to monitor and measure the plan for performance. You can measure progress by evaluating outcomes against objectives. In the example of the previously mentioned firm, the goals were to grow AUM to $400 million and revenue to $3 million and to double the average client size. These are specific and measurable, and the firm can easily track progress to ensure that it's moving in the right direction over time.

Measuring performance requires you to take a look at the underlying performance of the business in the areas that support its goals. We decided, in the case of this client, to closely measure a number of key performance indicators (KPIs) that provided insight into how the firm was progressing toward its goals, which included average fees, AUM per client, and revenue per advisor, among others.

For more in-depth discussion on measuring progress and performance, review Chapter 8, "Managing Business Performance."

CHAPTER 6

Living the Vision

Two books have influenced our thinking about the business planning process, and we suggest them for further reading: *Built to Last: Successful Habits of Visionary Companies* by Jim Collins and *Start with Why: How Great Leaders Inspire Everyone to Take Action* by Simon Sinek.[1] The concepts are similar to traditional texts on setting visions and establishing goals, but both authors have done an excellent job of researching what makes businesses and individuals successful, and they package their conclusions in ways that are engaging and easy to understand. We saw little value in reinventing the wheel, so this chapter reflects our interpretation of these concepts as we've developed them to fit our work with advisory firms over the years.

Pursuing a Purpose

The typical advisory firm seeks to serve its clients well, while achieving some measure of financial success. But neither of these objectives, in and of itself, is a purpose. Jim Collins defines purpose as what an organization stands for and why it exists beyond making money. Sinek defines purpose as our "why," as in "why are we here?" and "why do we do what we do?"

Your purpose is what makes you passionate about your work, what motivates you beyond financial products or profits. Some examples of purpose statements from some of our advisory firm clients include the following:

- Help our clients achieve financial security and well-being.
- Help Middle America achieve financial security and independence.
- Simplify our clients' financial lives.

Crafting Your Vision

A firm vision clearly articulates what your firm aspires to, a clear picture of where you want your firm to be at some specific time horizon. Some examples of vision statements are:

- Build the premiere wealth management firm and become the employer of choice in the Mid-Atlantic region.
- Become the most respected firm in Greenstone County.
- Become the firm of choice for medical professionals in the region.
- Build the industry's largest and most respected firm serving the needs of high-net-worth women and their families.

These aren't necessarily measurable goals, but the point of a vision is to state what a firm wants to become, not to define how that will be measured.

A clear vision focuses the firm's attention and motivates its members to take action. It provides drive and determination to succeed despite challenges. Without a defined vision, firms have a tendency to meander and lose focus. When you have clarity about what you want to achieve, you can marshal your time, resources, and energy to that cause.

Creating Clear Values

Values are the guiding principles that drive behavior. According to Collins, they are the essential and enduring tenets of an organization; they are a set of timeless principles requiring no external justification and having intrinsic value to those inside the organization. Just as with personal values, business values define and guide how a firm and the individuals within it will conduct business.

If a firm's vision is to be "highly respected," then values such as integrity and excellence come to mind as behaviors that support that vision.

We find values particularly useful in helping to promote cultural alignment between the firm's vision and the owners and the team members. If a firm selects "winning" as one of its core values, it is unlikely that individuals who are happy to go with the flow and see how things turn out will be a good cultural fit. If a firm believes in "constant improvement" or a "passion for excellence," there is a certain type of individual who will thrive in an environment that always challenges the status quo, and there are individuals who will struggle to survive in such a place.

What's crucial is not which values you choose, but the need for shared values among those who work in the firm.

To make your values flow through your company and become part of your belief system and business behavior, you not only have to communicate them frequently, you also have to believe in them yourself and hire people who are predisposed toward the same values.

Getting to Goals

Accomplishing measurable results helps define the visionary goal. Collins calls this the BHAG: the big, hairy, audacious goal. He notes that it should be big enough to be scary and should require a firm to galvanize around it, with everyone working hard to make it a reality. He also recommends against goals that are small or easily attained. We use the 50/50 rule when helping clients set goals: the goal should be big enough so that there is only about a 50 percent chance of achieving it, and yet reasonable enough so that there is at least a 50 percent chance of being able to do so.

The goal should be big enough to be inspiring but specific, clear, and easily understood. For example, one advisory firm's vision was to "build the industry's largest and most respected firm serving the needs of high-net-worth women and their families," with a goal of having "$2 billion in assets under management and four offices within seven years."

Big goals require a great deal of work. Don't expect to achieve them in a single step, but break them down into a series of manageable points. Collins refers to these incremental goals as base-camps, or goals that set out what you want to accomplish on your way to achieving the big goal and vision. In the case of a firm with a goal of growing to $2 billion, while serving high-net-worth women from four offices across the country, we defined clear and measurable goals that the firm could govern itself by:

- Grow revenue by 15 percent per year.
- Achieve an operating profit of 30 percent per year.
- Grow the average account size and revenue per client by 20 percent per year.
- Maintain a 98 percent client retention rate and a 4.0+ (on a scale of 5) client satisfaction rate.
- Achieve employee satisfaction scores of 4.0+ (on a scale of 5).

With goals in place, you can identify the key business objectives you need to achieve en route to accomplishing them and fulfilling your vision. The same firm mentioned earlier defined key business objectives and their deadlines this way:

- Refresh the firm brand, messaging and marketing collateral to strongly appeal to target clients (year 1).
- Institutionalize business practices to prepare for multioffice expansion (years 1–2).

- Successfully develop and implement a firm culture and a compensation plan that make us the region's employer of choice (year 3).
- Open the first satellite office (year 3), the second satellite office (year 4), the third satellite office (year 4), and the fourth satellite office (year 5).

Dreams with Deadlines

Why is it so important to create a vision and establish goals? One reason is that multiple studies show that people who write down their goals have a much greater chance of achieving them. Yet we've heard many an advisor say they're successful without goals and have never needed them. Once again, building a better advisory business isn't about being successful; you probably already are. Building a better advisory business is about being as successful as you can be, realizing your firm's full potential. Harvard University made the point better than we can.

Harvard surveyed one graduating class about its members' goals 20 years after graduation. They learned that 80 percent of the former graduates had no goals, 15 percent had goals but had not written them down, and 5 percent had written goals or dreams with deadlines. They found that those who had written down their goals achieved far more than those who had not. Yet it's the detail of this study that is so powerful. Harvard found that the total net worth of the 5 percent of graduates who had written down their goals exceeded the combined net worth of the remaining 85 percent of the graduates.

Advisors who establish a vision, values, and goals stack the deck in favor of their own success by applying their energies to a specific course.

It's important to be specific and focused. When you reach for too many, disparate goals, it's easy to steer off course. Improving a business is a lot of work, and people tend to take the path of least resistance. The first step in tackling goals, therefore, is to be absolutely clear about exactly what you aspire to accomplish.

In setting your goals, it's more important to worry about *what* you want to achieve than *how* you will achieve it. Advisors frequently give us reasons they can't meet the goals or why they won't work. It seems we have a tendency to stop ourselves before we ever get started. Our experience has been that if you pick a meaningful "what" (goal) and pursue it with passion, the "how" has a way of working itself out.

From Vision to Results

Bringing the purpose, vision, values, and goals together creates a compelling platform from which firms can set their course toward success. We find that once advisors get started, the path from vision to results flows naturally. In one large solo practice, the client's vision was to build an enduring firm that, after his retirement, would maintain the legacy he had worked hard to build. His goal was to build his business value to $2 million and transition to a part-time schedule after 5 to 7 years, with the ability to transition out completely within 7 to 10 years. Making these important strategic decisions led easily to a series of others. For example, the advisor then knew he would need to recruit, train, and transition to a successor during the next 5 years. We quickly were able to perform the math to model out how to make it happen. The information provided in this scenario gave us a concrete level of clarity needed to develop a plan.

A Catalyst for Change

There's another reason why being explicit about your vision, values, and goals is so critical. We've gone into many firms and asked team members, "What could the firm do to make you more successful and happy in your job?" Eighty percent of the time, people tell us that they don't know why they're at the firm or what the firm is trying to achieve.

In a 30-person firm on the East Coast, the employees reported being satisfied, fairly compensated, and treated well. Yet when asked what would make them and the firm more productive and successful, they unanimously answered, "We want to know why we're here and what we're trying to accomplish." When told that his people were confused about their purpose, the founder said, "Why in the world do they need to know that?" He knew why he was there. He assumed everyone else did, too.

If you want invested, engaged team members who passionately pursue their work, you must give them something they can invest in and focus their contributions on. Steve Jobs said, "If you are working on something exciting that you really care about, you don't have to be pushed. The vision pulls you."

It has to be about more than money. As management consultants, we are as attuned to financial goals as anyone; however, not many people we know wake up each day and say, "I'm so excited, if I work incredibly hard this year, firm assets will grow by 10 percent. I just can't wait to sprint out of bed and rush into the office." The vision has to be inspirational for you and your team.

Once you draft your vision, values, and goals, hold a meeting and share them with your team. Distribute a copy of your planning document, in whatever form it takes, and walk your team through it. You might introduce it by saying, "We're taking the firm to new heights, and your investment is key. Here's what we're doing, why we're doing it, and how we think the plan will proceed. This is the mountain we're going to climb. This is why we're here and what we want to become and achieve. This is how we will measure our progress, this is the reward we will receive when we get there, and these are the values that we will hold ourselves to as we do this important work."

Every firm has its own personality and style: reflect it in your decisions, in the document that captures them, and in how you deliver the message to your team.

Creating a Culture of Alignment

Many advisory firms have drafted vision or mission statements and goals, only to have them disappear and languish in bottom drawers. To become a great firm, you have to live your vision, values, and goals by making sure that everything you and your team do is in alignment with them.

Advisors and their staffs need to measure every action and decision against the standards set by the vision, values, and goals. You and your staff should repeatedly ask, "Does the action/decision align with our values? Will the action/decision result in getting closer to achieving the firm's goals?" An example of a common case of misalignment between action and goals: A client firm had a minimum account size of $750,000 and an average account size of $330,000. The stated minimum was more a desire than a standard. This firm's advisors made frequent exceptions to the minimum and took on nearly anyone who came their way. A quick review of the new clients from the previous three-year period revealed that 80 percent of them did not meet the firm's minimum. Following this planning process, the advisors recognized that their behavior did not align with their vision to become a boutique wealth management firm or their goal of increasing the average account size to $500,000 and their average account size for new clients to $1 million.

These misalignments don't exist because their values are false, but because years of ad hoc decisions and practices have become institutionalized and obscured the firm's underlying values. To uncover these, firms must measure their reality against their values by constantly asking, "If these are our core values and this is fundamentally why we exist, what are the obstacles that get in our way?"

It's crucial to enlist your team's help by creating a safe environment for them to point out misalignments. First, it's a good way to get the team invested in the firm's vision. Second, team members will no doubt see misalignments that you have overlooked.

For example, one firm's purpose was to simplify its clients' financial lives. Yet the staff pointed out that the firm started its planning process with a 17-page questionnaire. In another case, the staff pointed out that although the firm claimed to cater to sophisticated high-net-worth clients, the office had marks on the walls, mismatched chairs, and outdated furniture.

We suggest that you ask each individual on your team to identify something in his or her daily work that's inconsistent with the firm's vision, values, and goals. Once all of their input is gathered, create a list of the misalignments and inconsistencies. Then ask the team to come up with the three most significant misalignments pertaining to each core value from the list. Typically, each group will identify the same or similar ones. This process lets you quickly identify—without pointing fingers—the four or five most significant misalignments. Ask your team to suggest how to fix these. If you address and correct the problems promptly, that will go a long way to getting your firm on track and will show your team that you're serious about having a values-driven organization.

If your goal is acquainting new employees with the firm's culture, it's not enough to say it. True alignment would be to make a statement, followed up by a plan of action: "On their first day on the job, all new employees will receive an orientation on what this organization is about. They will study its history and learn its purpose, vision, values, and goals. At the end of the orientation, they will have lunch with a principal to explore what they learned and discuss what it means to their work, their position, and their team and what has now become their business as well."

Such an alignment process turns ideas, wishes, and wants into specific and concrete actions that drive a firm's ability to achieve its goals. In this case, a few hours of investment can transform what would be an ordinary employee into an individual who demonstrates an extraordinary investment in the firm's success.

Reinforce and Reward

When advisors ignore their business plan, mission statement, and goals, it's often because they think these are a waste of time. We find, in some cases, that although the work was completed, these plans never made their way into the ongoing behavior of the firm: there was a failure to adequately reinforce and reward implementation. Would you create a financial plan for a client and then never discuss it? In this sense, the documentation was merely a historical mile marker that captured a moment in time, a view of where the firm wanted to go, but was in no way used to evaluate and make decisions. In that sense, we would totally agree that the exercise was futile.

Define and document the exercise, then distribute across the organization, if it is to have meaning. Although there are as many ways to do this as there are firms, here are a few simple tactics that we've found particularly effective:

- Create a firm vision document that outlines the business strategy, purpose, vision, values, goals, and key business objectives for each year. Some firms choose to go a step further and provide a snapshot of their multiyear plan.
- Create a vision board and post it in a prominent place. This is typically a full-color, poster-size or larger Styrofoam board that outlines the firm's vision, values, goals, and key business objectives. Something of this size cannot get lost or unintentionally filed in a desk drawer. Making it large and prominent also signifies that you mean what it says. We have created many versions of

the vision board. Our favorites are living references, where people physically record updates as they occur. One firm had a thermometer on the board showing the firm's revenue goals. The team colored it red each quarter as the firm progressed toward its goals (it was with dry erase in case they had to take some of the progress back along the way).

- Create and distribute laminated reference cards or other desk reference material, which summarize the firm's purpose, vision, values, and/or goals that everyone keeps in his or her work space. Genworth recently created values boards that are eight-inch-square metal placards that stand upright on people's desks. Each board contains three magnets, reflecting the company's core values: heart, integrity, and excellence.

- Genworth prints and distributes values cards to employees—one color for each of the value statements. They fill in the cards in recognition of when other team members exhibit one of the core values. Each time an employee receives a recognition card, he or she receives a magnet that is one-third of a circle for that value. For example, they stamp the word *heart* on a circular magnet and break it into three pieces. An employee receives one of the three pieces upon recognition for upholding the heart value. Employees receive recognition three times to complete the word. To complete the full set of three values requires nine nominations. The inspiring thing about this approach is that the metal boards sit on your desk, so you see them and the employees around you see them every day, providing a daily reminder and ongoing reinforcement of why and how people work there and what their work helps to accomplish.

- Conduct progress and alignment reviews quarterly, in which you gather the team, share your progress toward goals, and discuss alignment. Take time to discuss and explore what is working, as well as where there is opportunity for improvement.

Having clear vision and values against which to measure decisions and behavior is one way best-practice firms become the best—and how they continue to get better.

CHAPTER 7

Building a Business Blueprint

The Winchester mansion is a California tourism staple. Sarah Winchester, the wife of William Wirt Winchester, the manufacturer of the famous Winchester rifle, fell into a depression after the death of her infant daughter in 1866 and never recovered from the death of her husband in 1881. Grief stricken, she consulted a spiritual medium. The premature deaths, she was told, were the direct result of angry spirits who died by the Winchester rifle, and she likely was the next victim. To avoid a similar fate, Mrs. Winchester was to move west and build a great house for the spirits. Mrs. Winchester followed this advice and moved to the Santa Clara Valley of California, where she secured a piece of property and began to build the mansion. With an unlimited supply of financial resources, Mrs. Winchester commissioned around-the-clock construction that continued without disruption until her death 38 years later.

This unrelenting effort created a sprawling mansion rambling over six acres and containing 160 rooms, 2,000 doors, 10,000 windows, 47 stairways, 47 fireplaces, and 13 bathrooms. It is a cacophony of architectural oddities, including one of its most notable architectural features: a third-story staircase that leads to a doorway opening directly to the outside, with no porch to stop one from falling to the ground below. Mrs. Winchester built based on her nightly séances and simple sketches of building ideas. There were never any blueprints drawn. Each day she and her foreman examined her newest ideas, making the changes or additions needed to accommodate her desires.

Many financial advisory firms take a similarly haphazard approach to building their businesses. Advisors forge ahead in the direction of their vision and goals, with no blueprint to guide their efforts. Again, many of these advisors are successful, but this book isn't about building a good practice: it is about following the best practices for building a better advisory business. More particularly, it's about how to build your very best business, whatever that means to you.

Unlike Mrs. Winchester, most advisory firms don't have unlimited financial resources. A detailed blueprint helps them focus and direct to the very best effect the time, resources, and energy they invest in building their businesses.

What is an advisory firm version of the Winchester mansion? It has a sprawling, eclectic mix of clients and staff members—all pulled together based on the demands of any particular day or period. The staff members do whatever work happens to come across their desks on any given day, and the advisors try to complete the day's activities as these unfold before them in real time.

Advisors certainly can reach their goals this way, but it will take much longer, create more confusion, and require more energy than if they were to begin with a clear plan of execution. Imagine deciding to drive from California to New York, confident in the general direction but without a map or a plan of where you'll go and what stops you'll make along the way. You will eventually get there but without knowing how long it will take and how much it will cost. It would be so much more efficient to let a GPS navigate your every move and not have to rely on your instinct and intuition.

A Blueprint for Your Best Business

Transforming a firm's vision and goals into a detailed set of directions for building the business and achieving the desired outcomes requires a business blueprint. The blueprint flows from a firm's vision and goals, breaking down the business into quantifiable, comparative, and measurable individual components.

The key components outlined in the rest of this chapter provide concrete details on how the moving parts of an advisory firm work individually and as part of an integrated whole. In this way, advisors can "run the numbers" to assess the impact a decision will have on the overall business plan and whether that component will distract from the firm's goals or build toward them.

The business blueprint spells out how to achieve each business goal. Ideally, we develop two blueprints for our advisory clients: one showing their current business construct, and one showing how their best business (as defined by the vision and the goals) should be constructed. From there, we can easily identify gaps that exist between the two and make key business decisions to address them.

Although firms may choose to build their blueprints differently, those we construct generally include the following components:

- *Business vision.* As discussed in the previous chapter, while keeping the end in mind, clearly articulate the business vision. In particular, we recommend defining a business value goal to help ensure that the firm builds and realizes maximum value.
- *Business structure.* Identify the business structure or practice model that you want for your firm. Whether it's a solo, a silo, or an ensemble, defining the

practice model ultimately determines the number of advisors you will have and the scalability of the business you are building. If you want to change your model by transitioning from a solo practice to a silo firm or from a silo to an ensemble firm, or expand your ensemble into a multioffice franchise, reflect this in the business structure.

- *Business strategy.* Business strategy describes what you do and for whom, how you do it, and compensation. If the goal is to be the dominant firm in your area, this suggests a very different size and scale of firm than if the goal is to be a specialized boutique. If a firm provides investment management services or comprehensive wealth management, if it services a niche of corporate executives or mom-and-pop business owners, all of these factors greatly affect the services delivered, how they are delivered, who delivers them, and what is charged in return for them.

- *Business planning.* Here, we establish the specific goals and objectives of the business so that they remain ever-present targets against which we measure progress and performance. They have specific and measurable time frames and are assigned accountability owners. As discussed in the previous section, business planning should organize around the idea of how to get from where you are to where you want to go. That is, how does the firm best leverage its time and talent to develop and drive toward successful achievement of a plan.

- *Financial model.* A firm's financial model consists of multiple parts working together to ensure the financial success and stability of the business. A more detailed summary of each component follows:

  - *Revenue model.* What are the firm's sources of revenue in terms of fee versus commission income, who is generating the revenue, and what is the goal for growth in revenue?

  - *Revenue mix.* This represents the firm's revenue stream, by type, in both percentages and actual dollars. For example, a Registered Investment Advisor (RIA) will have only fee revenue, where a hybrid RIA may have fee and commission revenue, and a commission-only advisor transitioning to fees will have a shifting percentage of each. Defining and measuring this mix, where it exists, against the goal is important to defining what services and clients the firm will serve.

  - *Revenue drivers.* Anyone who sources new business is a revenue driver or "income engine." Defining how many income engines exist and are desired in the future helps provide a framework for revenue growth. For example, the founder of a $1 billion firm was tired of being the only income engine. This portion of the blueprint exercise helped him set a goal of having another revenue driver deliver 30 percent of new revenue growth within a three-year period, which in turn made the path forward clearer.

    Such a level of clarity and specificity helps him develop a clear view of the desired position, including the qualifications, skills, and level of experience required for someone who could reasonably achieve this goal. We also set a clear goal to share with the new employee. He also could measure the hire against this. We looked at the financial implications in order to design an appropriate compensation plan for the position. The firm's blueprint denoted two revenue drivers and highlighted a transition of 100 percent from the founder to 70 percent during a three-year time horizon. By clearly defining that one simple component, the firm was able to intelligently engage in a series of decisions that would ultimately support its ability to meet the goal.

Without a blueprint, the advisor would probably say, "I'm tired of driving all of the revenue in this firm; I really need to get someone in here to help," and would either do nothing, hire someone whose resume happened across his desk, or start looking for someone without a full picture of the impact this new role would have. The approach we described isn't common, but it is a best practice.

- *Growth model.* This defines the firm's growth projections, including the revenue mix, the revenue drivers, and a projected growth rate during a specific time horizon. Firms can get even more detailed and categorize growth across the client base as well. During the blueprint process, one firm, for example, realized that it needed to decrease the percentage of clients under its minimum and drive all new growth from clients above the minimum.

This decision allowed the firm to project the growth model more accurately. For example, the advisors could see that revenue from smaller clients would decline, and they needed to pace this against new client inflow to maintain revenue and profit levels throughout the transition. The results suggested the process would take four to five years. The firm decided against transitioning smaller clients out gradually, in favor of bundling and selling them via a revenue-sharing arrangement to a younger advisor in the area. Because of the advanced planning, the process went smoothly and comfortably for the firm.

To determine whether the growth model would also meet the firm's profitability goal of 30 percent, we drew on information from the economic model section of the blueprint to estimate the amount of revenue available for direct and indirect expenses. Based on the economic model guidelines set by the firm—35 percent allocated to direct expenses, 35 percent allocated to indirect expenses, and 30 percent dropping to the bottom line—it became clear that if the firm were to grow as projected and incur the estimated staffing costs, it would not meet its profitability goal. That led the firm to increase its account minimums and fees to drive growth based on larger clients, not on more clients. That in turn reduced the numbers of advisors and staff required to support the client base. Without this information, the firm simply would have grown and its executives would have hired more people and wondered why the firm's profit margin wasn't also growing.

- *Economic model.* A firm's economic model clearly defines a firm's financial flow, that is, how top-line revenue flows to the bottom line. This includes the following:
  - *Revenue.* All money that flows into a firm from business activities, including fees and commissions, net of any broker-dealer fees where applicable.
  - *Direct expenses.* Rewards for professional labor, including base compensation for owner and nonowner professional staff. This includes both salary (fixed expense) and incentives or commissions (variable expense), as well as any referral fees, solicitor fees, or commissions paid for sourcing new business (certified public accountant [CPA] alliances, custodian referral programs, etc.).

    Many advisors aren't clear about just what direct expenses are and how they relate to total owner income. Direct expenses are professional labor costs associated with the performance of an advisor's duties, whether the advisor is an owner or nonowner. These expenses are not the same as profits taken by owners as a return for their risk taken. Total owner income is a combination of the owner's fixed and variable compensation, as well as profits distributed. We also recommend further breaking down this category to reflect owner expense and nonowner direct expense to appropriately classify and capture total owner's income.
  - *Indirect expenses.* Also known as overhead expenses, indirect expenses include nonprofessional labor costs incurred by a firm. So, for purposes of the economic model, we break indirect expenses into two categories:
    1. *Indirect—overhead.* All general and administrative expenses, including office facilities, technology costs, marketing costs, and the like.
    2. *Indirect—staffing.* All administrative and support staff (nonprofessional) compensation, including benefits.
  - *Operating profit.* Any cash flow that remains after all direct and indirect expenses are paid.

    The primary reason for categorizing firm financials this way is to help you manage your business and its financial health more effectively. This model, albeit simpler than the other financial reports we recommend that advisors review (income statements, balance sheets, cash flow statements), provides a relevant and straightforward view of the business that can be easily measured against goals and peer benchmarks. Advisors are often surprised when they learn how we build out the economic model for a firm. How much advisors take home is usually their only measure of success, but that can be simplistic.

    Perhaps the biggest obstacle to adopting the economic model is how advisors categorize and take their compensation. Many don't separate their advisor labor compensation, the pay for performing their professional role, from their ownership returns or the reward for risk taken. The result is that advisors often "take what's left," masking an unprofitable business. Some advisors take all or most of their compensation as profit distributions for tax purposes, showing that the firm has little or no professional labor costs. Still others take all of their compensation in wages and incentives, leaving the firm with no profits to report in its profit-and-loss (P&L) statement. Although these strategies can have tax advantages, they don't provide a realistic view of the business and can obscure whether a firm is spending appropriate amounts on professional wages and realizing a fair profit.

Tax returns aside, a good way to get a clear view of the health of a firm's financial model is to allocate to the direct expense and operating profit categories the total owner income taken, based on fair market value and circumstances.

For example, an advisor whose total owner income is $350,000, taken entirely in profit distributions (no W-2 wages), appears to have no professional labor costs and seems to be highly profitable, when in fact the reality might be very different. To get a better view of financial performance, the advisor might allocate $200,000 of the total compensation taken to direct expenses for owner/advisor compensation, leaving the $150,000 balance to show up as profits. This approach allows the advisor to consider the anticipated replacement cost of professional labor, while getting a clear view into the firm's profitability, which in turn drives value.

The advisor's total income is unchanged and more appropriately allocated within the financial model. This may not seem important, and if you're a solo advisor with no plans to sell or add other advisors, it may not be. But for advisors who wish to add other advisors and/or build and realize business value, these numbers have a great deal of meaning.

For example, if a firm spends 60 percent on direct expenses, when the industry average is 40 percent, and has a profit margin of 5 percent when the industry average is 18 percent, it would be clear that the firm was not generating an appropriate return on its professional labor costs. This quickly allows the firm not only to determine what is happening, but also to question and discover why it is happening. In this case, the advisors are clearly not managing enough revenue relative to their compensation. This leads to another series of questions: Is one advisor (often the founder) managing most of the revenue, with another, less productive advisor providing support? Are the firm's income engines driving insufficient revenue to bring the direct expense ratio into proportion? Or are the advisors simply overcompensated relative to the fair market value for their work?

Allocating revenue into a basic economic model (Figure 7.1) provides more insight than you might think. This fundamental information can lead to decisions that transform a firm's productivity, performance, and profitability.

FIGURE 7.1 The Economic Model

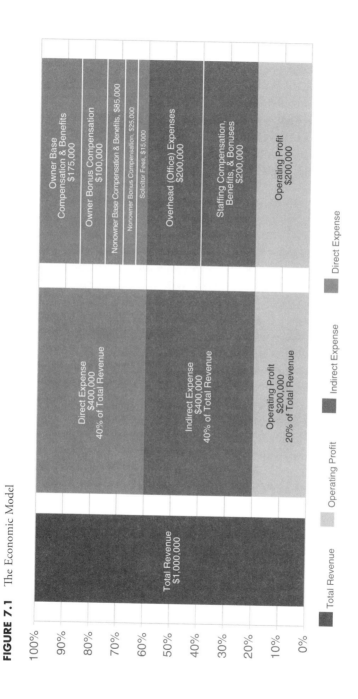

- *Client model.* The client model defines the type, number, and segment of the firm's client base, together with key ratios:
  - *Client type(s).* For whom does or will the firm provide its services? If a firm strictly provides investment management, it has only one type of client. A firm has distinct types of clients if the firm provides investment management services to some clients; hourly or fee-based financial planning services independent of investment management to others; and a comprehensive suite of services that includes planning, investing, insurance, tax, and the like to still other clients. We recommend categorizing clients by type and identifying the number of clients in each category, the percentage of revenue and/or assets under management (AUM) from each type, and other pertinent information. This allows the firm to determine which types of clients are most productive and most profitable, and that in turn can drive decisions on how to service clients and how to staff and grow the firm.
  - *Client segments.* Segmentation creates categories of clients based on a classification process. Firms commonly use categories such as A, B, and C clients or Platinum, Gold, and Silver. Alternatively, we have established an industry standard client segmentation tier system to allow for consistency across firms and the eventual development of benchmarks around client services and profitability.
  - *Client standards.* Using these client segment definitions, firms evaluate and establish appropriate standards or measures for their client base, such as account minimums, average account size, and revenue per client to provide additional insight into client base performance. We will explore account minimums and client benchmarks further, but the relationship between and among the client standards is as important in the blueprint process as the standards themselves. We evaluate this in the context of the remaining components of the business blueprint.

    One advisory client discovered through the blueprint process that the firm's account minimum was met by only 60 percent of the client base, and further review showed that two of the firm's three advisors were greatly skewing that number up by serving clients who didn't meet the standard, while the third held firmly to the minimum. The other two learned to their surprise that although the third advisor had fewer clients, he had greater revenue per client, resulting in fewer work hours and a more profitable client base. In this same firm, we established and evaluated client benchmarks to establish goals for growth in revenue per client and a decrease in the percentage of clients under the minimum for the two advisors who weren't making the standard.

- *Pricing model.* This is how the firm charges for various services and the associated benchmarks, such as average basis points (bps) charged to all clients, as well as different types or tiers of clients. With one advisory firm client, for example, we determined that the firm's average bps had declined each year for the preceding three years. Further exploration of the client base revealed that the firm had been taking on larger clients, and based on the breakpoints in the pricing model, fees were trending down. Yet revenue, assets, and profitability were trending up. When we analyzed what was going on in this four-partner firm and broke out the average fees per client tier per advisor, we discovered that one advisor was charging in line with the firm's fee schedule and the remaining three had average fees of 20 to 40 percent less. Interestingly, the advisors—who had formed an ensemble after a successful silo period—all had roughly the same asset base, yet the advisor with the higher average fees generated more revenue and profit.

In another firm, we determined that a comprehensive wealth manager was charging fees similar to pure investment managers, and that it actually cost $9,000 on average to deliver $11,000 worth of services to clients. All of the advisors were surprised to see this in the pricing model of the blueprint. As a result, the firm carefully designed and executed a pricing increase across the different client segments to bring each more in line with the firm's goals and industry benchmarks. The result was a 12 percent increase in annualized revenue. Only one client left because of the change.

- *Team model.* This section of the blueprint identifies key standards and thresholds for advisors and their teams, influencing how a firm structures its teams. This exercise is simple for a solo practice, because it has only one team, but perhaps not so for ensemble firms with distinct advisor teams and dedicated staff and specialist support. This component of the blueprint should be carefully crafted to meet the specifics of your firm and may include:
  - *Criteria per advisor/team.* This component establishes specific criteria (in revenue, assets, or profits, etc.) that advisors must reach to contribute to firm performance. One large advisory firm, for example, set the standard that a full client team would manage a minimum of $750,000 and would consist of a senior advisor or partner, a junior advisor, and a client service assistant. Revenue thresholds were then set to determine when a junior advisor would transition from being part of a team to starting his own, and after doing so, at what point he would be able to add staff and ultimately become a senior advisor himself.
  - *Team benchmarks.* Although different firms may choose different benchmarks, we calculate key performance indicators to show advisor and staff productivity, using them to improve growth and/or productivity. In one instance, we calculated team benchmarks such as clients per advisor, clients per staff, revenue per client (average), and revenue per staff (average). Armed with this information, we vetted the firm's growth goals against the team model and determined how many advisors and staff would be required to support the firm's projected growth.
- *Principal/Partner goals:* Because one of the objectives of the business is to deliver value to its stakeholders (owners), as well as to its clients, this component of the blueprinting process is critical. Although every stakeholder has his

or her own set of qualitative goals, we recommend defining and capturing any and all quantitative goals so that they can be evaluated, measured, and managed, including:

- *Total owner income.* Reflected in total income received from the firm in any form, it's the amount you want to withdraw from the business through wages, incentives, commissions, profits, and other personal expenses.
- *Time off.* Measure this by days out of the office when not engaged in business activity. One principal spent a lot of time out of the office but noticed she was always working and never had a chance to relax and recharge her batteries. To address her need for dedicated down time, we created "Out days" (days she was out but was available for contact) and "Off days" (days she was out and not available) and scheduled her calendar to reflect both, enabling her and her staff to determine when they could contact her and when they needed to let her fall off the radar. The simple act of defining the goal and distinguishing between the two types of days created a dramatic improvement in the principal's peace of mind and quality of life.
- *Client focus.* Define which clients you want to work with. In one advisory firm, after 16 years of supporting every client, the principal decided that he needed more of an intellectual challenge. To this end, he defined a category of clients he wanted to work with who would be more fulfilling to him. In defining this goal, the principal decided that it was time to advance a planning associate to a junior advisor and then to the associate advisor position. By identifying what he wanted to accomplish first, the blueprint process helped him decide how he would be able to accomplish it.
- *Activity focus.* Define how you spend your time. A partner in a large firm realized that he truly enjoyed and excelled at rainmaking, but that the firm's financial and compensation models were calculated based on revenue managed versus revenue sourced. After talking with the other partners about the importance and value of sourcing business, and the reality that this is perhaps the hardest skill set to acquire in a firm, the partner convinced the firm to redefine the financial, compensation, and team models. It quickly became clear that everyone benefited from this change. The advisor was able to capitalize on his talents, and the firm revenue improved as a result. The blueprint process let the firm evaluate what would happen if it changed its compensation model to value rainmaking as an activity separate and apart from servicing clients.

The business blueprint may seem like another form of a business plan. The key difference is that a business plan lays out the decisions, with no mechanism for vetting how they will affect one another and the firm. The power of the business blueprint process is not in any one component—although, from the examples provided, we suspect you can see the value in this function alone. The real power of the blueprint process is realized when the combined data are reviewed, evaluated, and used to make informed decisions across the business. As the previous examples show, there is almost never one piece of information that leads to one decision. Rather, a decision related to any component of the blueprint almost always requires reviewing other components as well.

In consulting engagements, we develop a written business blueprint that outlines all of the above, together with a detailed model that captures all of the quantitative data, reflective of both the current firm and the future firm, based on its vision and goals. In almost every case, firms realize that their decisions are not harmonious and congruent, and that the resulting friction is a source of lost productivity, performance, and profits.

Business Blueprint Case Study: Rising Tyde Advisors

To illustrate how the components of the business blueprint work, we have provided the following example.

John Rising and Dan Tyde are solo practitioners who joined forces in 2002 to form Rising Tyde Advisors. They operate under a silo model and now wish to merge into an ensemble firm to maximize their talents and expertise. John has 140 clients and annual revenue of $900,000, all of which is fee based. Dan has 160 clients and revenue of $1,200,000, 80 percent of which is fee based and 20 percent commission based. They are the firm's only advisors. They have a support staff of six, including a part-time intern, an administrative assistant, a client service manager, an operations manager, a portfolio manager, and a part-time research assistant. John is 58, and Dan is 53.

Business Vision and Goals
- Build a highly respected, boutique wealth management firm with a business value of $3 million within seven years.
- Grow fee-based revenue to $1.5 million over five years.
- Realize a 30 percent profit margin within three years.
- Double the average fee-based account size to $1 million.

Business Strategy
- Services: Boutique wealth management firm offering comprehensive, integrated advice to high-net-worth executives and their families.
- Position/Differentiator: Leading boutique serving executives in coastal southern California communities.

Business Structure
- Hybrid registered investment advisor (RIA), with the goal to transition to a pure RIA and fee-only model.
- Entity type: S corporation.

Financial Model
- Revenue Model: 100 percent fee-based business within five years.
- Economic model: 35 percent direct/35 percent indirect/30 percent profit.
- $775,000 in revenue per wealth management team.

Client Model
- Account minimum: $1 million.
- Average account size: $500,000 (current); goal $750,000.
- Number of clients served: 200 total, 100 clients per wealth management team.

Team Model
- Two partners to focus on tier 1 clients (largest) and rainmaking.
- One service advisor to support partners' tier 1 client relationships and manage all tier 2 and below client relationships (approximately 150).
- Two paraplanners to support service advisor in financial planning processes and investments (through a third-party asset manager [TAMP] relationship).
- One operations/business manager.
- One client service assistant.
- One receptionist.
- Two part-time "intern" positions.

Partner Goals
- Total partner compensation, excluding value, of $500,000 per year.
- Six weeks of vacation per partner each year.
- Focus on rainmaking, client meetings, and CEO functions.

Doing the Math

Typically, you need at least two data points to calculate how to make your strategy work, and more is better. Yet you can do it with only two. One of these must be the economic model, because this determines where and how much of the money can go to different parts of the business, and that is key in deciding how to put the pieces together.

Rising Tyde wants to build a business value of $3 million. Using a multiple of earnings (MOE) model to calculate how much they need to make to reach that goal, reasonably estimating six times earnings, to generate a $3 million sale price, the firm needs to produce free cash flow or pretax profits of $500,000 year.

When you do the math, the firm needs a $1.7 million practice, at a 30 percent margin, to produce $500,000 in earnings. If the firm's goal is to have an average account size of $750,000, then it's easy to see that it needs 200 clients to reach that revenue goal. The lower the average account size, the more clients the firm will need.

We can then quickly determine that at 35 percent of revenue going to direct expenses (advisor labor), this provides $595,000 for advisor compensation, including both owners and the service advisor. This also provides 35 percent for indirect expenses, including overhead and staffing. In this case, the firm's model allocated 20 percent to staffing, or $340,000. After the remaining 15 percent allocation to overhead, that leaves $510,000 for profits. Assuming the partners allocated 10 percent of this to an incentive compensation pool for their team, that would leave roughly $460,000 for the two partners.

With this information in hand, the firm can now decide if this is a model that works for them. This model has obviously been worked out so that the math synchronizes, but in the majority of cases, there is a process of checks and balances that helps a firm set its decisions in accordance with its goals. In the most common example, the number of clients, at the firm's average account size, almost never drives the desired revenue—resulting in an increase in average client size goals (which leads to a series of related business decisions around minimums, smaller clients, etc.) or in the number of clients (which has implications to the staffing model and the overhead structure that must be considered relative to the profit margin). One can quickly see how discussions of target clients, account minimums, pricing, staffing models, and levels of service—all in the context of realistic goals based on what the firm is willing to do—can quickly become center stage of this planning process.

The basic idea is that with a clear vision and goals, the framework for the business blueprint, and as few as two data points (assuming one of them is the economic model), you can calculate on paper what you need to do to accomplish your vision and goals.

Next, advisors have to calculate where they stand now, by doing the same exercise for their current business, and identify the gaps between the current firm and the goal. If a firm has revenue of $1 million and a goal of $2.5 million, that means it needs to add $1.5 million in revenue. If the current average client account is $400,000, however, and his future account size is $1 million, then the firm must either shift its focus to larger clients to make the blueprint work or adjust the goals.

Once you establish a clear blueprint, you can proceed on your path with confidence. The ability to plot progress relative to goals—as they shift and change—is important to effectively navigate the journey from where you are to where you want to be. This will help keep you on track and accountable for achieving your goals. When you combine your vision, values, and goals with this blueprint process and with benchmarking, which we will cover in the next chapter, you will have a model for success—a very powerful business management and information process.

CHAPTER 8

Managing Business Performance

For many financial advisors, the business is the largest asset they own. This asset generates both income and value:

- *Personal income.* Compensation for the role of financial advisor.
- *Business profits.* Free cash flow left after all income and expenses are met.
- *Business value.* The value of the firm realized upon sale or succession.

Most financial advisors spend their professional careers acquiring clients, gathering assets, and generating revenue. Like most entrepreneurs, they focus on what they do well and enjoy—rainmaking and managing client relationships. As a result, they tend to focus narrowly on top-line measures of revenue, assets, and compensation. Although this can generate a healthy income and a nice lifestyle, it does little to manage the business and make the most of it as an asset.

Few advisors have a disciplined process for managing their business financials and for using the resulting analysis to identify issues, recognize trends, and adjust their business practices based on what they learn. Yet the more information you have about what's happening in your business and why, from a financial perspective, the better able you are to adjust and make changes that maximize revenue, income, profits, and value.

Take Me to the Top Line

Shifting focus from top-line measures of revenue, assets, and clients to incorporate bottom-line performance will reveal much more about a firm's profitability. Top-line measures are important, but they are more a reflection of business strategy, sales, and marketing than of business management, operational efficiency, and financial performance. A firm's ability to establish financial management and controls to ensure effective use of revenue is just as important.

For example, we had a client firm that saw extraordinary year-over-year growth of greater than 50 percent. Driven by a desire to grow the firm, the owner unfortunately spent every penny of revenue. He continuously assured us that the firm would grow its way into profitability, just as soon as it reached the next revenue and asset goals. As they reached those targets, however, profitability failed to improve. Advisory firms can't grow their way to profitability if their original spending habits haven't changed. A healthy portion of fast-growing firms make the mistake of believing that, with higher revenue, profitability will follow. However, in the majority of cases we have seen, this has not happened.

And the firm continues to have a problem being profitable regardless of how much revenue they bring in. This problem does not affect only fast-growing firms; firms of any size can face the dilemma of how to best manage capital and resources as they grow.

Fundamentals of Financial Management

Financial management is a disciplined process for using financial data and information to evaluate business performance. Financial management gives advisors an objective way to gauge their business health, performance, and value.

To this end, best-practice firms will educate themselves and build business practices in two key areas:

1. Financial accounting and reporting.
2. Performance benchmarking.

The purpose of instituting financial management in a firm is to:

• Create an effective and objective review of the firm's financial performance and health.
• Identify business challenges, opportunities, and key trends.
• Objectively measure progress and performance against goals.
• Adjust business strategy and practices to maximize business success and financial performance.

With a disciplined financial management process that provides clear and objective data on firm performance, advisors have a wealth of information to help them make more intelligent and informed choices about how to build, manage, and grow their firms.

Fundamentals of Accounting

Given their profession, most advisors understand the basics of accounting, and some regularly review financial statements. Nonetheless, we find there is still a fairly large contingent of financial advisors who work hard all year, take out income as needed, and see what remains at year end with little or no regard for financial management and reporting.

An East Coast firm with a $2 million annual gross but no accounting software came to us for coaching. The owner's assistant wrote checks manually and manually entered them into a general ledger. She balanced the checkbook periodically and turned the check stubs over to the accountant at year end. Often, the owner's personal expenses commingled with the business accounts and the credit cards. With these antiquated accounting methods, the owner didn't realize he was withdrawing $1 million a year from the business. When funds were running low, the assistant would tell the owner, who would launch his considerable rainmaking prowess to produce new revenue. Before we could even begin to put financial management and reporting in place, we had to help the firm establish basic accounting procedures. We developed a plan to bifurcate personal and business expenses, bring in QuickBooks software, set up a chart of accounts, put the owner on a regular pay schedule, and hire a bookkeeper to maintain the accounting in coordination with the certified public accountant (CPA).

This section will briefly review the fundamentals of financial accounting as an effective starting point for financial management. We recommend that advisors consult with their tax and accounting professionals on this subject. In addition, for a thorough review of financial accounting and reporting, you may want to read *Practice Made (More) Perfect*, written by Mark Tibergien and Rebecca Pomering.[1] We offer a brief synopsis of their teaching in the following "Key Financial Statements" section.

Key Financial Statements

Advisory firms should produce three financial statements for monthly review:

- Balance sheet.
- Income statement, also referred to as a profit-and-loss (P&L) statement.
- Cash flow statement.

Each of these statements reports on different but related information, which, when viewed together, can transform financial data into a story about the underlying performance of the business. In *Practice Made Perfect*, Tibergien and Pomering accurately describe the typical situation: "Unfortunately, most owners of advisory firms regard the balance sheet as a cover page and the income statement as a scorecard. They look to either the bottom line or the top line to see how it tallies and then file the statement away."

The reality is that, in spite of their profession, most advisors find the financial side of their own business boring and laborious. We believe, however, that's because advisors don't recognize the rich story offered by the data contained in these statements and so set them aside for what they perceive to be more interesting and valuable activities.

Balancing Act

A balance sheet is a financial statement that summarizes a company's assets, liabilities, and shareholder's equity at a specific point in time. These three components provide a view into what the company owns, what it owes, and the amounts invested by the shareholders. A balance sheet must follow this formula:

$$\text{Assets} = \text{Liabilities} + \text{Shareholder equity}$$

It stands to reason the two sides must balance, given that a company has to pay for its assets by either borrowing money (liabilities) or by obtaining money from shareholders (shareholders' equity).

Each of the three components contained in a balance sheet will consist of underlying accounts that document the value of each.

The *asset side of the balance sheet* is comprised of current assets and fixed assets. Accounts such as cash, inventory, and property fall on the asset side of the balance sheet.

- *Current assets* convert to cash in one year or less.
- *Fixed assets* include items such as equipment, fixtures, furniture, leasehold improvements, and other assets necessary for business operations that do not convert to cash.

Work-in-process (WIP) is a recognizable asset when you perform billable work for a client but have yet to invoice it (a current asset). Tibergien notes that tracking WIP is important because the work consumes a lot of cash. In a financial advisory firm's working-capital cycle, it gets the client first, and then it produces the work, bills for the service, and collects the fee."

The *liability side of the balance sheet* consists of current liabilities, long-term debt, and equity.

Current liabilities are a firm's short-term debt or obligations due within one year. Current liabilities include short-term debt, accounts payable, accrued liabilities, and other debts. This includes retainer fees earned by advisors.

Long-term debt represents loans and financial obligations due in more than one year. It includes mortgages, notes, and obligations related to practice acquisitions; long-term financing for items such as equipment; and other obligations.

Equity represents the amount of funds contributed by the owners (stockholders), plus the retained earnings (or losses), and may be referred to as shareholder equity. New capital contributions or retained earnings (profits that are retained by the business and not distributed to owners) are the sources of equity.

Inside the Income Statement

The income statement, or profit and loss statement as it's more commonly called, is the measure of a company's financial performance during a specific period of accounting. Typically, financial advisors turn to the P&L to understand their revenue, expenses, and owner's income—that which remains after expenses are paid. This view provides basic information about your earnings, expenses, and profit or loss. Although it will tell you where the money went in terms of entries into the chart of accounts, it won't tell you where the money flowed across key categories and what that means to how you manage your business.

Most firms obtain information on revenue and expenses through their accounting software or from P&L reports provided by their accountants. If you don't have accounting software, you should immediately put down this book, leave your office, and buy a program. (QuickBooks is the most common.) The software is inexpensive, easy to learn, and even easier—and preferable—to outsource. Local bookkeepers and accountants can quickly set up your software and provide ongoing bookkeeping services.

Once your financial information is readily accessible, you can gain significant benefits by reviewing it on a regular basis. One quick and simple way to review this data and hence the health of your firm is in a view of the income statement we call the economic model, which we introduced in the previous chapter.

The economic model puts your P&L into distinct categories:

- *Economic model.* A firm's economic model clearly defines its financial flow, that is, how top-line revenue flows to the bottom line. This includes:
  - *Revenue.* All money that flows into a firm from business activities, including fees and commission, net any broker-dealer's fees.
  - *Direct expenses.* The cost for professional labor, including base compensation for owner and nonowner professional staff. This includes both salary (fixed expense) and incentives or commissions (variable expense), as well as any referral fees, solicitor fees, or commissions paid for sourcing new business (CPA alliances, custodian referral programs, etc.).[2]
  - *Gross profit.* The amount of cash remaining after direct expenses are paid. The gross profit is an important number because it determines the amount

of revenue required to cover professional compensation (the service firm's equivalent of cost of goods sold). The remaining cash flow covers your overhead expenses, including staffing costs, and produces a profit.

A simple formula calculates gross profit:

$$\text{Revenue} - \text{Direct expense} = \text{Gross profit}$$

- *Indirect expenses:* Also known as overhead expenses, Indirect Expenses include all nonprofessional labor costs incurred by a firm. For purposes of the economic model, we break indirect expenses into two categories:
  - *Indirect—overhead.* All general and administrative expenses, including office facilities, technology costs, marketing costs, and the like.
  - *Indirect—staffing.* All administrative and support staff (nonprofessional) compensation, including benefits.
- *Operating profit.* Cash flow that remains after all direct and indirect expenses are paid.

A simple view of the economic model would read as follows:

Revenue	All revenue flowing into the firm, net applicable broker-dealer fees
– Direct expenses	Owner and nonowner professional compensation, including salary, incentives, commissions, bonuses, and benefits
= Gross profit	Balance remaining after direct expenses have been covered
– Overhead expenses	All general overhead and staffing expenses
= Operating profit	

Let's review an example of how the economic model would look were a firm to perform in line with the industry benchmark of a typical advisory firm. Findings from our recent "Best Practices: Business Performance" study showed that the typical firm had average direct expenses of 43 percent of revenue, indirect expenses of 36 percent, and a profit margin of 22 percent. Moss Adams and FA Insight studies have consistently reported similar averages. The resulting industry average is 40 percent direct, 40 percent indirect, and 20 percent profit.[3, 4, 5] We'll discuss this more in the benchmarking section but will use it for the example in Figure 8.1.

We worked with a firm that, at first glance, appeared to be doing very well. The owner had a beautiful home in a very affluent neighborhood, sent his children to private schools, and had recently purchased a second lake-front home. Unfortunately, 2008 market downturn occurred, and the client's financial situation took a sudden turn for the worse. Apparently, he had relied on his

FIGURE 8.1 Sample Economic Model

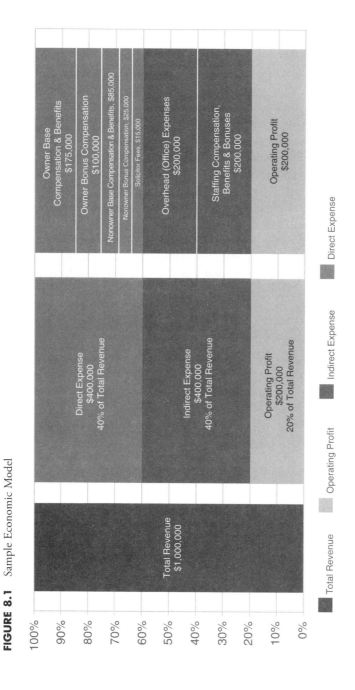

Total Revenue
$1,000,000

Direct Expense
$400,000
40% of Total Revenue

Indirect Expense
$400,000
40% of Total Revenue

Operating Profit
$200,000
20% of Total Revenue

Owner Base
Compensation & Benefits
$175,000

Owner Bonus Compensation
$100,000

Nonowner Base Compensation & Benefits, $85,000

Nonowner Bonus Compensation, $25,000

Solicitor Fees, $15,000

Overhead (Office) Expenses
$200,000

Staffing Compensation,
Benefits & Bonuses
$200,000

Operating Profit
$200,000

Total Revenue   Operating Profit   Indirect Expense   Direct Expense considerable total owner's income as though it were salaried wages, rather than basing the fixed expenses of his lifestyle on his wages and making discretionary purchases with the profits he withdrew at the end of each year. Instead, he took all of his profits as income along the way, leaving no retained earnings in the business for security during times of financial strain. Based on this experience and others like it, we highly encourage advisory firm owners to clearly distinguish between professional compensation for the job performed and owner's profits, and to manage their budgets accordingly.

The market downturn brought many painful lessons to seemingly successful financial advisors. Those who didn't set aside retained earnings (in personal or business accounts) in the good times suffered financial stress in the downturn. This is surprising, given that one of the first things financial advisors tell clients is to spend within their means, save first, and build up an emergency fund of three, and preferably six, months. Yet too frequently, advisors don't follow their own advice.

Every firm felt the effects of the market meltdown and the ensuing recession and market volatility. Yet the firms we had been working with that had put financial management practices in place were able to absorb the downturn with far fewer negative effects.

Imagine that the owner of a $1 million practice took out 40 percent of revenue in professional wages ($400,000), had staffing and overhead expenses of 40 percent (another $400,000), and was left with a profit margin of 20 percent ($200,000). Imagine further that the owner had set aside a percentage of profits for a retained earnings "safety net" to the tune of $200,000 over the previous five years. But what if the firm experiences a sharp asset decrease and revenue of 30 percent for a year? They could maintain the expense structure of the firm without sacrifice, as long as the owner is willing to reduce his compensation by 10 percent ($100,000). Given the firm's prior financial success, sound financial management, and retained earnings of $200,000 (still not equivalent to the minimum three months recommended for clients), the firm could maintain its operating model, including full owner compensation, without change for a full two-year period.

The reality is the above scenario is a far cry from what many advisory firm owners faced. Most had to significantly cut expenses and take a steep or complete cut in personal compensation to keep the staff paid and the doors open. If a firm has no profits and no retained earnings, something will have to give in any sustained revenue decline.

We suspect such circumstances would certainly undercut the firm's credibility with clients if they knew what was going on behind the scenes. If financial advisors sat across from clients and said that they spent their bonuses before they were earned, had no savings to speak of, had no defined goals, and had no real idea just how their money was being spent relative to budgets, the clients might find it prudent to seek out another financial advisor. Once again, we believe the best financial advisors are those who manage their own financial lives as well as they manage those of their clients.

The Rigors of Reporting

A sound financial management process will help you make a realistic, rather than an intuitive, assessment of your business health and will give you information to make informed, intelligent choices about how to grow. To do that, you need to review your financial information on a regular basis, just as you do for your clients. At a minimum, we recommend:

- Monthly reviews of the balance sheet, income statement (P&L), and cash flow statement, for that month and year to date.
- Quarterly reviews of the above, together with firm-specific benchmark reports comparing key performance indicators (KPIs) to peer benchmarks and firm goals. We cover KPIs in Chapter 9.

Unequivocally, every time we put this practice of monitoring and adjusting financial information in place, the result is increased financial performance. That's because when you start managing your financial performance with a goal in mind, you get a little more judicious about where you're spending money and why.

In one instance, as part of our regular financial reporting review, we noticed that a firm was spending what seemed to be an above-average amount on health benefits. When we asked about this, the owners attributed the expense to the fact that they were in a high-cost state (New Jersey). We had other clients in New Jersey who didn't spend as much on benefits, so we encouraged the owners to take a closer look at this expense. We soon found out that the firm, at the recommendation of its health-coverage provider, had enrolled in the most expensive premium plan available. This plan well exceeded the needs of an eight-person firm, and changing their coverage to a lesser plan that still provided good-quality care reduced the firm's expenses by more than $28,000 per year. Until we began to review their expenses, the firm never thought to doubt their assumptions.

Although $28,000 may not seem like a huge savings at first blush, when you consider what investments the firm could have made with that money, the value of those earnings during the business life cycle, or the increased business value they would drive, that amount is certainly significant.

Even good financial advisors who do excellent work for their clients often spend little time, energy, or effort managing the financial affairs of their own businesses. By employing financial management best practices, firms may gain valuable insight and information to make better financial decisions and drive improved results across the business.

CHAPTER 9

Benchmarking: Are You Making Progress?

Athletes continually strive for small increments of improvement, shaving a second off their time, maximizing the percentage of oxygen in their blood, increasing the angle of their swing by a fraction of a degree. Getting better at each of these components is what adds up to a championship game. For athletes and advisors alike, improved performance isn't about more overall effort; it's about being more efficient and effective with targeted, specific efforts. The journey from good to great or better to best isn't driven by an exponential leap, but rather by small, incremental improvements that, when summed, make a big difference.

Many financial advisors just work harder, longer hours to try to move their businesses forward, without any sense of whether and how the parts of their business are working to get them to where they want to be. Financial management is the first part of examining what's working and what's not. Benchmarking goes a step further.

By converting financial data into ratios and monitoring them over time by comparing them to meaningful benchmarks—such as best-practice firms, their peers, and their history—advisors can see precisely where they can gain those incremental improvements or where they are slipping behind.

The Benchmarking Process

A good benchmarking process will help financial advisors identify and understand how their firm is performing across key metrics. It helps establish goals for improved performance and regularly measures performance against those goals and against the standards set by top-performing firms. In short, business benchmarking is a process that helps you make faster, more insightful business decisions with specific business intelligence.

To incorporate the benchmarking process into their businesses, financial advisors can follow these three steps:

1. *Identify key performance indicators.* Create benchmarks by converting financial data into ratios. Establish a set of key performance indicators (KPIs), such as revenue per advisor, assets under management (AUM) per client, clients per employee, acquisition cost per client, and expenses per client, to include in benchmarking reviews. Use these metrics first to establish baselines.
2. *Measure and analyze performance metrics over time.* Monitor key performance metrics on a quarterly basis against budgets, goals, and peers to identify trends and areas of trouble or opportunities for improvement. Calculate the impact of performance gaps on business performance.
3. *Adapt business practices to improve performance.* Armed with sound business intelligence, you can confidently make changes to your business practices that result in big improvements. Continue making adjustments to business practices based on benchmarking reviews.

Each firm will want to identify the performance metrics that best suit its situation, needs, and goals. Figure 9.1 shows a view of the online Financial Dashboard we developed as part of our Best Practices Study Series and that we use with consulting clients. The online system automatically stores and calculates firm data and populates it to a personalized dashboard that benchmarks the firm's performance against its goals and peers.

As you can see, the dashboard provides a fairly exhaustive list of performance metrics as well as underlying metrics affected by changes within the firm.

Benchmarking analysis helps you make more informed and objective decisions about how to manage and grow your firm. For example, if actual revenue per client is $5,700 and the goal revenue per client is $7,500, an advisor might identify the need either to increase or perhaps adhere to minimum account sizes. When the next prospect with $300,000 comes calling, the advisor might decide not to take on this client because he recognizes that although top-line performance measures of revenue and AUM will increase, the revenue per client performance metric will decline, indicating a drop in performance in this area. The firm might examine its average fees and discover fees falling below the firm's goals or peer benchmark averages drive lower revenue per client.

The benchmarking process provides a critical view into the linkage between a firm's behavior (decisions) and its outcomes (results). Given that most financial advisors lack a clear way to define what behaviors and decisions they can change to achieve different results, benchmarking can be an especially valuable business process. It holds a mirror up to the firm that clearly reflects back the outcome of its business behavior and decisions. As advisors make adjustments based on what they learn from this process, benchmarking lets them monitor performance over time to ensure that those changes are in fact making the desired difference.

For example, one client firm set the goal of having every advisor maintain 100 clients and $500,000 in revenue. Benchmarking allowed the firm to see that its average advisor had 120 clients and $280,000 in revenue. Increasing the AUM and the revenue per client became a firm priority. As a result, the firm made a series of changes to drive performance toward this goal. The advisors raised account minimums, adjusted fees on underpriced client relationships, targeted their marketing efforts toward clients who fit their new profile, and modified the firm compensation plan to eliminate payments on incoming business that did not meet the firm's new standards.

By monitoring key ratios over time, the advisors were able to achieve their goals in about two years. There certainly were times they wanted to relapse into taking the easy, small accounts that came their way. Reinforced by the new business practices, they stuck to desired behavior to produce results and, through the benchmarking process, were able to highlight incrementally positive results. Any deviation from the firm's new practice standards was immediately recognized, and resulted in a meeting with the firm partners and denial of compensation.

Benchmarking showed the partners the underlying causes of the business performance. Knowing that, they could make changes to business practices that changed behavior and, in turn, the results.

The following example highlights why advisors should measure each of their key performance metrics on a quarterly basis to help ensure that they're progressing in the right direction. When the 2008 downturn hit, our clients saw a decline in their AUM and revenue metrics. Instead of throwing up hands and saying there was nothing to be done about market decline, we used benchmarking to carefully monitor performance in other areas and to determine change opportunities. In one silo firm, an advisor and his team had nonrevenue performance measures (such as clients per advisor, clients per staff) that were 20 percent better than the other two advisors. We found that his service and operations process made him more efficient. The other teams were able to quickly implement his process to improve their own client service and profitability.

At the same time, all three advisors recognized that their average revenue per client was below their target goal, which was now even lower due to the markets. The advisors had little time to deliver service to high-quality clients and almost no time to market for new clients. On the basis of the benchmarking information, the firm decided to hire a service advisor to support its smaller clients, so that the advisors could spend more time with larger clients to increase referrals and share of wallet. The three partners decided to share the service advisor and the related expense, resulting in a $25,000 per year cost each. In the

FIGURE 9.1 Genworth Online Financial Dashboard

Glossary · Print · PDF · Help · Benchmark: All, 1QA · Reporting: Q1 2009

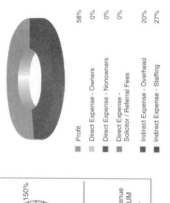

Economic Model

Profit	58%
Direct Expense - Owners	0%
Direct Expense - Nonowners	0%
Direct Expense - Solicitor / Referral Fees	0%
Indirect Expense - Overhead	20%
Indirect Expense - Staffing	27%

SAMPLE DASHBOARD FOR ILLUSTRATIVE PURPOSES ONLY

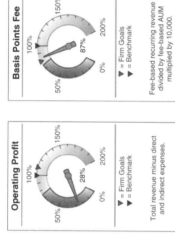

Total Revenue

130%

▼ = Firm Goals
▶ = Benchmark

Total revenue is the firm net of and applicable broker-dealer fees.

Fee-based AUM

85%

▼ = Firm Goals
▶ = Benchmark

Assets under management for which the firm receives recurring fee-based revenue.

Operating Profit

28%

▼ = Firm Goals
▶ = Benchmark

Total revenue minus direct and indirect expenses.

Basis Points Fee

87%

▼ = Firm Goals
▶ = Benchmark

Fee-based recurring revenue divided by fee-based AUM multiplied by 10,000.

Percentage to Benchmark

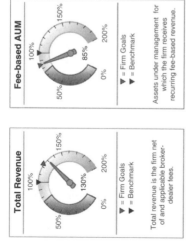

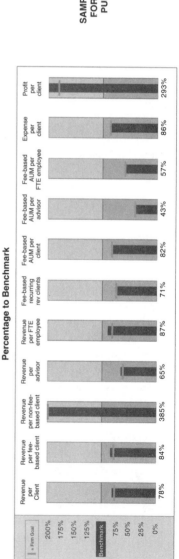

	Revenue per Client	Revenue per fee-based client	Revenue per non-fee-based client	Revenue per advisor	Revenue per FTE employee	Fee-based recurring rev clients	Fee-based AUM per client	Fee-based AUM per advisor	Fee-based AUM per FTE employee	Expense per client	Profit per client
	78%	84%	385%	65%	87%	71%	82%	43%	57%	86%	293%

= Firm Goal

200%
175%
150%
125%
Benchmark
75%
50%
25%
0%

80

Metric	2009 YTD Q1 Annualized	2009 Goal	% to Goal	Benchmark	Actual % to Benchmark	Goal % to Benchmark
Total revenue (annual)	$1,910,000	$1,810,000	106%	$1,464,100	130%	124%
Revenue per client	$10,324	$9,784	106%	$13,177	78%	74%
Revenue per fee-based client	$12,308	$11,538	107%	$14,641	84%	79%
Revenue per non-fee-based client	$5,636	$5,636	100%	$1,464	385%	385%
Revenue per advisor	$955,000	$905,000	106%	$1,464,100	65%	62%
Revenue per FTE employee	$382,000	$362,000	106%	$439,230	87%	82%
Fee-based recurring revenue clients	130	130	100%	$183	71%	71%
Fee-based AUM	$125,000,000	$125,000,000	100%	$146,410,000	85%	85%
Fee-based AUM per client	$961,538	$961,538	100%	$1,171,280	82%	82%
Fee-based AUM per advisor	$62,500,000	$62,500,000	100%	$146,410,000	43%	43%
Fee-based AUM per FTE employee	$25,000,000	$25,000,000	100%	$43,923,000	57%	57%
Expense per client	$3,784	$3,784	100%	$4,392	86%	86%
Profit per client	$4,292	$3,886	110%	$1,464	293%	265%
Clients per advisor	93	93	100%	$256	36%	36%
Clients per FTE employee	37	37	100%	$81	46%	46%
Fee for fee-based clients (basis points)	128	120	107%	$146	87%	82%
Total clients	185	185	100%	$256	72%	72%
Gross profit margin	100%	100%	100%	51%	195%	195%
Operating profit margin	10%	40%	26%	37%	28%	109%
Overhead expenses %	4%	18%	22%	37%	11%	49%
Operating profit per advisor	$397,000	$359,500	110%	$732,050	54%	49%
Operating profit per FTE employee	$158,800	$143,800	110%	$366,025	43%	39%
Gross profit per client	$10,324	$9,784	106%	$10,249	101%	95%

■ = 100% of goal/benchmark or better. ■ = 75% to 99.99% of goal/benchmark or better. ■ = Less than 75% of goal/benchmark or better.

All benchmark data has been calculated using medians.

© 2009 Quantuvis Consulting, Inc. All rights reserved.

TABLE 9.1   Benchmarking Case Study

DATE	TOTAL AUM	TOTAL CLIENTS W/OMP	TOP 10 CLIENTS % OF REV	TOP 20 CLIENTS % OF REV	BOTTOM 50% % OF REF	SEE REV	REV PER CLIENT	AUM PER CLIENT	ASSETS PER ADVISOR	CLIENTS PER ADVISOR	CLIENTS UNDER $75K
	2.2 × AUM	**22% fewer clients**				**2.2× total fees**	**2.5× revenue per client**				**63% fewer clients under $750K**
6/30/2006	$94,985,705	136	28.13%	42.84%	17.94%	$847,984	$6,145	$688,302	$52,769,836	77	97
3/31/2006	$98,886,594	142	26.58%	41.34%	17.36%	$849,412	$5,982	$675,257	$53,270,330	79	99
12/31/2004	$65,880,381	120	27.93%	44.95%	20.54%	$588,902	$5,453	$549,003	$36,600,212	67	94
10/3/2004	$43,019,163	167	25.12%	35.92%	23.23%	$404,615	$2,423	$257,600	$21,509,582	84	153+

following year, all three recouped their investment by getting more assets and referrals from their current clients. Along the way, their close monitoring of their benchmarking performance reinforced that their decision was paying off.

While firm revenue and assets were down, and revenue per advisor dropped further when they hired the service advisor, our quarterly benchmarking review showed that the affected performance metrics were improving at a rate that was faster than the markets. Once the market recovered, their AUM and revenue shot up far faster than those of their peers, because the market gains were a bonus to the gains they had driven internally. The benchmarking process helped them transform the market downturn to their advantage.

Business Benchmarking Case Study

Table 9.1 is an example of an actual case study in benchmarking from a consulting client. This firm began the benchmarking process with $43 million in AUM.

This was a firm where the principals had hesitated for years to do an analysis of their business because they loved their clients so much and didn't want to let any of them go. Yet after a few quarters of benchmark reviews, they could no longer ignore the numbers. Their performance wasn't improving as quickly as they wished, and they knew they had to take a more active approach to achieving their goals.

We surveyed clients to gauge their satisfaction, whether they had made referrals, and how well they understood the firm's offering, among other things. We also conducted a competitive fee analysis that revealed that the firm provided considerably more services than its competition for 15 percent less than the average for its competitors. Based on this information, we determined the number of clients the firm could lose as a result of the fee increase and still maintain its current revenue.

Armed with benchmarking data and deeper analysis, the firm concluded that it needed to rebrand itself to focus on higher-net-worth clients, increase its account minimum, increase its pricing model, increase fees for existing clients, and transition smaller clients to other advisors who could better serve them.

The snapshot of the firm's benchmarking report, seven quarters later, shows that the firm had more than doubled its AUM, to $94 million. The number of clients under the firm's minimum of $750,000 dropped from well over 150 to 97. Even though the firm had 22 percent fewer clients, it had 39 percent more in client revenues, 47 percent more in fees, and 45 percent more in AUM. Perhaps most shocking to the advisors was that there were no significant client losses. Several clients even said that they had been wondering when the firm was going to increase its fees.

Both advisors had been very concerned about alienating or hurting clients, but they were empowered by their improving benchmark reports. With useful and accurate business intelligence, they chose to take a disciplined approach to managing their business in order to build a better business.

By the time the 2008 downturn came, they had a very productive and profitable business, which they were able to sustain with minimal impact to partner compensation. Today, they manage nearly $200 million in assets and continue to improve their performance so that they can meet their eventual goal of selling the business and realizing maximum value.

These are just a few examples of benchmarking benefits. When a firm integrates benchmarking into business practice—not so much the specific information—it becomes a powerful business process. It can show firms how they are performing, how they can improve, and how those improvements play out in real time.

PART II

Business Development

CHAPTER 10

The Business Development Landscape

Whether a firm has lost its pipeline of new clients due to a market downturn or they just want to ramp up their business, they need to focus on business development. Targeting clients, creating a compelling brand, and developing consistent marketing and referral processes to get new business are the lifeblood of an advisor's business.

To grow, advisors need to be able to reach prospects, clients, and centers of influence with a clear, consistent message about who they are, what services they provide, and to whom. Many advisors understand this but don't do it in any systematic way.

During an up market, financial advisors often let their marketing muscles atrophy while they enjoy the trifecta of market appreciation, client contributions, and client referrals. So the business isn't prepared if the market tanks and clients recoil. Although the retiring Baby Boomers represent a substantial market opportunity for advisors today, advisors clearly recognize that growth in the future will require a more proactive approach than in the recent past.

Paths to Growth

While most advisors think of various marketing tactics as the way to grow their firms, business development is in fact a lot larger category that contains not only marketing but also branding, cross-selling, ongoing quality client service, referrals, and more. Indeed, best-practice advisors see the greatest growth opportunities in developing systematic, efficient approaches that focus on existing client service and attracting new clients. Though responses varied, three paths to growth dominated in our recent "Business Development Findings" study of more than 3,000 advisors:

- Eighty-three percent of top-quartile advisors say the biggest opportunity lies in getting the service proposition right and delivering a better standard of service.
- Sixty-eight percent of top performers say the opportunity lies with scaling the business by building and maintaining more efficient systems.
- Fifty-nine percent of top-quartile advisors say that looking to the Boomer generation will drive growth, and they suggest that our focus should be on our nation's 76 million Baby Boomers.

Secondary growth drivers included:

- Fifty-six percent of top-quartile advisors note that leveraging technology is a significant business opportunity, which we believe helps advisors provide higher-quality services more efficiently, improving productivity and freeing time to focus on business development.
- Forty-seven percent of top performers indicate that investing in business is an opportunity; our findings indicate that top-quartile advisors invest more in business operations and business development.
- Seventeen percent, 22 percent, and 22 percent of top-quartile advisors, respectively, reported that acquisition, mergers, and industry consolidation were growth opportunities; our report *Business Performance Findings 2009* further supports this.

Overall, the strategies that advisors identify as driving growth can best be summarized as:

- Have a marketing plan and invest the time and money to execute it. The real challenge advisors face is transforming business development from an organic, founder-driven talent to a firm-driven business system that will create steady growth.
- Buy growth by acquiring another practice or hiring another advisor. A significant number of advisors are considering, if not actively preparing, to buy future growth, through buying either practices or advisor talent that will support growth.
- Leverage existing resources by hiring additional business development staff. Firms with $1 million-plus in annual revenues are leading the way by taking steps to retain business development professionals to represent the firm and drive business growth, independent of the principal, the founder, or the partners.

In most of the categories that are important to business development, top-quartile advisory firms are further along than other advisory firms.

Marketing: Starting with a Plan

Marketing is much more than an activity or an event; it is an organized business system that consistently creates and drives growth. An effective marketing plan is the link between a firm's growth goals for the future and the advisor's "to do" list. Although a vast majority of advisors accept this and believe that creating a plan will drive growth, only 32 percent of the best firms have created such a plan, as depicted in Figure 10.1.

Implementing a plan is even more difficult for most advisors. Of the 32 percent of advisors with a clear plan, only about half say they have mostly or fully implemented it. Even among the most successful firms, only 11 percent have a fully implemented plan.

Finding the Right Audience

Many advisors don't understand how important it is to know their audience. Developing and implementing a marketing plan can and should differ from firm to firm, based on an advisor's target client profile.

Targeting a specific profile may not drive firms into the top performer category, but data suggest it is a contributing factor. As shown in Figure 10.2, 68 percent of top-quartile advisors meet their defined client profile, compared with only half for the remainder of the advisor population.

The difference between 50 percent and 68 percent may not seem significant, but it shows that top performers have over 30 percent more target clients. If you were to replace 18 percent of their smallest, or even average-size, clients with

FIGURE 10.1 Percentage of Participants Who Do or Do Not Have a Marketing Plan

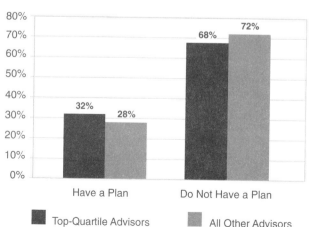

FIGURE 10.2   Percentage of Active Clients Who Meet the Target Client Profile

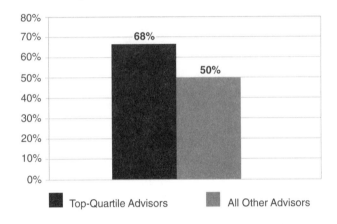

target clients, the resulting revenue increase would likely be significant. The research shows that little changes can make a big difference.

Based on the data and our consulting experience, there's no one best target client. Rather, what profile an advisor chooses is less important than the act of choosing one. Simply put, those advisors with a higher percentage of target clients were considerably more profitable.

Referrals: The Conductor of Growth

Developing a plan and focusing on an audience are key components of sustainable marketing, but what are the components and activities that drive growth? Although no one tactic works for everyone all the time, referrals come close. As seen in Figure 10.3, top-quartile advisors indicated that 60 percent of new business came from client referrals and, though that number dropped to 50 percent for other advisors, client referrals still drive the majority of their new business. Professional referrals represent a smaller contribution to growth, at 20 percent and 10 percent of new business for both top performers and other advisors, respectively.

Again, the difference between top-quartile advisors and the remaining advisory firms may not seem significant, as the difference between 50 percent and 60 percent is 10 percent. If every advisor went back 10 years and added an additional 20 percent more clients every year for that period, the result would be a major boost in revenue. Additionally, the difference between 10 percent and 20 percent represents double the number of referrals. If every advisor firm went back 10 years and doubled the number of professional referrals they had received

FIGURE 10.3   Primary New Business Sources

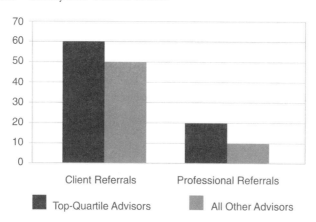

each year, another major boost in revenue would result. Simply put, the difference in the numbers doesn't accurately highlight the significance of the missed opportunity.

Advisors agree that asking for referrals directly is best, but a majority indicate they do so only occasionally, with a mere 20 percent asking for referrals systematically. This is another huge opportunity cost for most.

While the majority of top-quartile advisors have a process in place to thank clients for referrals, nearly half of advisors do not place a call or send a thank-you note for every referral. These findings suggest that 50 percent of advisors do little or nothing to encourage referrals. Given that referrals are most responsible for growth, this makes little sense.

The challenge with referrals is that, for the most part, advisors are uncomfortable asking for them—understandable, given that no one wants to seem needy. Advisors also want to avoid putting clients in an uncomfortable situation. Still, we often challenge this thinking. Advisors, without exception, ask prospects to entrust to them the prospects' financial assets, which represents a significant act of trust and confidence. Advisors do this with great comfort and without hesitation because they believe they can add tremendous value to their clients' lives. Yet, in spite of this, once the prospect has converted to a client and realized the value of the relationship, the advisor suddenly feels uncomfortable asking the client to consider referring anyone else who would benefit from a similar relationship. In this context, advisors' hesitation to ask for referrals seems less than logical.

We propose that the issue isn't asking for referrals but, rather, *how* to ask for them. Understandably, few advisors are comfortable with sliding a piece of paper across the table and asking their clients to write the names of people they know who might be interested in their services. However, it should be noted that this strategy, while sales oriented in nature, has actually worked, not because it's a great method but rather because it creates a *system for asking*, and therein lies the secret.

The firms best at generating client and professional referrals aren't necessarily better at asking for them, but they do tend to have a system for doing so, and it is part of their regular business behavior—which is why it works. The reality is that a systematic approach with poor quality is likely to outperform an inconsistent approach of high quality. In most cases, we recommend that firms focus less on asking for referrals and more on making clients aware of the value of referrals, the process for making them, and the benefits to the referring party when they do so.

Most of the common approaches to referrals focus on why it is good for the firm and how it is an important way for the firm to make money, but never approach the real reason. Clients want their friends and family to have the same positive experience and opportunity to meet financial goals. Think of the last good restaurant you went to: did you keep the experience you had to yourself, or did you share it with those you know, like, and care about? The better your experience and value, the more likely you are to endorse it to others. When advisory firms do not receive a considerable number of referrals, we look at areas such as client experience, relationship management, and value delivered, as well as referral awareness and education strategies, to determine the real reason behind the lack of referrals.

Return on Marketing

Although at first glance, even top-performing firms do not appear to be attracting more clients than their counterparts, this is an issue of quality over quantity. Note that top-performing firms attract larger clients, focus more consistently on their target client group, and ultimately see as much as a 63 percent return on their marketing dollars, while others may see no return at all.

As shown in Table 10.1, the median top-performer dollars spent on business development are three times the typical advisory firm spend. Even during the market downturn, top-quartile advisors spent considerably more on marketing, in absolute terms, than their counterparts did. On average, firms indicated that they invested a median of 2 percent of revenue in marketing activities, with budgets ranging from less than 1 percent to about 4 percent of revenue.

To see whether this money was well spent, we calculated the return on marketing (ROM) by comparing new revenue generated to the amount advisors spend on marketing. We compared the same year for top performers and typical advisors. ROM for top performers was $1.63. We found $1.63 in new revenue generation for every marketing dollar spent. For typical advisors,

TABLE 10.1 Marketing Expenses

	2011 MARKETING EXPENSES	2012 YTD MARKETING EXPENSES
Top	$15,000	$9,000
Other	$4,750	$2,500

TABLE 10.2 Return on Marketing

QUARTILE	ROM
Top	$1.63
Other	$1.00

ROM was a 1:1 ratio, with every marketing dollar generating $1 in new revenue (see Table 10.2).

Again, the 63 percent difference between the two groups may not seem like much, but it represents a difference that, in the case of recurring revenue, repeats itself year after year.

Spending more on marketing affects other high-level performance measurements, in addition to ROM. At the end of Q2 2009, the median new revenue generated by top-performing firms was $20,000, twice that of average firms. At the same time, top-quartile firms generated a median of four new clients, compared to five for average firms. This is probably because top-performing firms focus on a wealth management offering and higher-net-worth clients, according to our 2009 business performance study.

We're not implying that if you throw money at marketing, it will create new revenue. Marketing is less about what advisors do and more about how they do it. Advisors are beginning to understand that they need to engage in systematic marketing for future growth. Of the respondents, 73 percent linked their growth to marketing investment, and 71 percent said that developing a marketing plan was the key, as shown in Figure 10.4. Consistent marketing plan or referral program execution may do wonders for business.

The Challenges

Advisors face serious challenges when it comes to these business development steps, including:

- *Lack of focus.* Although a majority of advisors say they have some way to identify their target clients (typically, assets), typical advisory firms indicate

FIGURE 10.4   Business Development Strategies to Drive Firm Growth

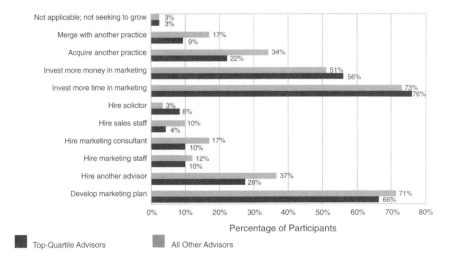

that only half of their clients fit the bill. Top-performing firms demonstrate stronger focus, with 68 percent of clients in the target client category.

- *Failing to plan.* Fewer than one-third of advisors indicate they have a written marketing plan in place, and fewer still have fully implemented a plan.
- *Using an ad hoc approach.* Many advisors take an ad hoc approach to marketing and communications; only a few indicate they have systematized their business development process.
- *Overlooking key stakeholders.* Fewer than one-third of advisors have formally asked for feedback on what clients need, want, and expect. Yet those same advisors indicate that focusing on client service is essential for driving growth.

The Yo-Yo Effect

Most advisors do some form of ad hoc marketing. From experience, we've found three basic kinds of marketing implementation: event driven, cycle driven, and process driven (Figure 10.5).

The event-driven advisor responds to a single event, such as a referral call or an invitation to speak at an event. This is an isolated opportunity, driven by an outside source or the advisor's own idea, but unrelated to any broad strategy or effort. It is marketing driven by incident or intuitive forces, and not by intentional design.

The cycle-driven advisor represents many practicing advisors, who focus on business development sporadically. The advisor engages in a series of one-off

FIGURE 10.5 The Phases of Marketing: Event Driven, Cycle Driven, and Process Driven

activities, such as hosting client events or having lunch with centers of influence for intense but relatively brief periods. This usually leads to one of two results: once new business comes in, advisors spend all of their time integrating the new clients, which prevents the advisors from continuing to market, or the advisor gets no immediate results and stops marketing.

Both event- and cycle-driven advisors fall prey to a "yo-yo effect"—either advisors ignore marketing or they engage in temporary and unsustained flurries of it. By contrast, a process-driven advisor develops an ongoing business development plan that involves systematic marketing, a referral management process, and a client feedback process. A series of simple, consistent steps implemented over time may generate growth and expand the firm's client base. Marketing a practice is not easy; it requires effort. That said, there are some basic concepts that can dramatically improve advisors' ability to successfully market their firms. We will explore these concepts in detail in the chapters that follow.

CHAPTER 11

Target Clients and Niche Markets

The first step in developing a consistent marketing strategy is to choose a target client profile by defining what kind of clients you serve and want to serve. It's almost impossible to approach a market effectively if you don't know whom you are trying to reach.

There's also a financial advantage to having a specific target client. When we look at other professions for best practices, there's a strong correlation between pay and client profile. In legal firms, accounting firms, and doctors' practices, specialists make more money than generalists do. Yet in financial services, advisors staunchly resist specializing. That's often because they approach their work with a fear of scarcity. Choosing one group of people excludes others, thereby "limiting" their opportunity to grow the client base. This can be scary if you think each new client represents new revenue. As we saw in the last section, however, *taking all comers may increase top-line revenue, but it frequently erodes bottom-line profits*. Conversely, the deeper you dive into the interests or needs of a common group of clients, the better able you are to serve them, increase the percentage of assets they place with you, and get referrals.

Being a generalist can be hard on your revenue stream, and it can detract from the quality of your working life. When advisors have to meet the needs of a diverse client base, they tend not to develop any particular expertise that could engage them more in their work and differentiate them from the competition. Trying to be all things to all people also tends to result in generic, sometimes even superficial, service. As generalists, advisors frequently have to cater to the least common denominator.

Choosing a target market makes it easier to define and offer the most appropriate services. The more specifically advisors can meet their clients' needs, the more satisfied the clients will be and the more rewarding the advisor's work will become. Moreover, the more satisfied your clients are, the more referrals they

97

are likely to make and the more word will spread about your services to other people in that niche.

For example, Sally is a horse owner in ranch country and has become the advisor of choice for her target audience: wealthy cattle ranchers and farmers. She stays on top of their trends and problems and can be very specific in how she addresses their needs. On a typical day, she will spend the morning meeting with a cattle rancher and the afternoon meeting with a horse breeder. Her knowledge of their issues makes it easy for her to wow them with information on the specialized feeding, housing, breeding, and medical costs related to their industry. Not only is Sally's information highly targeted, but she also shares their interests, which elevates her credibility and their trust—not to mention her enjoyment of the business.

Another example is an advisory firm client of ours that specializes in technology executives with stock options. The advisors study the tech sector, staying abreast of trends and developments that matter to their clients. They have an advanced understanding of stock options and a profound feeling for the considerable challenges and opportunities faced by tech executives. They have become experts in this area and therefore easily attract new technology clients who need and value their expertise.

Whatever your niche, having one makes it easier to develop a compelling brand and value proposition that is highly attractive to your target client because it shouts out, "We are all about you! No other financial advisor knows your needs better." Choosing a niche requires knowing yourself and your audience and having the confidence to proclaim openly and boldly who that audience is. We often suggest that advisors start by simply describing the group of people with whom they do their best work. For example, a firm that specializes in the technology sector can have this as their statement of their target audience: "Over the years we have found that we do our best work with highly paid executives in the technology sector. These individuals have complex financial needs and very specific issues they need to address. Because we focus our work exclusively on these individuals, they benefit from our specialized knowledge of how to make, manage, and maximize their highly concentrated wealth."

More often than not, it is a lack of confidence that prevents advisors from focusing their experience, expertise, and efforts on a target client group.

Define Yourself

You can get a better picture of what kind of clients appeal to you by defining yourself and your interests. Ask yourself the following questions:

What type of personality do I have?
What are my career goals?

What are my personal goals?
What are my interests/hobbies?
What areas of expertise do I have?
What market do I truly enjoy working in?
What type of clients do I work best with?

Define a Target Audience

The next step is to find groups of people who are in sync with these interests and goals.

- *Know your marketplace.* What will your particular target area encompass? For example, a large metropolitan area may offer better niche opportunities than a rural community. Do you prefer to work with lawyers over the age of 50? Are they few and far between in your immediate region, or is every advisor in the area targeting these lawyers? In determining your specialized market, ensure that you can deliver unique value that differentiates you from the competition.
- *Know your client base.* Evaluate your current client base and isolate your favorite clients—what do you and this group have in common? Are they your most profitable clients? What characteristics do they possess to link you—age, profession, hobbies? By narrowing down the clients with whom you regularly work, and enjoy working with, you can better identify your target client base.

  When they explore their client base, many advisors find that they already have a niche without realizing it. One advisor found that 80 percent of his clients were doctors, which made them a natural target market. Other advisors may want to remake or add to an existing niche. One client firm specialized in widows because the owner naturally seemed to attract them as clients over the years. His business was successful and he liked his clients, but he had considerable knowledge and expertise he wasn't using, and he needed a bigger challenge. He found it by creating a new niche for female executives, which meshed with his firm's identity as serving women.
- *Do some research.* Examine where your referrals come from—who are your best referral sources? Recognizing a consistent client source is a good way to identify markets in which to focus.
- *Refine the market.* After studying the preceding three elements, you should have a clear idea which niche markets are in line with your business goals and objectives. Once you define this, you can further drill down within the markets and specifically target the clients you prefer. For example, as shown in Figure 11.1, you may be interested in working with highly educated people who have advanced degrees. Narrow that to medical professionals, for example, and then

FIGURE 11.1 Defining a Target Client Profile

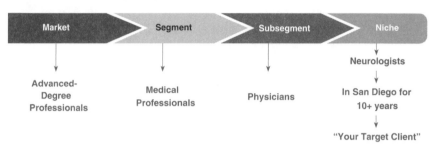

again to physicians. Can you go further and identify a group of physicians who are geographically and financially desirable? A good niche for someone in southern California may be neurologists who have been in San Diego for 10 years or more. The time requirement increases the likelihood that the clients have built up a certain level of wealth. With this criterion in mind, identifying these target clients is infinitely easier, and so, too, is marketing to them.

Be the Go-To Person

Your goal within a niche market is to become the expert—the go-to person with whom everyone wants to work, who has the breadth and depth of knowledge to offer value. If you do your homework and find a niche that meshes well with your personality, personal interests, and goals, this should come naturally. To achieve trusted-advisor status, advisors must stay focused on trends in that market and anticipate client needs. If the market is doctors, the advisor should be learning everything about health care, Medicare, HMOs and malpractice insurance, pensions, and partnership issues.

It's much easier to develop a brand and marketing materials when advisors have a specialty. In the case of the client whom we identified as having 80 percent of his clients in the medical profession, we developed the brand WealthRx®. His marketing materials come in a folder with a notepad that looks like a prescription pad, and a design of molecules on the inside flap represents the components of the wealth management process. Another advisor client likes to travel in his RV. He meets people at high-end campgrounds, who meet other people in RVs, and these have become a nationwide source of clients for him. They plan trips together and do most of their meetings via Skype. Yet another advisor was interested in antique cars, allowing him to advertise in appropriate magazines and meet new clients at car auctions, while engaging in his own favorite pastime.

In this way, serving clients who have similar interests allows advisors to have some fun pursuing their hobbies or interests along with their clients. A natural shared interest or affinity builds trust. This is a lot more rewarding than advisors trying to remake themselves for each client who walks in the door.

Any fears of not having enough clients should quickly evaporate when advisors see that they're penetrating their niche much deeper than they could a general market.

The Financial Side of Target Clients

Common interests and compatibility aren't the only factors that should define target clients. They should mesh with the firm's financial goals and client segmentation:

- Client size (e.g., net worth or investable assets).
- Client needs (e.g., age or specialized needs).
- Client affiliations (e.g., lifestyle or profession).

If a certain account minimum is necessary to meet a firm's financial goals, advisors need to make sure their target clients meet those minimums.

How many clients a firm can support profitably varies, depending on the offering, the available support, client expectations, and efficiency drivers such as technology and process. At Genworth, we find it helpful to think about capacity as a number of seats on a bus. If your business is a bus with 100 seats, one for each client, whom do you let on? In best-practice firms, advisors fill those seats with their target clients.

Capacity also raises the question of how many clients are "active"—households or institutions the firm actively serves. Inactive clients can limit growth and drain profitability. Overall, top-performing firms have a higher number of active clients and fewer nontarget clients than their peers, contributing to better overall performance. Depending on the practice model, the number of active target clients managed by top-quartile firms ranges from 60 to 75, compared with 24 to 52 for typical advisory firms (Table 11.1).

Study participants identified many ways to target new clients, including net worth, investable assets, profession, age, lifestyle, interests/hobbies, specialized needs, and other (Figure 11.2 and Table 11.2). Yet client size dominated: About three-quarters of advisors used investable assets as the primary determinant of a target client. About half used net worth and just less than half used age.

TABLE 11.1 Number of Active Target Clients by Practice Model

	QUARTILE	SOLO	SILO	ENSEMBLE
Active target clients	Top	62	60	75
	Other	24	36	52

TABLE 11.2   Percentage of Other Responses for Primary Factors Used in Target Client Profiling

PERCENTAGE OF OTHER RESPONSES	OTHER RESPONSES	TARGET CLIENT ANALYSIS AND THOUGHTS
10.2%	Business owner	Arguably a target client factor, but could also be included in the "Profession" category, increasing its overall importance in client profiling.
7.0%	Personality/Likeability/ Fun to work with/Nice/ Behavior	While psychometrics are a more subjective category, they clearly play a role in defining an ideal client. Experience has shown us they are important to advisor satisfaction as well.
7.0%	Referrals	The old standby of referrals has surfaced, yet this characteristic is often hard to quantify at the onset of a prospect relationship and may not translate to actual referrals after a prospect becomes a client.
5.5%	Willingness of client to do something . . .	The conditional factor of willingness to listen, learn, and so on, is used as a gatekeeper for advisors to weed out possibly difficult clients. While effective in developing a stronger client relationship down the road, it can be a difficult factor to measure.
4.7%	Income	In the same general categories and tied to net worth and investable assets, this is an easily defined and measureable target client factor.
0.8%	Worldview	While not statistically relevant, we thought you might enjoy learning that psychometrics such as worldview and culture may be up and coming target client factors.

FIGURE 11.2   Primary Target Client Factors by 1QAs and <1QAs

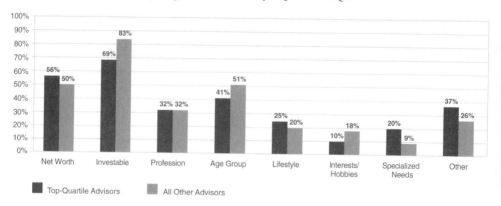

FIGURE 11.3 Primary Reasons Advisors Accept Referrals that Do Not Meet Their Target Client Profile

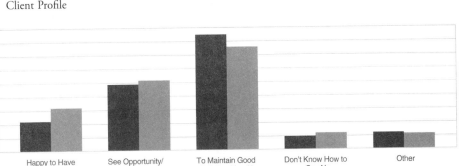

Still, many advisors accept clients who do not meet their target profile, as you can see in Figure 11.3. The primary reason they accept these clients is to maintain a good referral relationship or because they see a potential opportunity in the client.

It is, of course, important to protect referral relationships. When a client (or a professional) goes out of his or her way to make a referral, advisors don't want to offend the client by not taking on the person referred. Yet advisors have to decide whether possibly offending a current client outweighs the opportunity cost of taking on a less profitable client and affecting overall financial performance.

We will explore the opportunity costs of doing this in greater detail in later chapters.

As you take the steps described in this chapter—defining yourself and your interests, choosing your target clients, defining and claiming your niche—you'll find that each step leads to the next on the road to building not only a better business but also a more satisfying one.

CHAPTER 12

Landing Your Brand

An out-of-towner drove his car into a ditch in a rural area. Luckily, Farmer Jones came to help with his horse named Hobo. Farmer Jones hitched Hobo up to the car and yelled, "Pull, Nellie, pull!" Hobo didn't move a muscle. Then Farmer Jones hollered, "Pull, Buttercup, pull!" Again, Hobo didn't move. Once more, the farmer commanded, "Pull, Stetson, pull!" Nothing from Hobo. Then the farmer nonchalantly said, "Pull, Hobo. C'mon, boy, pull!" And the horse easily dragged the car up and out of the ditch. The motorist was appreciative but curious. He asked the farmer why he called his horse by the wrong name three times. Farmer Jones answered, "Well, ol' Hobo here is blind as a bat. If he thought he was the only one pulling, he wouldn't even try!"

Many a savvy marketer would agree with Farmer Jones, noting that potential clients and referral sources are like Hobo: what they perceive drives their reality. Yet many firms are failing to define the perception of their brand in the market-place. Creating a brand is more than images and words; it is a clear, concise, and compelling message that defines the value you provide. It should be different and genuine enough to stick in people's minds. When done right, rebranding your firm can relocate you from the "land of bland" to the "land of brand"—a far more desirable neighborhood.

What Is a Brand?

When we ask advisors what their brand is, they often say it's their logo, brochure, or website. These are physical manifestations of a brand that promote a firm's message, but they are not a brand. A brand is the key message the firm is sending to the marketplace about the value it offers.

Automobiles provide a simple illustration of a brand and brand differentia-tion. Consider Mercedes and BMW. Both are aluminum shells with four wheels and engines, much like other vehicles. But Mercedes and BMW are high-end automobiles, with one synonymous for luxury and the other admired for performance. They represent different and distinct associations that stick in customers' minds, and customers gravitate to the brand that best reflects their style.

Here are some basic definitions of how a brand does and does not work.

- *Your brand is a promise you make to the marketplace.* This promise should stand out and drive every aspect of your messaging, marketing, and client experience.
- *You can have only one brand promise.* You want one promise that is crystal clear, compelling, and aligned with your firm's values. When you try to convey a series of promises—for example, smart, personal, and premium—your message becomes diffused and hard to remember.
- *A brand promise should differentiate the firm from the competition.* Again, BMW and Mercedes are good examples. They are both high-end cars, but their marketing has clearly differentiated them. What do you offer that is truly reflective of your firm?
- *The brand promise must align with what the firm delivers.* A firm whose brand is simplifying clients' financial lives isn't conveying a consistent message by using a complicated 17-page client intake questionnaire.
- *Attributes are not a brand.* Often, when advisors try to explain what makes them "better" or "unique," they say some version of "we care, we have integrity, and we provide great service." These attributes don't describe the brand promise; they merely describe how the firm delivers on the brand promise.

Case Study: Building Brand Architecture

Following are the elements that make up brand architecture, which is the foundation of any good marketing strategy. Defining each of these elements in a coherent, consistent message lets the right people in the right markets know that an advisor is there to serve their needs. Let's review each of these steps to see how one client firm, FP Financial Services, was able to develop a meaningful brand that resonated with its target audience.

- Target clients
- Firm name
- Client motivators
- Market position
- Brand identity (corporate identity)
- Brand promise
- Value proposition

Target Clients

We discussed target clients at length in Chapter 11 because knowing and defining a target market are essential to conveying the right message for your audience. Although we first tried a brand promise for FP Financial of "peace of mind," it quickly became clear that this wasn't consistent with the firm's target clients: middle-America accumulators who were unlikely to ever have enough capital to gain true peace of mind. At some level, these individuals would likely always need to carefully manage their capital and lifestyle in order to maintain a good quality of life in retirement. A better fit was the notion of "guiding clients," helping them understand where they are in relation to where they want to be, and enabling them to maximize their resources to enjoy life's journey along the way.

This message appealed to the firm's audience of people who were, essentially, financial delegators. They lack either the time, talent, or temperament to manage their own finances and so choose to rely on a trusted guide—a partner—to help them define and pursue the path that is right for them.

Firm Name

Named after the founder, FP Financial sends the message that the firm is founder focused, and ties perceived value to him. If the goal is to build a firm that extends "beyond" the owner, both while he or she is working and certainly afterward, then a more firm-centric name is appropriate. FP Financial's owner wanted to add advisors and prepare for his eventual transition out of the business, even though that was more than 10 years away.

FP Financial decided to change the name to be more "firm-centric" and transitioned focus from the owner to the role it plays in the lives of the clients: Guidant Wealth Management.

Client Motivators

Client motivators are the reasons that target clients engage an advisor. They can be positive motivators (hopes and dreams) or negative (fears and concerns).

Based on emotion, they are powerful and compelling. An effective brand will speak directly to the client motivators of an advisor's target market, thus ensuring that you get people's attention. Guidant had a list of client motivators:

- Wanting to make the most of their financial situation.
- Needing guidance to make the right decisions and direction to avoid financial pitfalls.

- Wanting to know where they are and what is possible.
- Seeking clarity and confidence.
- Wanting a firm they can trust (advice, experience, ethical).

Guidant determined that its marketing message needed to consistently reflect the needs, goals, and motivators of its clients "to ensure that they recognize that we relate to and understand their situations, bringing comfort in knowing we have the experience to meet their needs."

Market Position

A good market position differentiates a firm and is memorable, staying in the mind of the target audience. Designed to identify and retain information that is unique and different (good and bad), the human brain must filter background noise while attempting to understand your message. This highlights why effective positioning is important. A firm needs to stand out among the crowd, just as "We're no. 1" or "the un-cola" does. These slogans not only position the firms they represent, but they also ensure that the competition cannot own this space.

Guidant's market position was "The Trusted Firm," based on the premise that when you hire a guide, trust is essential. You can't comfortably follow a guide who doesn't inspire confidence. As the trusted firm, Guidant was able to articulate its role: "We help bring comfort to our clients through our knowledge and experience and also in the personal approach we take. We listen, we care, and—of utmost importance—we always act in our clients' best interest. We guide them through a process that brings value to their life by giving them the confidence of knowing they have a trusted partner to work with them each and every step of the way along their life's journey."

Brand Identity

Brand identity (corporate identity) should consistently communicate intangible attributes in all of the firm's messages and materials. At a firm that caters to high-net-worth clients, marketing literature should reflect affluence and luxury. If the brand is innovation, a website that's indistinguishable from its competitors' is out of alignment. Brand identity includes your firm's color palette and imagery, which should run consistently through your stationery, documents, logo, décor, and office. All interactions and experiences with your firm should reflect your brand identity, including but not limited to:

- Website
- Marketing materials
- Building, office space, meeting areas
- Furniture and décor

- Staff appearance and demeanor
- Amenities (reading materials in the waiting room, refreshments, etc.)
- Meeting materials
- Performance reports

One client, whose branding is "helping people make the right moves," uses a chess piece as a logo and has a chess board in his waiting area. If your clients are high-net-worth and they vacation in such places as the Ritz Carlton and Four Seasons, this is the experience you're competing with, not with the financial advisor down the street. If you have a mom-and-pop clientele, an office with 16th-century furniture would be intimidating and would strike the wrong chord. If clients feel awkward and uncomfortable, they will never open up to the advisor.

To convey guidance, leadership, and trust, Guidant chose a brand identity we titled "Calming Finance," composed of a muted palette of blues and gray-greens, with black and beige neutrals, and a burgundy accent. This brand style includes a calming color palette and iconic symbols to evoke a connection to the historical area in which the office was located.

Brand Promise

This is the promise that your firm makes to the marketplace. It acts to present a singular, compelling theme that symbolizes what your firm represents (luxury, performance, peace of mind). Your brand promise serves as the cornerstone of your firm brand and brand architecture. It is the basis of the reputation you want to build for the firm.

Whatever values a firm brand claims in the brand promise requires diligence at every contact point with clients, prospects, or spectators. Translating a qualitative brand promise into a meaningful experience requires full understanding of the brand across your firm.

Guidant's brand promise reflects the financial-planning process and the role the firm plays in navigating clients through their financial lives, providing leadership and direction, support and counseling, and working to ensure that the best possible course is followed.

Here's how Guidant described its brand promise: "You rely on a guide for their knowledge, expertise, and experience. A guide's job is to help you through a journey; ensuring you have the best experience and helping you avoid any potential problems along the way. In the context of financial planning, the firm's role is to apply its knowledge, expertise, and experience for the benefit of each client's financial success. We help them make the most of the good times and help them navigate the challenging times. They rely on us to help them make the most of their financial success and future, while allowing them to enjoy their life along the way."

Value Proposition

This is a clear statement defining what a firm's target market can expect from its services. Most companies have value propositions that focus on the firm's unique qualities (firm-centric), rather than on the client (client-centric). Given that your target market is seeking to address its motivators, describing the qualities of a firm requires clients to stretch and connect the dots between their needs and your services. By contrast, client-centric messaging directly addresses the client motivators and thus clearly communicates the reasons for working with the firm, with little or no interpretation required.

When firms focus on the emotional benefit or value delivered to the client, there's no doubt about the benefit the client can expect. An awareness of an unfulfilled benefit encourages the client to assess the need for that benefit and how the firm can satisfy the need. They can then make a positive connection with the firm. This gets prospects emotionally invested in exploring a relationship.

Guidant's value proposition is "A Tradition of Trust." It focuses on their target clients' need for ethical, reliable service: "A key concern and motivator of clients when selecting a financial planning firm is the integrity and ethics of the firm. We choose to boldly proclaim that we are a firm that can be trusted to ensure clarity around this very important value."

Brand architecture provides advisors with a meaningful framework for promoting, advertising, and marketing their value to the desired audience. Leveraging this potential requires advisors to execute on the brand consistently and across as many aspects of their firms as possible.

CHAPTER 13

The Elevator Speech

One area where your brand should stand out strong is your "elevator speech"—whenever people ask you what you do, your response should be a quick, succinct description of your services and value, covered in the time it takes an elevator to move a few floors. You may not have your audience for longer than that, and even if you do, their interest may wane quickly.

The best elevator speech starts with why you do what you do and briefly covers what you do and whom you serve best.

Over the years, we've found the traditional elevator speech to be firm focused, not client focused, and rather lacking in its ability to create an interesting interaction. With this in mind, we suggest that advisors expand their thinking to build more effective elevator speeches, or whatever one wants to call the answer to the "what do you do?" question.

Here's a quick checklist:

- *It's clear, compelling, and concise.* The message must be relevant and sticky; the brain notices and remembers words, images, or events that are different or out of the ordinary. People remember that 7-Up is the "un-cola" because it strongly advocates what it is not, which is different from most advertising, and thus sticks in people's minds. The elevator speech needs to differentiate you with a clear image that stands out in your audience's mind.
- *It defines your value.* The elevator speech should illustrate how the firm benefits clients. An advisor who works with women after divorce may say that he or she "works with women who are suddenly single and ready to take charge of their life and finances." What this advisor is selling is far more interesting and valuable to the recipient of the message than "financial planning" or "investment management."
- *It contains effective ambiguity.* Effective ambiguity develops curiosity in your listeners, so they want to learn more. By being somewhat mysterious and open-ended, effective ambiguity invites listeners to "come into the advisor's

space for a visit" and ask questions. In the process, they give the advisor permission to market to them.

- *It differentiates the firm and avoids stereotypes and misconceptions.* This short introduction shouldn't be so generic that it doesn't differentiate an advisor from the crowd or that it locks him into a specific position. For example, the term *financial planner* isn't a great differentiator, and *investment manager* may stereotype you in a role that doesn't interest the audience.

Consider which of the following elevator speeches best meets these criteria and creates a more attractive opportunity for the financial advisors.

Two financial planners, both of whom specialize in working with doctors, are attending the same medical conference to build their reputations in the space. At an evening reception, they are discussing the day's sessions when a doctor/attendee walks up. She recognizes that the two planners aren't wearing the typical attendee badge and inquires what they do.

The first advisor says, "I am a financial planner." The doctor nods politely, smiles, and turns to the second advisor. This advisor smiles on cue and says with confidence, "I help doctors develop an RX for their retirement and make sure they can enjoy it fully by solving the three most common problems they typically face as they retire." If you were the doctor, which advisor would you want to pull aside later to discuss your financial future?

Simply saying, "I am a financial planner," is a conversation killer for most people. Although it's an important profession, we've never heard anyone within earshot respond, "That is so interesting! Please, won't you tell me more?" More often than not, the interest generated by the first example is a quest for free financial advice, and that's not the conversation we are looking to initiate.

The second advisor's answer touched on all of the key components of an effective elevator speech. It was clear, compelling, and concise. It was differentiating, in that it told us precisely who the advisor's target market was and that there were deliverables involved. Finally, it created effective ambiguity by giving just enough information to make us want to know more.

If the attendee/doctor is at all interested in planning for her retirement, she will probably ask about the three most typical challenges. She is responding to the effective ambiguity. This makes the doctor more likely to invite the advisor into her space and ask him to spend some time there because the advisor has implied that he knows more about the doctor's financial future than the doctor does.

Effective ambiguity is compelling because it creates intrigue. It also tells your audience that you know the answers to questions and/or challenges that concern them, but of which they may not be aware. In this way, the advisor who uses effective ambiguity has moved from telling his audience whom he helps to getting them to ask how he can help them.

On a very basic level, effective ambiguity allows you to qualify or gauge the interest of a prospect. In our example, if the doctor has no interest in preparing for her retirement or learning about the three challenges she will likely face, she probably isn't the right client for this advisor.

One advisor told us she had a five-step process for helping financially independent women. Although that's close, it doesn't invite the listener in. Yet a small tweak of this elevator speech created effective ambiguity and marketing permission: "I help independent women understand the five most important things they need to know to be financially smart and successful." This statement directs the message to unmarried, divorced, or widowed women, appealing to their need to feel smart and successful about their finances and raising questions to which they are likely to want the answers.

Practice Makes Perfect

Because the elevator speech is a first face-to-face impression with prospects and potential referral sources, how you deliver your description is as important as its context and substance. Give the speech with confidence and conviction—you may want to practice the speech until it becomes second nature to you. It does not matter whether someone else is listening as you practice. Focus on becoming comfortable delivering your brand message and sounding natural as you do.

CHAPTER 14

A Marketing Plan

A successful brand organizes all of your messages so that they are consistent and address the values and desires of your target audience. Marketing is the process of getting those messages out to potential and existing clients, centers of influence, and strategic partners. An effective marketing plan is the link between your growth goals for the future and your daily to-do list. The most common misconception about marketing is that it is a thing—an event, a catchy jingle, a flashy website. While these are all arrows in a marketing quiver, marketing at its core is a systematic process for cultivating new business. This process outlines each of the marketing activities, from client events to drip mailers to center-of-influence lunches, with clearly defined details on implementation. Mapping out a plan should change how you run your business and, as a result, requires real commitment. Although this may be the reason marketing plans aren't universally implemented, the benefits of doing so can't be understated.

The Challenges

Typically, so many good ideas emerge from the creative process that no firm could possibly implement all of them effectively. Our best advice is to pick a few ideas you can execute well and then repeat them over and over. This may be boring, but it works. Once the system is set up, it's relatively easy to continue, and by repeating it on a regular basis, advisors can trade in yo-yo marketing for a steady stream of prospects.

In many firms, marketing occurs "naturally" and is largely driven by advisors' rainmaking abilities. Yet, ultimately, successful firms want to establish thoughtful, disciplined, and effective marketing strategies that are not dependent on advisors' rainmaking abilities alone. A simple marketing plan that can be consistently implemented is a highly effective way to generate new business. Moreover, it creates value when the owner wishes to leave, merge, or sell the firm. The goal is to transition from informal marketing to intentional marketing, and to take a proactive approach to growth. Over and over again, we have seen simple plans that are consistently implemented over time outperform big efforts that are engaged in occasionally.

Marketing may even be daunting, due in part to some common misconceptions. Advisors believe they have to be "great marketers" or "marketing experts" to get clients and that they have to make a great investment of capital. These ideas are unfounded. There is no mystery to successful marketing, and it requires no particular talent. Again, it is a simple, systematic, sustainable process that is repeated over and over again.

The most common reasons that advisors fail to design and implement effective marketing plans include:

- They fail to do the necessary "homework" required for a good plan.
- They lack the information or the ability to easily compile information that supports a sound plan design.
- They don't have a simple way to establish goals and design their plan.
- They don't distinguish between systematized and specialized marketing.

Getting with the Plan

What's the key to a good marketing plan? A good plan is not sexy and does not sizzle. The reality is that an effective marketing plan is boring, merely a carefully crafted exercise consisting of three essential elements: It should always be simple, systematic, and sustainable.

1. *Simple.* Develop a plan that's easy for you to implement and commit to. And within your plan, continue to keep it simple. A workshop called "Are You Retirement Ready?" might be more compelling and simpler to market to the average Baby Boomer than "Learning How to Use Investments to Reduce Taxes." Effective marketing is not about sexy ideas or the latest thing. It's about picking a few simple messages that fit your firm and your audience and repeating them in various ways to the right people. Advisors tend to overcomplicate marketing by searching out the latest, greatest idea to turbocharge growth, instead of implementing the simple idea that's right in front of them. Simple isn't sexy, it doesn't sizzle, but it is the ultimate sophistication.
2. *Systematic.* In the advisor community, marketing is generally based on instinct, not on institutionalization, and is driven by people, instead of by processes. What really works, however, is not a particular idea, seminar, or brochure but an ongoing disciplined approach. In its best form, marketing is the repetitive process of sending out educational or informational materi-

als on a regular basis that is planned in advance, following up on all referrals and referral sources in an organized way, and coming through on commitments exactly as promised.

In our experience consulting on practice management, advisors have a strong tendency to struggle with business systems. That may be because systems seem to rein in the independent, entrepreneurial spirit that defines this profession, or it may be simply that advisors don't know how to build them. Yet systems—whether in marketing or other areas of your firm—are key drivers of success. You don't have to like them, but when you experience how well they can drive efficiency, effectiveness, growth, and profits and free you from the everyday details of the business, you learn to love them.

3. *Sustainable.* Exhaustive lists and complicated plans are difficult to sustain, but plans that are simple and systematic are, above all, do-able. That makes them sustainable, and sustainability is the single biggest driver of marketing success or failure in advisory firms. Advisors never lack for ideas, but they struggle persistently with developing a plan and following it through.

At Genworth, the process of developing a firm's marketing plan starts with listening to the advisor's numerous ideas, sharing our ideas, and researching what options and activities are best for a specific firm's situation and goals. The next step is to develop a list of possible activities, a schedule, and a related budget—and then we cut out 80 percent of it. Why? Because our next conversation is what you just read: Effective marketing must be simple, systematic, and sustainable.

If a Tree Falls and Nobody Hears It . . .

Ask yourself the following questions:

- If I live in your area, and I have money to invest, do I even know who you are?
- If I am a professional in your area, with clients who need your services, do I know who you are?
- If I am a client, can I clearly and simply articulate the value you deliver in a way that makes other people want to learn more?

If you answered no to any of the above, you likely have marketing opportunity in your business. The next step is to understand what marketing is and what it is not, so that your marketing is effective.

To clarify a misconception, rainmaking and marketing are not the same things. Many advisors are powerful rainmakers. Right now, though, even the best rainmakers are trying to figure out what dance to do. Should they advertise?

Should they start having lunches? Do they ask clients for referrals? Do they hold seminars? Yes and no.

Yes, these options and others might be right for you. No, these options and others may not be right for you. Are we speaking in contradictions? No. We're trying to make the point that you must customize your marketing to your firm's strategy, goals, target markets, and resources. Here are a few marketing principles that are far more important than what you do, or don't do, to market your services.

Sales versus Marketing

"Sales" refers to a specific activity focused on a narrow target, typically a single individual. For example, a meeting in which you discuss the potential use of your services with a prospect is a "sales" activity. Sales will focus on creating a specific opportunity for someone to work with you.

"Marketing" refers to an activity that focuses on broader exposure, typically aimed at a group of individuals. For example, mailing an article you wrote to certified public accountants (CPAs) in your area is a "marketing" activity. As a general rule of thumb, marketing will seek to build recognition and credibility and promote need.

A common mistake is to focus on sales activities without building the credibility that comes from broader marketing activities. For example, if you do an annual financial planning seminar for a local company, some employees are likely to attend. If, however, you send a series of quarterly mailings to these employees on financial planning, preparing for retirement, or commonly asked questions, you'll draw a bigger audience because you have established recognition and credibility and worked to promote need.

Types of Marketing

Marketing can be categorized into two basic styles: systematized marketing and specialized marketing.

Systematized marketing is based on systems and scalable activities and tools. The up-front effort is multiplied over a large audience. Typically, the impact is lower, but the scale is high. Articles, newsletters, mailings, e-mail commentary, and staff-supported activities are good examples of systematized marketing.

Advisor time is leveraged by promoting a single instance of work effort to a broad audience. Here are some examples:

- Twice-a-year mailings of a white paper to professionals in your area.
- An annual letter to clients about what happens when they make a referral.
- Mailing a presentation you gave on "Impacts of Divorce on Financial Plans" to family law attorneys in your area.

Specialized marketing focuses on personal interaction with the advisor and therefore requires a commitment of direct time and energy, such as the time spent writing an article or in personal meetings, at events, and at speaking engagements.

While the scale of specialized activities is lower, the impact tends to be high. Here are some examples:

- Wine sommelier dinner with four top clients and their select guests.
- Sending a gift certificate for two to an upscale country club to a CPA who has referred three clients this year. Attached is a note: "Many thanks for your ongoing confidence. I only hope the number of referrals next year matches your golf score."
- A special event with a top client and 10 "near retirement" executives from his or her company.

Successful advisors spend, on average, 30 percent of their time on marketing, while the typical advisor spends 10 percent or less on marketing. Yet many advisors fail to recognize opportunities to leverage their marketing time. As a general rule of thumb, 70 to 80 percent of your marketing plan should center on systematized efforts and only 20 to 30 percent on specialized efforts. This way, you spend less of your valuable time on personal activities and more of it on achieving a greater reach and impact overall.

Visibility Equals Credibility

The number one reason financial advisors do not attract clients consistently is that they don't commit themselves to marketing consistently. Consistent marketing is crucial because trust is based on familiarity. The more potential clients hear or see your name and your brand, the more they will consider you as a possible advisor—but they must have seen your name and heard your message more than once. Advisors need to develop a long-term marketing message and a plan that consistently delivers your message to a targeted set of potential clients, over and over again.

Consider this: It takes five to seven contacts to "move" a prospect to become a client. Each of those contacts needs to reinforce the firm's brand and thereby the advisor's credibility through a clear and consistent message. None of these individual interactions may lead the prospect to pick up the phone and schedule an appointment, but the person does start to listen. The firm gets on the individual's radar, and the advisor has taken the first step toward being a familiar and trusted resource. This familiarity is part of the decision-making process. If prospective clients don't see or hear an advisor's name now and repeatedly, that advisor stands less chance of getting the call when the prospect needs advice.

It takes on average four to six contacts with a potential referral source before the person will consider sending you a referral. Be sure to spend time each month or quarter deciding what information, material, or message you will send to your potential referral sources and then commit to following through on the activities that will drive the relationships forward and deepen them over time.

Visibility builds credibility: If prospects and professionals do not truly believe in an advisor's credibility, they will not contact the advisor or refer clients to her. By creating a culture of marketing at the firm, advisors can increase both, with credibility built one step at a time through a process that consistently reinforces the firm's targeted message to its core audience.

Communication Schedule

An effective marketing plan is built on a month-by-month schedule that identifies what marketing activities and communications will be distributed to whom—prospects, clients, referral sources, other client advisors, and community leaders—by when and by whom. Advisors decide which communications will go to each audience group, each month. This can be prepared months, if not years, in advance. Advisors can send the same communications to every audience group or send more targeted messages to particular audience groups, such as referral sources. Advisors often do both.

Again, consistency is the single biggest factor in keeping an advisor's firm name and message in the public eye, reinforcing the view that you are the go-to expert for your audience. Few things so simply, inexpensively, and efficiently drive and deepen a relationship better than consistent, credibility-building communications.

Marketing Strategies

What strategies are advisors using to market their firms? One way to find out is to look to the firms that have done it best. The Genworth/Quantuvis Best Practices Study Series has conducted surveys on more than 3,000 advisors during the last two years to explore the difference between top-performing firms and the balance of the advisor population.

One-on-One Contact

We asked advisors about the effectiveness of a range of marketing activities, from drip mailers to newsletters to client events (Table 14.1). Direct contact is, not surprisingly, seen as most effective—a position also held by clients.

TABLE 14.1 Effectiveness of External Marketing Activities

	QUARTILE	EXTREMELY EFFECTIVE	HIGHLY EFFECTIVE	EFFECTIVE	MILDLY EFFECTIVE	NOT EFFECTIVE	DOES NOT APPLY
Newsletter	Top	3.4%	10.2%	28.8%	22.0%	10.2%	25.4%
	Other	0.6%	9.8%	17.8%	29.9%	6.3%	35.6%
Educational calls	Top	0.0%	11.9%	22.0%	10.2%	1.7%	54.2%
	Other	1.7%	3.4%	18.4%	18.4%	4.0%	54.0%
Educational meetings	Top	1.7%	15.3%	15.3%	22.0%	0.0%	45.8%
	Other	2.3%	12.6%	21.8%	17.8%	2.9%	42.5%
Market commentary, email	Top	1.7%	13.6%	18.6%	20.3%	1.7%	44.1%
	Other	0.6%	12.6%	17.2%	21.8%	6.9%	40.8%
Market commentary, mail	Top	0.0%	3.4%	20.3%	10.2%	5.1%	61.0%
	Other	0.0%	5.2%	8.0%	17.2%	5.2%	64.4%
Phone calls from advisor	Top	16.9%	39.0%	23.7%	8.5%	0.0%	11.9%
	Other	10.9%	25.3%	32.8%	16.7%	1.7%	12.6%
Phone calls from staff	Top	1.7%	15.3%	22.0%	16.9%	3.4%	40.7%
	Other	4.0%	6.3%	15.5%	13.2%	3.4%	57.5%
Client events—formal	Top	3.4%	13.6%	16.9%	13.6%	0.0%	52.5%
	Other	2.9%	6.9%	13.2%	10.3%	4.0%	62.6%
Client events—informal	Top	3.4%	16.9%	11.9%	16.9%	3.4%	47.5%
	Other	2.9%	7.5%	12.1%	11.5%	4.6%	61.5%
Client dinners	Top	6.8%	8.5%	13.6%	15.3%	0.0%	55.9%
	Other	2.9%	6.3%	13.8%	9.2%	4.0%	63.8%

After that, educational communications tends to dominate, with newsletters seen as effective to extremely effective for 42 percent of advisors.

We believe that using staff to enhance direct communications is a missed opportunity for many advisors. Well-trained staff can engage clients by proactively reaching out with "touch base" or "check-up" calls. This would drive a higher level of client satisfaction, determine whether any client needs have changed, and keep the firm at the top of the client's mind without taking up advisors' time.

Written Materials

Printed information offers greater credibility than the spoken word. Always provide a brochure or marketing materials to establish credibility and set expectations. E-mail communications are efficient and well received, but do not underestimate the perceived value of hardcopy mailings.

Send out some communication to each group each month. Research shows that clients desire 18 to 24 "touches" a year. A monthly communication drip easily covers 12 touches and demonstrates that the advisor is doing the work clients pay for: staying abreast of issues, providing value-added information, and generally thinking and working behind the scenes.

Alternate between different types of communications. We generally suggest the following types of communications:

- Technical expertise (e.g., "All About the Roth").
- Value-added information (e.g., "Learn about how LifeLock can protect your credit").
- Relationship-building pieces (focus on something happening within your firm, share special events happening in your area, or include a piece on talking about financial legacy with family members).
- Brand building or communications about the target client. If your firm focuses on single women, you might want a "Singles Series" of pieces focused on never-marrieds, widows, and divorcees.

Send at least one substantive piece each year. This builds your reputation as a technically proficient expert. You can contract this writing out, reconstitute articles or information you glean from the industry, or purchase content from providers.

Newsletters provide a simple, systematic way to deliver consistent client touches, but be leery of the "canned" version. People recognize these for what they are, which dilutes their effect. The content is often too general because it needs to appeal to everyone and therefore isn't highly relevant to anyone.

Newsletters work best when they're relevant and relate to their intended audience, creating a personal connection between advisor and clients.

We aren't suggesting that advisors shouldn't use newsletters or that they write their own. Each firm must determine what works best for its clients, budgets, and goals. Advisors should explore their alternatives, such as developing a number of simple, cost-effective methods for drip communications with clients and centers of influence, personalized to the firm and client base.

Frequently and regularly communicate your target client to your clients, alliances, referral sources, and others. For example, case studies indirectly and credibly communicate whom the firm works with and what value it can provide.

To do a case study, create a document that outlines the two or three client types you work with most successfully, with a few bullets underneath each client type heading to convey more detail. For example, "Widows" is a header, then add bullets, such as these:

- Help educate on financial options.
- Bring order to the financial situation following the death of a spouse.
- Provide financial guidance during an emotionally difficult time.

Keep this document in your lobby, mail it to your clients and referral sources periodically, and give it to your referral sources to remind them whom they should be referring.

Client and Center-of-Influence Events

Hold regular client events. Client events can be costly, so focus them on clients and areas that are most valuable to your business. Best-practice firms create leverage by focusing their marketing efforts on the interests or hobbies of their "Influentials" or top referrers. If your top referrers are wine lovers, a wine tasting might be a good idea. If they are families with young children, a family-style picnic might be more appropriate.

Some examples of client event ideas include:

- Summer barbecues for clients with families, including "bouncy tents" and other child-friendly activities. Families with children are always looking for fun things to do, and attending an event of this nature is likely more appealing to them and their friends than attending a seminar on investment strategy.
- Conduct client workshops two to four times per year on nonfinancial subjects, such as establishing relationships with grandchildren in a tech-driven society, how to build a family legacy, how to pass personal and financial values on to

children, the best places to vacation this year, or how to select charities for giving.

- Hold hobby/interest events for groups of clients. If you can, identify and track client interests, such as reading, wine tasting, golf clinics, or foreign travel. Clients enjoy attending events tailored to their interests. Choosing the right client event seems to depend on truly understanding your target clients.
- Conduct continuing education (CE). As do financial advisors, other professionals have CE requirements. Conducting CE courses is an effective way to engage a professional audience. This inherently builds credibility and provides a forum for developing relationships based on expertise, not on marketing. Some sources of information on CE (all of which are readily accessible on the Web) include:
  - For CPAs, your state board of accountancy.
  - For attorneys, your state bar.
  - For insurance agents (if you are fee-only), your state department of insurance.
  - Other professional information is easily located on the Web using a Google search for "[name of profession] and continuing education."

Media

Media, advertising, and PR activities (see Table 14.2), often employed by traditional businesses, have yet to gain traction or prove highly effective for financial advisors. Larger firms benefit more from these traditional marketing avenues because they help build recognition, brand awareness, and dominant positioning when used consistently over a long time. Smaller firms often can't afford to do so. Engaging in any of these activities sporadically has, in our experience, not proven to be highly effective.

Authoring a financial-focused article or engaging in an interview is a good use of media to build credibility. The public will see the advisor as an expert, and the media source as endorsing the advisor.

Marketing as a Major Player

Marketing is as important to your business and your success as your core services are, so treat it accordingly. Successful firms treat marketing with the same care as investments or financial planning, giving it the same time, talent, and resources. Some ideas include:

- Establish a marketing team or manager.
- Compensate for marketing performance.
- Establish marketing meetings and processes.

TABLE 14.2 Level of Effectiveness of Marketing Activities Used in the Last 12 Months

	QUARTILE	EXTREMELY EFFECTIVE	HIGHLY EFFECTIVE	EFFECTIVE	MILDLY EFFECTIVE	NOT EFFECTIVE	DOES NOT APPLY
Passive referrals from existing clients	Top	11.9%	11.9%	25.4%	42.4%	3.4%	5.1%
	Other	2.3%	9.8%	22.4%	45.4%	16.7%	3.4%
Actively market to clients to generate referrals	Top	5.1%	11.9%	18.6%	11.9%	11.9%	40.7%
	Other	2.3%	4.6%	16.7%	24.7%	12.1%	39.7%
CPA and attorney relationships	Top	5.1%	10.2%	18.6%	28.8%	18.6%	18.6%
	Other	3.4%	9.2%	16.1%	35.1%	20.7%	15.5%
Financial advisor/broker relationships	Top	0.0%	0.0%	6.8%	8.5%	10.2%	74.6%
	Other	2.3%	1.1%	6.9%	8.0%	21.3%	60.3%
Direct marketing (mail, fax, e-mail, Internet)	Top	0.0%	1.7%	3.4%	13.7%	20.6%	60.5%
	Other	0.0%	1.1%	4.0%	13.2%	24.1%	57.5%
PR/media coverage—retain firm	Top	0.0%	0.4%	3.0%	6.9%	6.0%	83.7%
	Other	0.0%	0.0%	1.1%	6.9%	5.2%	86.8%
PR/media coverage—internal	Top	0.4%	1.7%	3.0%	7.3%	7.3%	80.3%
	Other	0.0%	0.6%	2.3%	5.7%	5.7%	85.6%
Radio/TV shows	Top	0.0%	6.8%	1.7%	6.8%	8.5%	76.3%
	Other	0.6%	0.6%	1.7%	2.9%	6.3%	87.9%
Seminar marketing	Top	0.0%	5.1%	6.8%	20.3%	3.4%	64.4%
	Other	1.1%	5.2%	9.8%	17.2%	5.7%	60.9%
Professional/trade groups	Top	0.0%	0.0%	3.4%	13.6%	10.2%	72.9%
	Other	0.6%	1.1%	5.2%	17.2%	8.6%	67.2%
Referral/networking groups	Top	3.4%	0.0%	0.0%	13.6%	16.9%	66.1%
	Other	1.1%	1.1%	6.9%	17.2%	13.2%	60.3%
Cold calls/solicitation	Top	0.0%	0.0%	3.4%	5.1%	3.4%	88.1%
	Other	0.0%	0.0%	4.0%	12.1%	10.3%	73.6%
Advertising	Top	0.0%	0.0%	1.7%	10.2%	15.3%	72.9%
	Other	0.0%	0.6%	1.7%	13.2%	20.1%	64.4%
Internet presence	Top	0.0%	0.0%	3.1%	6.3%	43.8%	46.9%
	Other	0.0%	1.1%	3.2%	8.4%	40.0%	47.4%
Community involvement	Top	0.0%	6.8%	13.6%	32.2%	5.1%	42.4%
	Other	1.7%	4.6%	16.7%	26.4%	10.9%	39.7%
Charitable involvement	Top	0.0%	8.5%	8.5%	30.5%	5.1%	47.5%
	Other	1.7%	5.2%	10.3%	14.4%	12.6%	55.7%
Niche marketing	Top	3.4%	11.9%	3.4%	15.3%	3.4%	62.7%
	Other	5.7%	5.7%	10.9%	8.6%	7.5%	61.5%
Other	Top	18.2%	0.0%	9.1%	9.1%	0.0%	63.6%
	Other	8.3%	4.2%	8.3%	12.5%	4.2%	62.5%

- Treat marketing as a client, allocating the same time to marketing that you would to one of your best clients (e.g., four hours of meetings per year, monthly communication, quarterly rebalancing).

Once advisors have developed a predictable, process-driven marketing schedule, they can truly leverage their time by delegating the driving to a team member, a part-time person, or even an independent contractor. The advisor's job is to set the strategy, develop the plan, and then turn it over to the team or a business development person to make it happen, while he or she plays a part in the process.

CHAPTER 15

Referrals: An Untapped Opportunity

Referrals may be a silver bullet for those who actively pursue them within a growth strategy, and they will likely continue to be the main source of new clients going forward. Advisors rate client referrals as a highly effective source of new business, according to our business development study (Table 15.1).

Client Referral Appreciation

While one might expect top-quartile advisors to outperform on referrals, this was not the case in 2009. Although they estimated higher numbers, both top performers and typical advisors attracted only two referrals in the first half of 2009. As the Best Practices Study Series continues in the future, we will better be able to determine potential causes or correlations for this finding.

The referral numbers suggest that a better follow-up process should lead to more referrals. If top performers estimated five new clients from referrals in 2008 and two in the first half of 2009 (Figure 15.1) and we take into account their referral follow-up statistics (Table 15.2), it stands to reason that increasing the frequency of sending thank-you notes and gifts and notifying the referral source of the outcome would increase the number of referrals.[1] To create a truly active referral market, advisors have to develop and follow a consistent process that encourages more referrals.

Although client referrals are the single biggest driver of new business, only 20 percent of advisors ask for referrals systematically. Worse, a majority indicate that they address referrals only occasionally in client meetings (Figure 15.2). Only half of advisors always place a call or send a thank-you note to a referrer. Only about 14 percent of firms, however, even those at the top, indicate that they follow a formalized referral process.

TABLE 15.1 Level of Effectiveness of Marketing Activities Used in the Last 12 Months

	QUARTILE	EXTREMELY EFFECTIVE	HIGHLY EFFECTIVE	EFFECTIVE	MILDLY EFFECTIVE	NOT EFFECTIVE	DOES NOT APPLY
Passive referrals from existing clients	Top	11.9%	11.9%	25.4%	42.4%	3.4%	5.1%
	Other	2.3%	9.8%	22.4%	45.4%	16.7%	3.4%
Actively market to clients to generate referrals	Top	5.1%	11.9%	18.6%	11.9%	11.9%	40.7%
	Other	2.3%	4.6%	16.7%	24.7%	12.1%	39.7%
CPA and attorney relationships	Top	5.1%	10.2%	18.6%	28.8%	18.6%	18.6%
	Other	3.4%	9.2%	16.1%	35.1%	20.7%	15.5%
Financial advisor/broker relationships	Top	0.0%	0.0%	6.8%	8.5%	10.2%	74.6%
	Other	2.3%	1.1%	6.9%	8.0%	21.3%	60.3%
Direct marketing (mail, fax, e-mail, Internet)	Top	0.0%	1.7%	3.4%	13.7%	20.6%	60.5%
	Other	0.0%	1.1%	4.0%	13.2%	24.1%	57.5%
PR/media coverage — retain firm	Top	0.0%	0.4%	3.0%	6.9%	6.0%	83.7%
	Other	0.0%	0.0%	1.1%	6.9%	5.2%	86.8%
PR/media coverage — internal	Top	0.4%	1.7%	3.0%	7.3%	7.3%	80.3%
	Other	0.0%	0.6%	2.3%	5.7%	5.7%	85.6%
Radio/TV shows	Top	0.0%	6.8%	1.7%	6.8%	8.5%	76.3%
	Other	0.6%	0.6%	1.7%	2.9%	6.3%	87.9%
Seminar marketing	Top	0.0%	5.1%	6.8%	20.3%	3.4%	64.4%
	Other	1.1%	5.2%	9.8%	17.2%	5.7%	60.9%
Professional/trade groups	Top	0.0%	0.0%	3.4%	13.6%	10.2%	72.9%
	Other	0.6%	1.1%	5.2%	17.2%	8.6%	67.2%
Referral/networking groups	Top	3.4%	0.0%	0.0%	13.6%	16.9%	66.1%
	Other	1.1%	1.1%	6.9%	17.2%	13.2%	60.3%
Cold calls/solicitation	Top	0.0%	0.0%	3.4%	5.1%	3.4%	88.1%
	Other	0.0%	0.0%	4.0%	12.1%	10.3%	73.6%
Advertising	Top	0.0%	0.0%	1.7%	10.2%	15.3%	72.9%
	Other	0.0%	0.6%	1.7%	13.2%	20.1%	64.4%
Internet presence	Top	0.0%	0.0%	3.1%	6.3%	43.8%	46.9%
	Other	0.0%	1.1%	3.2%	8.4%	40.0%	47.4%
Community involvement	Top	0.0%	6.8%	13.6%	32.2%	5.1%	42.4%
	Other	1.7%	4.6%	16.7%	26.4%	10.9%	39.7%
Charitable involvement	Top	0.0%	8.5%	8.5%	30.5%	5.1%	47.5%
	Other	1.7%	5.2%	10.3%	14.4%	12.6%	55.7%
Niche marketing	Top	3 .4%	11.9%	3.4%	15.3%	3.4%	62.7%
	Other	5.7%	5.7%	10.9%	8.6%	7.5%	61.5%
Other	Top	18.2%	0.0%	9.1%	9.1%	0.0%	63.6%
	Other	8.3%	4.2%	8.3%	12.5%	4.2%	62.5%

FIGURE 15.1 Number of New Clients Generated from Client Referrals for Top-Quartile Advisors and Other Advisory Firms

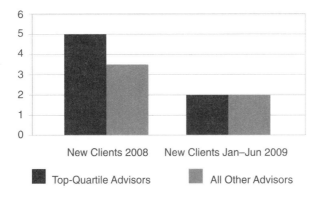

TABLE 15.2 Referral Follow-up Activities by Top-Quartile Advisors and Other Advisory Firms

REFERRAL FOLLOW-UP	QUARTILE	ALWAYS	MOST OF THE TIME	SOME OF THE TIME	RARELY	NEVER
Place a thank-you phone call	Top	47.5%	15.3%	15.3%	16.9%	5.1%
	Other	42.0%	20.7%	21.8%	9.8%	5.7%
Send a thank-you note or letter	Top	54.2%	15.3%	20.3%	6.8%	3.4%
	Other	40.8%	26.4%	18.4%	9.2%	5.2%
Send a thank-you gift	Top	10.2%	5.1%	28.8%	28.8%	27.1%
	Other	10.3%	12.6%	23.0%	27.6%	26.4%
Involve referral source on ongoing basis	Top	13.6%	28.8%	32.2%	13.6%	11.9%
	Other	9.8%	23.0%	33.3%	22.4%	11.5%
Notify referral source of result of referral	Top	35.6%	27.1%	20.3%	10.2%	6.8%
	Other	36.8%	31.6%	17.2%	8.6%	5.7%
Follow formalized referral process	Top	13.6%	20.3%	13.6%	23.7%	28.8%
	Other	9.8%	16.7%	23.0%	21.3%	29.3%

When we asked the top 400 advisors at a major broker-dealer about referrals, 54 percent said they sent thank-you cards or made a phone call in response to a client referral.[2] Our informal polling of thousands of advisors also supports the finding that about half of advisors have a specific response to client referrals.

We can't explain why half of the advisor population wouldn't respond to the one event that drives most of their growth, but can conclude that few advisors actually maximize the referral opportunity. In fact, a very small percentage of advisory firm clients have actually provided a referral opportunity.

FIGURE 15.2 Active Marketing Practices Engaged In to Obtain Client Referrals

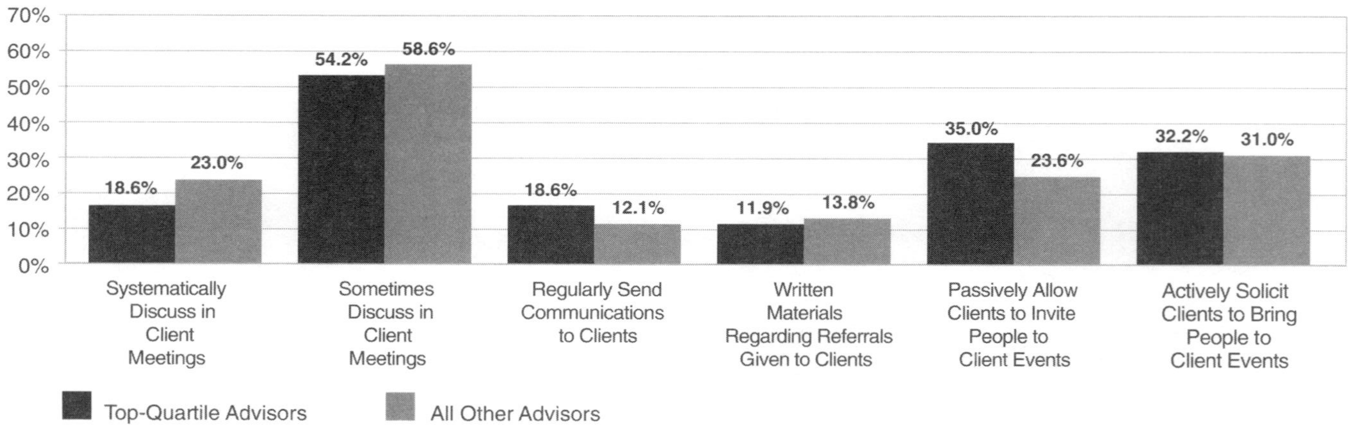

■ Top-Quartile Advisors	▨ All Other Advisors

Systematically Discuss in Client Meetings: 18.6% / 23.0%

Sometimes Discuss in Client Meetings: 54.2% / 58.6%

Regularly Send Communications to Clients: 18.6% / 12.1%

Written Materials Regarding Referrals Given to Clients: 11.9% / 13.8%

Passively Allow Clients to Invite People to Client Events: 35.0% / 23.6%

Actively Solicit Clients to Bring People to Client Events: 32.2% / 31.0%

We believe when advisors are busy managing growth they don't pay much attention to maximizing growth through referrals or otherwise. Since markets have become more volatile and client referrals have declined, we are urging advisors to focus on reinforcing referral behavior in their client base.

Yet taking a proactive approach to marketing and referrals is difficult for even the most successful firms, and few know where to start, much less how to do so effectively. This is particularly interesting because most advisors are natural marketers. Perhaps that's why they don't see the need to systematize these talents into processes. In our survey of the broker-dealers' top advisors, the results supported this view:

- 39.6 percent of advisors did not ask for referrals.
- 38.5 percent have no system for referrals.
- More than 75 percent of new businesses are referrals.

Obviously, most advisors aren't proactive about referrals, which means there may be a wealth of untapped opportunity waiting for you.

Using the Right Net

How can advisors tap into this potential opportunity? What works best to capture client referrals? There is a wide range of approaches, from indirect questions in client communications to client events to asking directly. The clear standout is discussing referrals in client meetings and calls (Figure 15.3). This is by far the easiest and most cost-effective way to generate referrals. It also allows advisors the time and opportunity to educate current clients on the type of referrals they seek.

We found that top-performing firms augment asking for referrals in client meetings with other communications. Notably, they are more likely to send referral communications to clients, thus reinforcing the preferred behavior. Top-quartile advisors are also slightly more likely to use client events to promote referrals by actively encouraging clients to bring people to these events. We would not expect to see these strategies used in isolation. Those advisors who are using client events, for example, are more likely to address referrals directly during personal meetings and calls as a starting point.

The best client events, as we mentioned in the previous chapter, depend entirely on the interests of the client base. Best-practice firms understand their clients and focus on affinity groups within their target client base by creating separate marketing activities for their top referrers. If their top referrals like art, maybe touring an artist's studio or a gallery would be rewarding; if they like cooking, maybe a dinner with a specialized cuisine.

FIGURE 15.3 Primary Activities Used to Generate Client Referrals

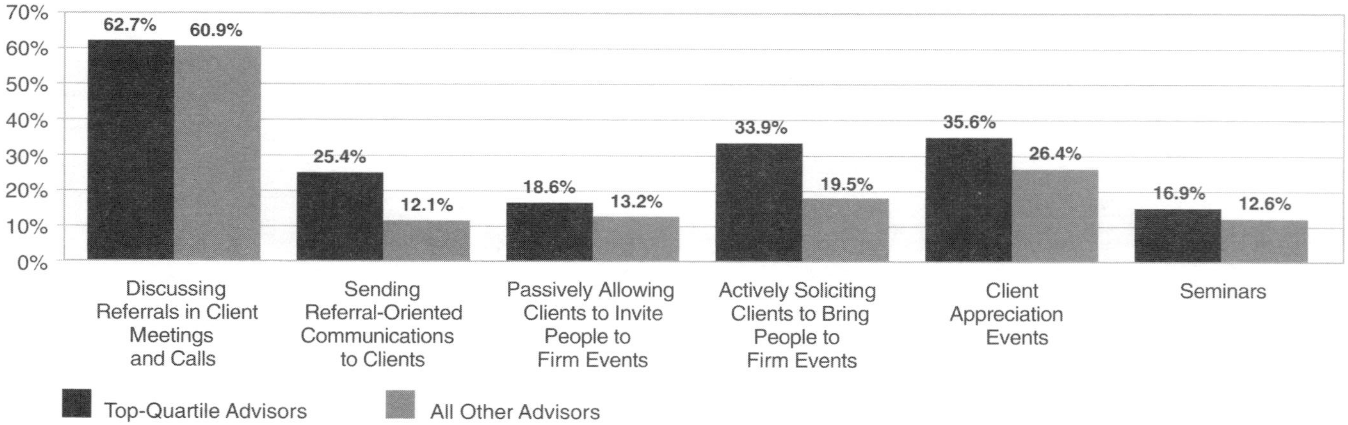

- Top-Quartile Advisors
- All Other Advisors

Activity	Top-Quartile Advisors	All Other Advisors
Discussing Referrals in Client Meetings and Calls	62.7%	60.9%
Sending Referral-Oriented Communications to Clients	25.4%	12.1%
Passively Allowing Clients to Invite People to Firm Events	18.6%	13.2%
Actively Soliciting Clients to Bring People to Firm Events	33.9%	19.5%
Client Appreciation Events	35.6%	26.4%
Seminars	16.9%	12.6%

Fear of Asking

When it comes to the number of referrals received, insurance firms win the race, probably because they have successfully incorporated referral marketing as a systematic task into their ongoing process; asking for referrals is an ingrained part of their culture. We can see this outperformance on referrals both with insurance firms and independent broker-dealer advisors with an insurance affiliation (Figure 15.4).

Insurance advisors, for example, may be more comfortable asking for referrals given the sales-focused nature of their core business. By contrast, an overwhelming majority of fee-based or fee-only independent firms view themselves as service organizations (which we do not dispute), and this can make them reluctant to ask for referrals. They tell us they don't want to appear to be selling something or to put clients on the spot, and they don't want to look like they need the business.

During the past decade, many advisors were told to pass a blank piece of paper across the table to clients, while confidently saying, "Can you give me the name of five people you know who . . . ?" Many successful advisors tell us that this simply does not feel like the right style for them. That's understandable, but what we like about this approach is that it tends to work because it gives advisors a simple, systematic way to ingrain asking for referrals into their business behavior. The point is that finding some way, whatever that may be, to make referral-seeking a part of the firm's business behavior will yield far more referrals than not asking or asking occasionally.

Developing Strategic Alliances

Professional referrals are a good way to grow the business; however, many advisors get frustrated because they don't see results fast enough. Working with centers of influence (COIs), such as certified public accountants (CPAs) or attorneys, is a long-term process. Nurture these relationships to establish credibility and build trust with the COI. None of this happens quickly. Further, advisors have to be careful that they are working with the right professionals, which means that they share a similar service ethic, target the same clients, and are open to reciprocal referrals.

By and large, advisors market to COIs (Table 15.3) using the same communications they use with clients, and they consider direct contact most effective. Ongoing communication with professional referral sources is clearly important to maintain the relationship and articulate your ideal client profile.

Having professional referral sources know and truly understand what you do as an advisor—and whom you do it for—is an important strategy. The better the referring professional understands the advisor's process, the more conviction

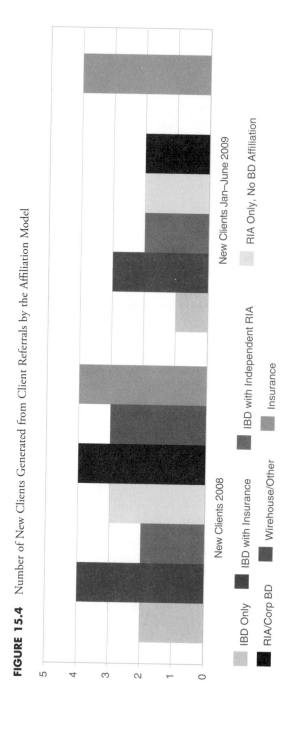

FIGURE 15.4 Number of New Clients Generated from Client Referrals by the Affiliation Model

TABLE 15.3 Effectiveness of Marketing Activities to Maintain a COI Relationship and to Clearly Articulate Your Ideal Client Profile

	QUARTILE	EXTREMELY EFFECTIVE	HIGHLY EFFECTIVE	EFFECTIVE	MILDLY EFFECTIVE	NOT EFFECTIVE	DOES NOT APPLY
Newsletter	Top	1.7%	1.7%	11.9%	32.2%	13.6%	39.0%
	Other	0.0%	3.4%	12.6%	28.2%	10.3%	45.4%
Educational calls	Top	0.0%	3.4%	5.1%	22.0%	5.1%	64.4%
	Other	0.0%	1.7%	9.2%	19.5%	4.6%	64.9%
Educational meetings	Top	0.0%	5.1%	8.5%	16.9%	8.5%	61.0%
	Other	0.6%	4.0%	14.4%	17.2%	4.6%	59.2%
Market commentary, e-mail	Top	0.0%	7.7%	23.1%	50.0%	19.2%	0.0%
	Other	2.7%	6.7%	26.7%	44.0%	20.0%	0.0%
Market commentary, mail	Top	0.0%	1.7%	3.4%	18.6%	3.4%	72.9%
	Other	0.6%	0.6%	5.2%	10.3%	6.9%	76.4%
Phone calls from advisor	Top	5.1%	16.9%	27.1%	8.5%	5.1%	37.3%
	Other	4.6%	12.6%	24.1%	21.3%	4.0%	33.3%
Phone calls from staff	Top	0.0%	3.4%	10.2%	15.3%	5.1%	66.1%
	Other	1.7%	1.1%	8.0%	8.6%	4.6%	75.9%
Client events, formal	Top	0.0%	6.8%	13.6%	16.9%	1.7%	61.0%
	Other	2.3%	2.3%	10.3%	9.2%	4.0%	71.8%
Client events, informal	Top	0.0%	10.2%	10.2%	22.0%	0.0%	57.6%
	Other	2.9%	2.3%	8.0%	12.1%	3.4%	71.3%
Client dinners	Top	1.7%	5.1%	13.6%	20.3%	1.7%	57.6%
	Other	3.4%	5.7%	16.7%	19.0%	1.1%	54.0%

FIGURE 15.5 Top-Quartile Advisors and Other Advisory Firms Inform Professional Referral Sources of Their Target Client Profile

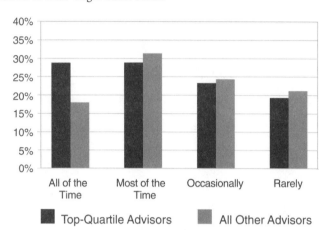

he or she will convey to prospects. This reinforces your position as the expert and the "go-to" resource for prospective clients. Note that top performers understood the importance of communicating their value, with a higher percentage indicating that they always inform professional referral sources of their target client profile (Figure 15.5).

It's imperative that firm leadership champions a formal process to build strategic relationships or risk limiting possible referrals. A good starting point is to review the firm's top 10 or 20 clients and identify their CPAs, attorneys, or other professional advisors. Introduce yourself to these COIs as one of their clients' key advisors and arrange a breakfast or lunch meeting to get acquainted.

It generally takes a series of lunches or meetings to get to know each other well enough to establish comfort on the part of the referral source. Expect to start out giving more than you receive. Once you build a rapport, however, the tide may turn. Successful professionals, just like you, are busy! You may be able to help by giving them useful information or support in serving their clients.

Bear in mind that CPAs are risk averse by nature. They're not salespeople. They tend to be logical, analytical, and fact driven, the opposite of intuitive financial planners with a vision for big ideas. So advisors want to be very transparent about their process. CPAs love processes and want to know exactly what's going to happen and when. Talk about what you're doing with the client and how it may affect the CPA and keep him or her in the loop. Ask whether you can come to the CPA's office and show him or her exactly what steps you take clients through. It helps to have a visual piece or a diagram that explains what you do.

You can explain what you're doing for the COI's clients and say that if he or she has any other clients who want some clarity around their financial future, please feel free to make a referral. You want the COIs to think of you every time one of their clients is about to retire or is unhappy with another financial professional. You have to be at the top of the COI's mind when his or her clients need something you have to offer.

Ultimately, the goal is to be consistent with current and potential COIs. Firms that follow a consistent process for how they handle referrals, regardless of the source of the referral, have more and better-qualified referrals. For an ongoing process, see the section "Five-Step Referral Process for Professionals" in Chapter 16. By focusing your time and attention on a few key areas in business development, such as establishing COI relationships and following a documented referral process, you should quickly realize increased return on investment for the time. The efficiency gained by establishing and following these processes will ultimately help you reach your goals.

The Referral Management Process

By handling referrals in a simple, systematic, and disciplined way, advisors can promote meaningful growth at a limited cost. The referral management process is just such a system. It can help to:

- Increase referrals.
- Decrease marketing costs.
- Increase profitability.
- Positively enhance client and professional relationships.
- Create a referral culture throughout your organization.

Most advisors recognize the value of referrals, but few seem to understand the psychology and the processes that promote referrals. We have developed a five-step referral process for working with professional sources and a three-step referral process for referrals from clients. These can help advisors systematically manage these important sources of new business and increase the quality and quantity of referrals made. Both processes should achieve the maximum result from the minimum amount of time and effort.

Process versus Result

Most often, both parties in a referral situation measure the success of the referral by the outcome: If the prospect becomes a client, the referral was successful. Advisors need to understand that the most important part of a referral is the behavior. *It's the referring behavior—not the outcome of the referral—that you want to promote and reward.* It's more important to focus on the process than on the result to improve the quantity and quality of referrals you receive.

Advisors can proactively design and manage referral activity with a referral management process. Items to consider using include:

- Cover letter addressing the method of introduction.
- Brochure or other materials about your firm.
- Current materials and process expectations (here's how it works).
- Referral letters.
- Thank-you letters.
- Referral introduction letter.
- Referral procedure form.
- Referral scripts/dialogue points.
- Follow-up process.
- Referral tracking form.

For the referral management process to work, it must become a standard part of the firm's business practice and a priority. To this end, we recommend that once advisors tailor this process to their firms, they hold a meeting with their staff to share its purpose, design, and use in their practice.

The Five-Step Referral Process for Professionals

The five-step referral process for professionals is for use with professionals, such as attorneys and certified public accountants (CPAs), who refer clients to you. The goal of this process is to enhance the role and value of the professional in the referral process. Each step in the process has a specific goal to help promote and reward the referral behavior.

Step 1: Recognition

Once a professional such as a CPA or an attorney has made a referral to you, make it a priority to communicate a few key points:

- Thank you for your confidence.
- I will give it my immediate attention.
- I will keep you posted.

These points send the message that you appreciate the person's trust, that you will act professionally and give the referral priority as a result of your relationship with the referrer, and that the referrer is a valued participant in the process. Do this by telephone shortly after receiving the referral, if at all possible.

During the developmental stages of a relationship, keep this call brief. It's important to recognize the referral source's contribution and then move on, giving you an opportunity for future conversation about the referral. Relationships with professional referral sources take time to build and require ongoing interaction, which is a goal of the process.

Step 2: Enhancement

When the prospect makes contact with your office, send the referral source a "thank-you" note. This establishes the "team approach" you desire and reinforces the key points of step 1 (I am touched by your confidence).

If you set up an appointment with the prospect, send a copy of the appointment confirmation letter to the referral source (if you currently do not send such a letter, you may wish to reconsider your procedure). Write a hand-written note directly on the letter, saying:

- You look forward to meeting with the prospect.
- You value the referral source's input on this matter and will be contacting him or her to discuss the referral in further detail.
- One or more of the following:
  - You are touched by the referrer's confidence.
  - You will do your best to be of help.
  - You will ensure that the referrer's relationship with his or her client is enhanced by your contact.

For example, your note might read:

> Bill, I appreciate your confidence and look forward to meeting with John and Mary. I'll give you a call to learn more about their situation and needs. As always, I'll do my best to ensure that my meeting with them reflects well on you.
>
> My best,
>
> Robert

Step 3: Participation

The "participation" step is generally a phone call to learn more about the prospect's situation.

Plan your call a few days before your prospect appointment to allow for missed connections or "phone tag."

There are two purposes for this telephone call:

1. To learn more about the referral's financial status, personality traits, likes/ dislikes, and special needs so that you are fully prepared to address his or her personal situation.
2. To communicate important messages to the referral source.

Learn as much about the prospect as you can, so that you are fully equipped to influence the outcome. In addition to common discovery questions such as financial condition, personality traits, and who participates in the decision-making process, the following are also important to know:

- The prospect's motivation for learning about financial planning/investment management. This establishes what's important to the individual and will help you influence the value he or she sees in retaining you. For example: "What prompted the Joneses to take an interest in financial planning?"
- How the subject came up. This will provide some indication of whether the referral source mentioned the subject or if he or she makes a referral only when the client requests one.
- The referral source's motivation for making the referral. Does he simply feel this prospect will benefit from further information, or does he see a specific need that is cause for concern? For example: "What financial planning issues or concerns do you think John and Mary have?"

Use this time to communicate important messages to your referral source. The previous questions, through dialogue, style, and tone, need to communicate to the referral source that:

- He or she is an important member of the team—equally as important as you in the process.
- You understand that this is the referral source's client and that you are being trusted.
- You believe in the team approach, are a team player, and will act accordingly.
- You will do your best to enhance their relationship by your contact.

Step 4: The Initial Prospect Meeting

Have a standard format and agenda for your initial prospect meeting that should include several reference points related to the referral source and the process. Remember, this is an opportunity to improve your relationship with the referral source, which is more important to your ongoing success than whether this particular prospect becomes a client.

Consider what discussion points to include in the initial prospect meeting that will enhance your referral source relationship. For example:

- "I receive a lot of referrals from CPAs, but Jack is one of the best. He always takes time to make sure his clients know about financial planning."
- "I'm sure you enjoy working with Jack. Not a lot of CPAs take the time to make sure their clients do good financial planning, and I'm always impressed by how thorough he is with his clients."

You obviously don't want to overdo it, but this is an opportunity to reinforce the prospect's choice of professional. At some point, follow through on your commitment to ensure that your interaction with the referral reflects well on the referral source. You'll want to share this with your referral source in the future to further enhance your relationship (typically, in step 4 of the process).

Step 5: Follow-Up

The follow-up step ensures that you tell your referral source the result of your meeting as soon as possible. The goal, once again, is to create positive relationships based on the process, not on the result. If you believe the messages you communicated to the referral source about including him or her in a team approach (or if you expect the referral source to perceive that you did), you should include him or her in every step of the process.

If you hold a prospect meeting in the morning, notify the referral source of the outcome that afternoon. If the meeting is in the afternoon, update the referral source no later than the next morning. We call this the "AM/PM" rule.

Your prompt update will show that you both understand and practice the "team approach," and you communicate important messages that support your relationship. Someone will update the referral source about the outcome of the meeting—either you or the prospect. If the advisors do this before the prospect does, they protect their professional relationship with the referral source. If the prospect notifies the referral source after the meeting that he or she has decided not to do planning with the advisor, the prospect will undoubtedly give some reason—such as high fees—that in no circumstance will reflect well on the firm and that may harm the advisor's relationship with the referral source. If, however, the advisor is the one to notify the referral source that the client didn't see the value in a financial plan or seemed sensitive to fees, the referral source is more likely to think it was his client's issue and not the advisor's fault.

Proactively communicating the meeting result, positive or negative, focuses on the partnership and the process and not the outcome. Over time, this helps ensure an ongoing relationship with the referral source and more referrals.

Through the five-step referral process, the referral source fosters a vested interest in the result of the meetings, making him more likely to work with the advisor to achieve the desired result. There will be a stronger sense of "team" and a desire to see the team succeed. If the prospect later calls the referral source for advice and reports that he or she liked you but found the planning fees higher than expected, the source is prepared because you already revealed the outcome and he is more likely to advise the prospect (his client) that this is important work, which is well worth the fees.

The Three-Step Process for Client Referrals

Acknowledge client referral sources in a similar, but abbreviated, manner: Thank them, show that you value their trust, and encourage future referrals. We use the following three-step process.

Step 1: Recognition

The first step is a brief telephone call to tell referring client how much you appreciate the referral. For example, tell your client:

- You are touched by his or her confidence.
- You will give the referral your immediate attention.
- You will do your best for the referral.

In addition, to show your appreciation to clients for their confidence in referring someone to your firm, send an appropriate gift.[1] Gifts that show knowledge of your clients' tastes and interests are the best relationship builders, while sending such gifts to their business address may make the gift more visible and provide them with the opportunity to explain why they received the gift and from whom they received it.

One of the more common mistakes advisors make is not doing enough to reward the referral behavior of their clients. Making a referral, particularly the first referral, is not common behavior and thus should be highly recognized and rewarded to encourage positive feelings and repetition of the behavior.

We've noted that many advisors send a thank-you note if the prospect doesn't become a client and will send a thank-you gift only if the prospect becomes a client. Again, this implies that the result of the referral is more important than the referral behavior. Making a referral, particularly the first time, requires your clients (and professional referral sources) to extend themselves beyond their comfort zone and place tremendous confidence in you. Your resulting actions should at least equal that effort.

To the degree allowable, reward client referrals regardless of the outcome of the referral. Some tips and ideas include:

- Send a unique/interesting client gift on receiving a referral, even if the referral isn't a good fit. We've found that Sherri's Berries (chocolate-covered strawberries) always seem to go over well and are within the available allowance. There is no lack of ideas available by doing some research on the Web.
- One firm sends an apple pie or a chocolate cake (depending on client preference) with every referral. This makes the activity memorable and enjoyable for clients and seems to keep generating more referrals.
- One firm has Tiffany boxes with small gifts, such as key chains or small vases, on a table at its annual client event. At the end of the evening, the principal calls up clients who have made referrals during the year and hands them each a Tiffany box. Interestingly, clients are always looking for referrals so they can get the Tiffany box next year.
- One firm sends two sets of golf balls with its logo to clients who golf, with a note that they can keep one set and pass one on to the next referral.
- One firm gives clients wine goblets with their initials engraved, with a note about how great it will be to complete the set.

There is no end to the ideas for rewarding referral sources; just be open-minded and creative.

Step 2: Enhancement

Enhance your relationship with the client referral source by encouraging referral behavior. Draft a hand-written thank-you note instead of copying the client prospect confirmation letter (also, not appropriate unless the client is also a professional referral source). Use the talking points identified in Step 1: touched by their confidence, you will do your utmost for the prospect.

If you have scheduled a meeting with the referral, let your client know because this will reflect positively on you and the process. Even more important, if the referral was not a good fit for your firm, the "enhancement" call provides the perfect opportunity for you to educate your client on whom he or she should be referring.

Step 3: Follow-Up

As with professional referral sources, proactively communicating the outcome to your client, prior to the prospect's doing so, has important relationship implications. If you are not the one to share with the client the outcome of the referral, the prospect undoubtedly will.

If the prospect chose not to work with you or you with them, and you are not the first to share this information with your client, it will not likely reflect positively on you and may ultimately harm your relationship with the client. In addition, openly communicating with your clients why a prospect was not an appropriate fit would give you an additional opportunity to share your value proposition and target client profile. In this way you will be further reinforcing your value to the client while teaching him or her whom you do your best work with.

Best-Practice Ideas

Track and Monitor Client Referrals

Consistently update contact records to track key referral information. Include a method for identifying and tracking the number of referrals made, the name of the person referred by the client, the date of the referral(s), and the results. Many firms develop a referral report to monitor and review on a quarterly basis. This keeps advisors aware of who is referring actively to their practice so that they can promote an overwhelmingly positive experience for the referrers through ongoing acts of appreciation. It also helps firms to identify the number, type, and quality of referrals, so they can actively address changes or improvements desired. Additionally, it provides a view of what percentage of the client base is referring, highlighting how effective a firm's referral awareness and programs are.

Make Referring a WOW! Experience

Although the manner and the method vary from firm to firm, many advisors make referring a WOW! experience that goes way beyond thank-you notes for the person referring. Creatively think of ways to make the experience so positive that those who refer can't help but want to do it again. Make the experience memorable by making it extraordinary.

Generate Referrals, Don't Wait for Them

Here are several events to host to encourage an introduction to new clients ("future friends of the firm"). The ideas range from very upscale to "mom and pop." The point is that the type of event or activity should reflect the style and nature of your clients and practice. Your interest or comfort will depend on the nature of your client relationships (business formal or more personal). That could also vary by client, so you might want to segment clients into groups for different types of activities.

- *Fireside chats.* Held in the office, these quarterly client meetings discuss market conditions and other relevant topics. Clients get used to them and find it easy to bring friends, family, or colleagues.

- *Life-enhancing meetings.* One of our client advisors, who emphasizes enhancing clients' lifestyles, has started a series of quarterly meetings focused on nonfinancial subjects. For example, he is having a family therapist discuss how to create family traditions in an age of latchkey kids and television. He plans to have a travel agent discuss wonderful vacation destinations at another meeting. The general premise is to provide a consistently interesting format. Regular meetings make clients more comfortable and more likely to bring others.
- *Summer picnic series.* A client firm in the Midwest that has many clients with children and grandchildren hosts a summer barbecue complete with food and child entertainment (a clown, balloon tents, etc.). The idea is that families with children know other families with children, and families tend to attend child-centric activities.
- *Golf getaways.* Invite golfing clients to a golf outing, providing the opportunity for them to bring "future friends of the firm." A foursome a month or a quarter could generate some good prospects.
- *Charitable events.* Gather clients to participate in charitable events, such as a tree-planting day or working on houses for Habitat for Humanity. This might be worthwhile as a community involvement activity.

Categorizing Referral Sources

Part of an ongoing process for managing referrals from either clients or centers of influence (COIs) is what we have come to call the rule of influentials, which suggests there are three ways to group people who could give you referrals:

1. *Influentials.* These are individuals who presently have a positive impact on your practice by having referred someone to you within the last two years. This group includes clients, professionals, or anyone else who champions your cause or otherwise has had a positive marketing impact on your business. For example, a larger advisor who refers small clients to you (or vice versa) could be an Influential.
2. *Incubators.* These individuals *could* have a positive impact on your practice, but they need nurturing to get there. This would include clients who have the potential to refer, other professionals who work with your clients (automatically a warm relationship), or people in your COI who have responded positively but have not as yet made a referral.
3. *Popeyes.* These are individuals who are not likely to refer anyone, regardless of how hard you try. We call them Popeyes, because, like the cartoon sailor who frequently said, "I am what I am, and that's all that I am," these people are not likely to change. These are clients who like, respect, and trust you and who think you're doing a great job, but they will never refer someone

to you because it simply isn't in their nature. This is also true of some professionals or others with whom you may have tried in vain to establish relationships.

Categorizing your clients and professional contacts by how likely they are to refer clients helps you identify who might be important to your marketing and referral efforts. It also tells you who is, perhaps, not the best use of your marketing dollars and time.

Once you designate your client and referral lists by group in your database (feel free to change "Popeye" to something more practical), you can market more easily and effectively, increasing the probability that you will sustain the effort.

Keep track of referrals from the Influentials and the Incubators and monitor them in two-year increments. If someone in your Influential group hasn't made a new referral in two years, put him or her in an "alert" group for about 90 days, and try to figure out what's going on. For example, it's perfectly appropriate to ask a CPA who has stopped referring clients whether anything has changed in his practice or yours that would cause fewer referrals.

If, during the alert period, no improvement results, move the CPA to the Incubator group. This is not exile: They receive attention even in this group. You simply are making the best use of your resources. Alternatively, if someone in the Incubator group makes a referral, this person should be promoted to the Influential group. Even if the referral prospect is unsuccessful, the source has positively influenced your business.

CHAPTER 17

Unlocking Client Feedback

In a recent study of investors, research and feedback firm Advisor Impact proved that there is a clear and enduring link between the quality of advisors' client relationships and their ability to grow profitably.[1] Any growth strategy, therefore, must build on the strength of your relationship with existing clients. This will allow advisors to focus organically on cross-selling, gaining share of wallet, and referrals.

Although a majority of advisors agree that creating and maintaining a satisfied client base is essential, few formalize the process by asking for feedback. Client feedback is seen as "nice to have" when, in fact, it can fundamentally affect overall profitability and drive growth.

Executed well, a client feedback strategy not only tells advisors whether clients are satisfied but also uncovers detailed information on what they need, want, and expect—all of which link directly to revenue and referral opportunities.

A relatively simple client survey should help you meet at least four core objectives:

1. Building deeper relationships.
2. Structuring and streamlining client service.
3. Cross-selling more effectively.
4. Increasing referrals from both existing clients and centers of influence (COIs).

The data suggest that there's a great opportunity here. Figure 17.1 shows that a minority of firms have conducted a client survey in the past three years. Notably, top-performing firms are more likely to have asked for client feedback, suggesting a stronger focus on understanding the needs of clients.

FIGURE 17.1 Percentage of Participants Who Have or Have Not Conducted a Client Survey in the Past Three Years

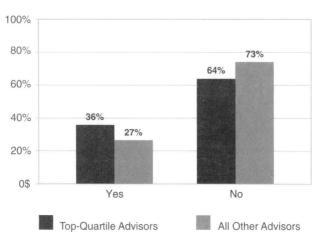

Client feedback is a very personal process, and many advisors are afraid of getting negative feedback. Our position has always been that fear of negative feedback is more harmful than soliciting feedback that's negative. Once advisors recognize negative feedback, they can remedy any problems, which would clearly impress clients and increase the value of the business.

The fact is, actual satisfaction ratings suggest that this fear is without basis. For advisors who had conducted a client survey, satisfaction ratings were 4.5 out of 5 for top performers and 4.55 for other advisors. These high scores occur across the industry, according to Advisor Impact, which reports average satisfaction ratings of 4.6 across the tens of thousands of clients it has surveyed on behalf of financial advisors. As Figure 17.2 suggests, however, advisors want more—they covet overall satisfaction ratings of 5.0, and the perfect score is elusive.

Are advisors who solicit client feedback more confident about their service offering and client satisfaction and thus more likely to get high ratings? Would less confident advisors be less likely to do surveys, and would they get lower scores if they did? We'll never know. Delivering financial advice is a deeply personalized service, and we firmly believe that conducting client surveys is a best practice every advisor who wants to deliver a high-quality client experience should embrace.

The frequency of surveying clients is a clear differentiator between top performers and typical advisors. Thirty-three percent of top-quartile advisory firms conduct surveys annually versus 17 percent of other firms (Figure 17.3). Only about 15 percent of advisors from both groups conducted client surveys as a one-off event. The point is that the majority of firms conducting client surveys

FIGURE 17.2   Client Satisfaction and Goal Satisfaction Ratings Based on a Scale of 1.0 to 5.0: From Highly Dissatisfied (1.0) to Extremely Satisfied (5.0)

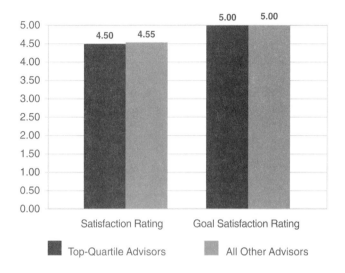

FIGURE 17.3   Frequency at Which Client Surveys Are Conducted: Results Are Only for Firms That Have Conducted a Survey in the Past Three Years

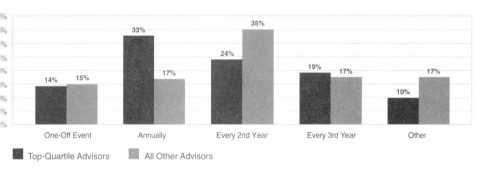

are doing so with some frequency, learning from them, and instituting changes when necessary.

Making Clients Matter

The very process of asking for feedback can help deepen client relationships. We believe, however—and the data support this—that actually using that feedback is what matters most, whether it's to follow up on a question or on a revenue opportunity.

The importance of providing input is the reason client advisory boards work; people want to feel that they matter, and giving them a say in their experience at the firm level provides that sense of significance. Like most initiatives, though, it takes a commitment not only to ask the questions but also to respond to the answers. Clients want to hear your response to their feedback. If you fail to explain your position, you defeat the purpose. Conducting a client survey and not responding to the results is the equivalent of getting a client referral and not saying thank you. It's simply poor taste and judgment.

According to research from Advisor Impact[2]:

• Sixty-one percent of the most engaged clients say a request for feedback is somewhat or very important; 68 percent of those with $1 million or more in investable assets agree.
• Seventy-two percent of the most engaged clients say that the feedback they provide actually makes a difference.
• While the benefits of client feedback can be compelling, there is both an art and a science to getting it right. As a result, many advisors outsource the process, because the money they save by doing it internally may represent a false economy if the questions aren't right and the analysis doesn't clearly link to practical and actionable outcomes.

Driving Growth

Any client feedback program should, of course, reflect a firm's unique business objectives, but here are two approaches to using client feedback to increase revenue.

1. *Increase awareness of existing services or improve cross-selling.* A good client feedback program can uncover opportunities to build deeper relationships with COIs, increase share of wallet, improve cross-selling, and increase referrals from existing clients. You can uncover cross-selling opportunities by simply asking clients which services, from, say, charitable giving to estate planning, they're interested in learning more about.
2. *Increase client referrals.* No matter what range of services you provide, referrals are always a key driver of growth. A client survey can ask a simple question: "Are you comfortable providing referrals?" Advisors can then focus their referral efforts on those who say yes.

These are just the basics—the core of any good client feedback program.

Yet there are many other objectives advisors can meet, using carefully crafted questions and a good process to analyze and use the information. For example, advisors might want to gather feedback on services provided by support staff and link that to their bonuses. Advisors might be interested in testing client reaction to a new workshop series they want to hold or evaluate how well positioning statements are working. Regardless of how advisors use the feedback, it is a frequently overlooked way to deepen and enhance client relationships.

We prefer to use Advisor Impact to survey clients, as they have developed an online client survey capability that meets the criteria we've established: ease and affordability, as well as help ensuring that thoughtful surveys are designed, that meaningful evaluation of feedback results, and that the information is translated into actions. The latter includes help with both process and tools to give firms and their clients the maximum opportunity to benefit from this important work.

PART III

Harnessing Human Capital

CHAPTER 18

The Value of Human Capital

Any firm that wants to grow needs to consider how to best manage one of its key assets—its people. Unfortunately, although most advisors are great entrepreneurs and visionaries, they are not necessarily good people managers. They know how to bring in and service new clients, but they often don't realize that how they hire, train, promote, and pay their people are interrelated functions and not isolated activities.

As a result, advisors avoid or severely limit creating teams because they find that adding new staff and/or advisors creates as many problems as it was meant to solve: employees don't do what you want them to do the way you want them to do it; teaching them how to do it "right" takes time away from rainmaking and spending time with clients; employees don't live up to your expectations or seem invested enough in the firm; they expect raises and too often leave as soon as they're good at their jobs.

The best way to manage these problems is to institute a sound human capital program. The goal of a human capital program is to align employee motivation and performance with the goals of the firm so that everyone is pulling in the same direction to create a successful, sustainable, profitable firm. A human capital program codifies exactly what employers and employees can expect from one another.

In this sense, an effective program creates a common language among all of the members of the firm so that everyone can strive for a common goal. All of the employees in an organization have expectations about what their responsibilities and roles are and what they should receive in return. Yet managing these expectations may be a nightmare unless everything is clear to all involved. The point of the program is to codify these expectations so that everyone understands his or her responsibilities and rewards.

Our research shows that neither top-quartile firms nor the 75 percent balance of firms are terribly good at implementing the components of human capital programs. Yet top-performing firms are slightly further along.

Key findings show that top performers:

- Have a higher head count, which better leverages advisor time.
- Hire additional advisors to support owners and drive revenue growth.
- Are willing to invest in additional staff and higher compensation spends.
- Focus on hiring more experienced and licensed staff members.

On the whole, top-quartile advisors outperform their peers on implementing best practices for human capital by only about 10 to 20 percent on average. These aren't earth-shattering differences, but when you add up all of the small steps top performers have taken in the right direction, that incrementally higher investment yields exponentially better performance.

Note that top-performing firms achieve five times greater total owner(s) income, six times more revenue, and seven times greater profit than their counterparts. In fact, top-quartile firms demonstrate greater performance across every performance metric related to a firm's human assets (Figure 18.1).

Although not the only contributing factor, these gains come from better use of the firm's human capital. With larger and better-deployed teams, top performers can create sustainable and scalable growth by efficiently focusing their time and energy on revenue-producing activities.

We defined key elements that constitute a solid human capital program and listed them below:

- *Firm vision and goals.* Building a team, whether it consists of 1 person or 100, begins with a clear vision and goals. Many advisors hire in response to a specific need (e.g., so they can stop doing administrative work) without thinking through the objectives and outcomes they want to achieve with their investment in new hires. In hiring, promoting, and paying people, advisors need to consider both their quantitative and their qualitative definitions of success.
- *Organizational model*: An organizational model formally defines the framework, form, and functions of roles within a firm. This includes how the organization allocates relationships, rights, and responsibilities. A significant number of advisory firms lack formalized organizational structures and struggle to define the roles of, and relationships between, positions within the firm. Irrespective of firm size, creating clarity around roles and responsibilities encourages improved performance and establishes a clear path for how and when to hire as the firm grows.
- *Job descriptions.* A job description is a list of duties, responsibilities, and functions attached to a specific position that, if spelled out properly, forms the basis for tracking job performance over time. Our research shows that a sig-

FIGURE 18.1 Human Capital Performance Metrics

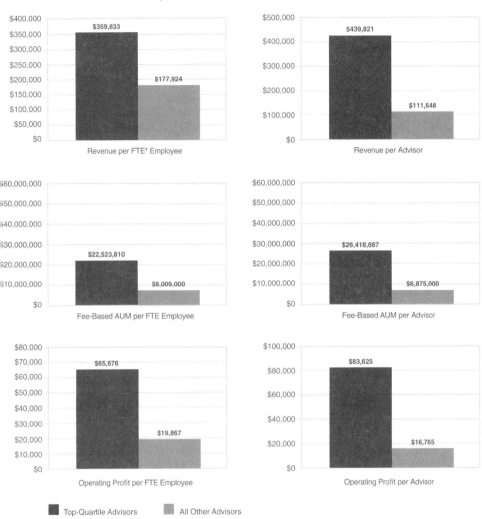

Top-Quartile Advisors   All Other Advisors

* Full-time equivalent.

nificant number of firms don't have or fully use job descriptions as a business tool to measure, manage, and maximize job performance. Effective job descriptions should do more than define tasks; they should clearly define the outcomes expected of each position and create a yardstick to measure and manage ongoing performance.

- *Career ladders.* Career ladders establish a path for advancement within a position and/or an organization. They define the responsibilities, pay range, and additional functions required to move up within that pay range and beyond it. Defining the roles, responsibilities, and rewards at each level creates clarity for both individuals and the firm, addressing many of the conflicts and the challenges firms face over raises and advancement.

- *Firm compensation plan.* Compensation plans define, document, and formalize a firm's compensation philosophy, policies, and practices. They spell out how the firm will distribute compensation to motivate employees, control costs, and ensure an equitable exchange between individuals and the firm. Effectively designed compensation plans create a common language to define and align goals, promote employee investment in those goals, and attach compensation rewards to achievement of desired outcomes.

- *New-hire process.* Most advisors make new hires in reaction to some event at the firm and base their choices on intuition. A new-hire process formalizes a consistent methodology for choosing a new team member. It defines the steps to create a new position and the process for seeking out and evaluating candidates. Given the investment made in new hires and the hard and soft cost of mistakes, an objective process can help increase the probability that hires will be successful.

- *On-boarding and training programs.* On-boarding is a new-employee orientation-and-mainstreaming process, ensuring that new hires are welcomed to the firm and eased into their responsibilities. Simple on-boarding methods help new hires integrate quickly and effectively.

  Training programs provide a systematic way for new hires to learn their responsibilities so that they can more quickly perform them independently and successfully. The cost savings is considerable, given the potential cost of undermining new-hire success with the prevalent "just figure it out" approach to training.

- *Performance reviews.* Performance reviews are opportunities to summarize and evaluate employees' progress, motivate them to continue doing well in their areas of strength, and build up areas where they can improve. To be productive, the reviews should be two-way exchanges that promote the objective evaluation of performance based on job descriptions and career paths. Through this process, you are better able to determine raises, define expectations, and promote professional development. Reviews should reinforce open communication by clarifying expectations for both parties. Rather than alienating and confusing employees, performance reviews can make them feel valued and encourage them to want to enhance their contribution to the firm.

In our experience, regardless of size, services, or style, most firms want to create a positive work environment that promotes the success of both individuals and the firm. Defining and developing a human capital program that formalizes these key elements will help firms measure, manage, and maximize their teams to promote greater success and satisfaction.

CHAPTER 19

Making the Successful Hire

Most advisors we work with recognize that they don't particularly like hiring and training people. Sure, it's work, but it can be work in the best sense. Just as losing an employee can be a painful experience, hiring an employee can be exciting and hopeful. Almost without exception, advisors who make a successful hire—whether a new one or a replacement—say they wish they had done it sooner. The key, of course, is that the hire be successful.

Understanding how firms hire is an important first step in creating a high-performance team. A number of advisory firms implement a hiring process (Figure 19.1) but are inconsistent in how they formalize the process. In general, firms have hiring processes that are informal, though similar each time. More top-performing firms have developed a formalized process for hiring, in part contributing to their ability to recruit and hire the right people.

Most advisory firms hire in a reactive and rushed way when someone leaves or when they get busy and need help. Advisors then typically follow an informal process of resume-interview-and-you're-hired. They don't have an intentional formalized hiring strategy involving an intentional search-and-selection process.

The interview is often the least effective way to hire someone. If interviews were truly reliable, there would be no need to engage in the hiring process, as employees would stay. Candidates put their best foot forward and tell the advisor what they think he or she wants to hear, and the advisor tends to talk more than listen. Advisors often don't check references or make sure the candidate has the skills listed on his or her resume. Under these circumstances, whether the hire will work out is little more than luck.

The final decision usually stems from the advisor/owner's gut instinct: Do I like the person? Are they a "good fit" for the team? Gut instinct does play a crucial role in hiring a good fit, but it shouldn't be the determining factor. Just

FIGURE 19.1 Percentage of Firms That Have Developed a Hiring Process

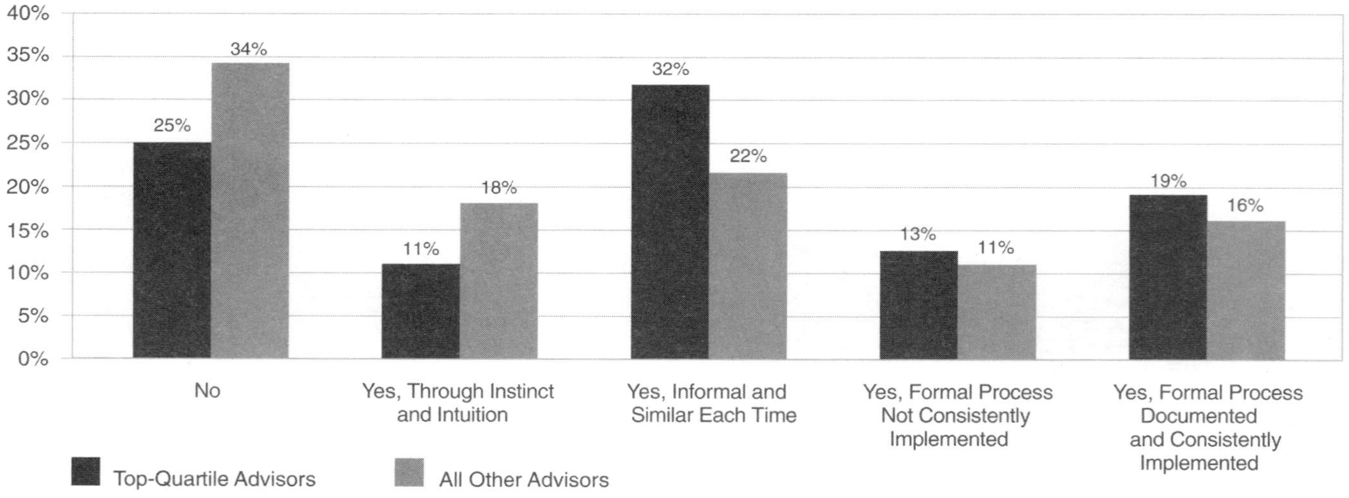

Yes, Formal Process Documented and Consistently Implemented — 19%, 16%

Yes, Formal Process Not Consistently Implemented — 13%, 11%

Yes, Informal and Similar Each Time — 32%, 22%

Yes, Through Instinct and Intuition — 11%, 18%

No — 25%, 34%

■ Top-Quartile Advisors   ■ All Other Advisors

as important is whether this person is right for a clearly defined position the firm wants to fill.

The first step is due diligence. You need to make sure the candidates are who they say they are and can do what they claim. Given that talk is cheap and people aren't, it seems worth spending some time on this process.

Of course, before any hiring process is necessary, advisors must make the decision to hire, whether to fill an open position or to create a new one.

Determining when to create a new position ideally should be a function of the firm's goals and financial circumstances. You want to have both additional work and the revenue to pay someone to do it. We received more than a few calls from advisors looking to create a position for somebody great who has come along when no positions were open. We call this a missing-the-boat hire: the reason for the hire isn't need but fear of passing up a good person. Hiring decisions should flow from business strategy and the ideal organizational model and should define every position in the firm, even those that may not be filled for some time.

The Six-Step Hiring Process

Our experience in helping advisors hire over the years suggests two very important concepts. First, there is no perfect process for predicting a successful long-term hire. Second, there are steps firms can take to increase the probability of a successful hire. That starts by supplementing gut instinct with a robust set of objective information. After helping advisors fill hundreds of staff and professional positions over the years, we've learned that a well-defined process built on a series of disciplined criteria and steps serves as a best-practice standard.

Step 1: Establish Meaningful Criteria

Once you've determined it's appropriate to fill or create a new position, develop a thorough job description and a pay package in advance of the hire so that you have clear parameters for the hiring process. A detailed job description makes it much easier to select a candidate who meets the written requirements. Compensation parameters are equally important. Too frequently, firms set compensation based on the person they hire, rather than setting compensation that is appropriate for the position.

Step 2: Post the Position

The job posting can be as important as the interview process, because it alone may determine (outside of a referral) whether someone, and specifically the right someone, will apply for your position. The posting, if created strategically, can increase your chances of attracting the most qualified candidates.

- The posting sets out specific criteria highlighting the desired qualifications for consideration. One firm hiring an administrative assistant knew it would be overwhelmed with resumes. The advisors mitigated this by listing three essential candidate criteria: a cover letter outlining compensation, specific experience working in a financial service organization, and the willingness to work a few extra hours on a regular basis. This significantly limited how many resumes they had to sift through.
- The posting should also be exciting and attractive to the right candidates by including why someone would want to work at your firm: "If you want to be part of a great team of people who are passionate about their work, are committed to the highest standards of excellence, and are recognized and rewarded for their contribution . . ." Such wording is far more enticing than "financial planning firm seeks operations manager."

Where should you post your job listing? In our "Best Practices: Human Capital 2010" findings, local/regional job search websites and schools/universities proved the most successful at producing candidates, followed by print media, recruiters, and recruiting from the competition (Figure 19.2). Our research also shows that no one site was more successful than others. After all, one of the

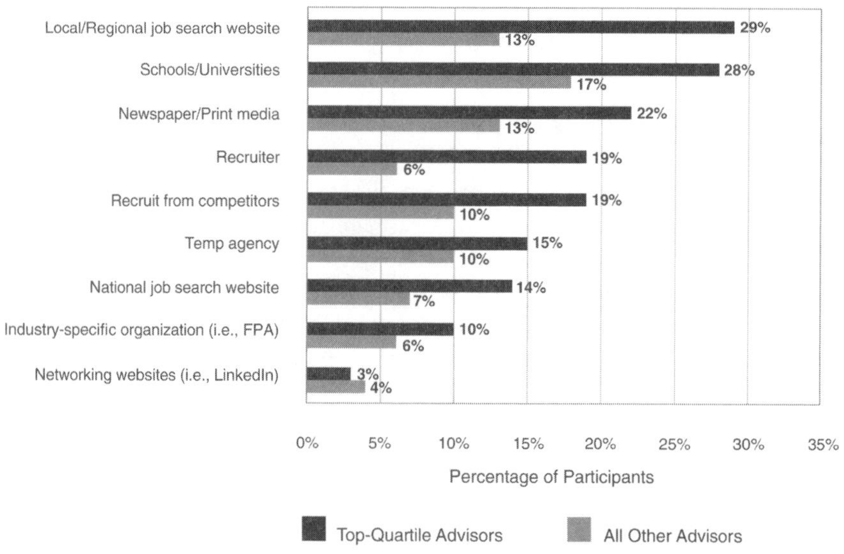

FIGURE 19.2 Job Search Resources That Resulted in a Successful Hire

popular general job sites might be fine for finding an administrative assistant, whereas more professional websites make more sense for hiring an advisor. Personal referrals often produce qualified candidates, but they should not be the sole search mechanism.

Our research did reveal that top-quartile firms are more likely to engage multiple resources when conducting their search. They therefore cast a wider net to attract a broader pool of potentially attractive candidates. The added expense of posting on multiple sources may well be the reason average advisory firms turn to fewer resources for hiring.

Step 3: The Screening Process

One way to make the interview process more productive is to create a list of revealing, behavior-based questions that you use consistently with each candidate in the interview process. This promotes a more objective evaluation and helps you more easily compare candidates by their responses.

In general, you want to ask questions that tell you (1) whether the person has the skills needed to perform the job, (2) his or her values and belief systems, (3) how the individual functions best, and (4) how well he or she will fit into your team. More specifically, good interview questions will:

- *Be precise.* There should be a specific reason to ask each question, a specific piece of information the answer should reveal. Do not waste time with questions you and they know the answer to or that everyone anticipates with a pat answer. For example, we know someone who always asks, "What is your superpower?" They feel it's an effective way to gain insights about the candidate that they wouldn't get with a traditional interview question. Another firm asks, "What is one thing we could tell you that would definitely make you not want to work here?"
- *Be open-ended.* This is actually a complement, rather than a contradiction, to the above. The question should be precise in what it seeks to learn but open-ended in order to encourage someone to share information that will be revealing. No one ever learned anything from a yes or no answer. For example, advisors often ask candidates whether they perform well under pressure, and every time the candidate says yes. If this is an important criterion for the position, a better question might be, "Give me an example of a time you performed well under pressure, and how did it positively affect the situation?"
- *Be behavior-based.* Beyond skills and abilities, you want to learn what behaviors you can expect when someone joins your firm. Someone may have the skill to do the job but be behaviorally incompatible. For example, a client service candidate may have the ability to communicate with clients but might not enjoy spending hours on the telephone.

Make sure that your questions explore all of the areas of importance: the candidates' skills and abilities, attitudes and values, working behaviors (how they work and how they feel they work best), and cultural fit. At one firm with the established value of "winning and competitiveness," we helped frame the following interview question: "We win here at Madison Wealth Management. We're playing for people's financial security. Losing is not an option. Prove you are a winner." Candidates were able to provide some revealing insights as a result of this demand.

If you're hiring for a technical position, be sure to ask specific skills-based questions. For example, if you're hiring a paraplanner to perform financial plan input and want to know whether the person has real experience doing this (beyond that claimed on his or her resume), ask the candidate questions such as "What inputs will you need to complete a financial plan successfully? When establishing annual rates of return in a plan, what are the considerations? What typically gets you hung up so that you have to consult with the advisor in order to move forward?" If the person can't answer these questions adequately, he or she is unlikely to have the skills and experience he or she claims. If the individual can answer the questions to your satisfaction, you can be reasonably confident that he or she has a good probability of fulfilling the technical requirements of the position.

Once skills and experience are covered, move on to values, sociability, and self-awareness. For example, when exploring values, you might ask, "If you could choose between more pay, a better title and/or office, or time off as a reward for a job well done, which would you choose?" If you need to know about how the person interacts with others, ask questions about interpersonal relationships, such as, "Which coworker at your last job did you get along with least well, why, and what did you do about it?" If you want someone who is truly open to input and self-aware, ask him or her, "What is the worst professional mistake you have made in the last five years?" Even the best of us make mistakes, real ones, so if someone says they never make mistakes, it may mean he or she is not being forthcoming or doesn't take ownership of mistakes.

If you expect people to perform well under pressure, ask tough, challenging, and even stressful questions. For example, ask a candidate for his or her thoughts about your website. This will not only reveal whether the person took the time to visit your website, it will demonstrate what he or she took away. Too easy? Ask the candidate, "If you could change one thing about our website, what would it be?" Nothing may be more revealing than asking a candidate to be critical of a firm he or she wants to join.

Explore the candidate's most effective work environment. If the position calls for frequent interaction with people, it's crucial to hire someone who enjoys this. Does the position require constant change and priority shuffling? If so, find a candidate who is task driven and enjoys uninterrupted time to complete projects.

Step 4: Aptitude and Attitude

It's essential to have a process that measures the education and experience but also the skills, aptitude, desire/drive, and other qualities of a potential hire (Figure 19.3). Having the functional ability to do a job doesn't mean you want to do the job, are driven to achieve success, or have a passion for excellence. Firms that use a systematic process that goes beyond interviews and reference checks to include the following tools tend to have more success in hiring candidates that fit in all of the ways that matter:

- *Psychometric profiling.* Personality profiling can dig deeper into a candidate's suitability for a position. Profiles such as Kolbe, DISC, and Myers-Briggs will help assess the behaviors you can expect once someone is on board. Knowing what's lurking behind the smile is more important than the presentation.

  For example, if the profiles determine personal motivators—money, knowledge, social contributions, or personal recognition—the scope of the tests can be tailored to specific positions. Most of these tools, however, don't account for experience or emotional and professional maturity. Though helpful, they do not represent the whole of a person and, thus, should never be the only deciding factor in hiring.
- *Ability/aptitude tests.* General skills testing can provide important information about the abilities of candidates. Do not assume candidates have abilities and/or aptitudes based on their resumes—or that they don't have certain abilities because these are absent.
- *Job-specific skills testing.* When hiring for a position that requires expertise (e.g., financial analysis or delivering client advice), job-specific skills testing can help. Consider giving a prospective advisor hire a case study to gauge his or her approach and advice-giving and presentation abilities.
- *Multiple visits.* Having candidates come to the office a few times gives you a chance to get to know them. People tend to let their guard down over time, so the more you interact with them, the more likely they are to be themselves. Often, advisors feel they don't have the time for such a thorough process, but then they find they have to make time to deal with the results of an unsuccessful hire.
- *Reference checks.* Though most firms don't invest the time in reference checks, and many employers will share only basic information, we strongly encourage firms to take this step. Human resources departments often provide only clinical information upon inquiry. That shouldn't stop you from expecting to reach someone who can be more helpful. Quality employees should be able to produce at least one or two direct managers who feel strongly enough about them that they will say a few words on the employees' behalf. And you can always ask for nonmanager references, such as former clients, colleagues, or

FIGURE 19.3 Methods Used when Assessing New Hire Candidates

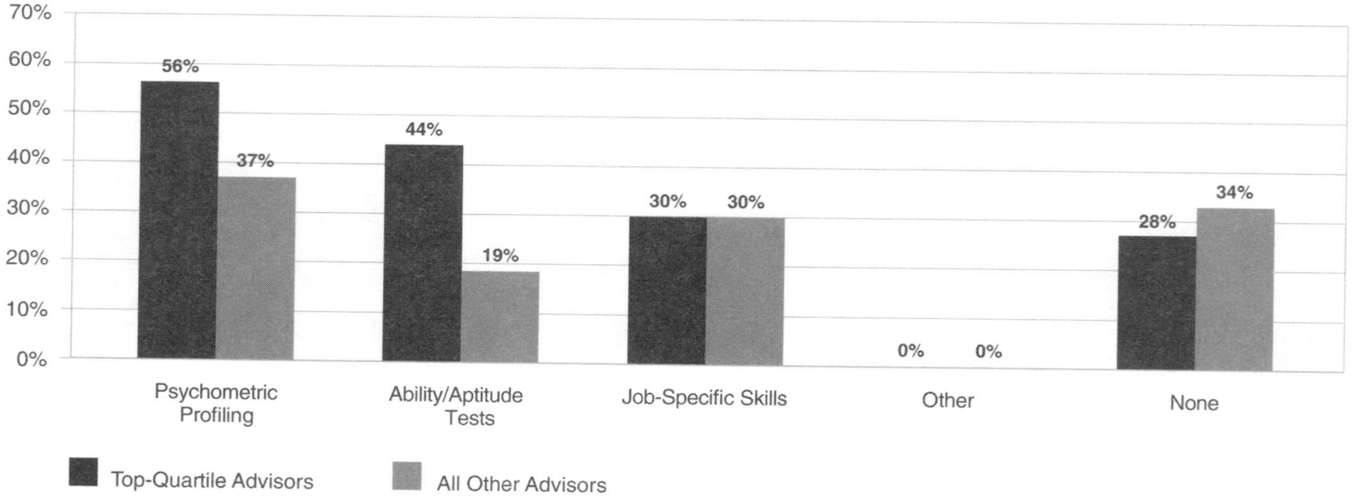

Legend:
- Top-Quartile Advisors
- All Other Advisors

Categories and values:

Psychometric Profiling: Top-Quartile Advisors 56%, All Other Advisors 37%

Ability/Aptitude Tests: Top-Quartile Advisors 44%, All Other Advisors 19%

Job-Specific Skills: Top-Quartile Advisors 30%, All Other Advisors 30%

Other: Top-Quartile Advisors 0%, All Other Advisors 0%

None: Top-Quartile Advisors 28%, All Other Advisors 34%

professional contacts who can speak to the character and caliber of the candidate.

- *Clue into culture.* Once a firm feels that a candidate is in the running, the advisors should share a deeper view of the firm culture with the candidate, so that both sides can evaluate it for fit. We have our advisory firm clients share their firm vision, values, and goals documents and discuss why and how these are important. We will show candidates an overview of the compensation plan and the career ladder for their position. We tell candidates what the firm's "best" and "worst" days are like so that they have a realistic expectation of life beyond the interview and you will have a basis for managing expectations once they are on board.

Step 5: Engage in Thoughtful Evaluation

Engage in what we like to call "equal and objective" evaluation of candidates. We create standardized documentation for each step in the process, from the phone interview questions to the in-person interviews, to the skills testing, and so on. We then develop a scoring system that allows us to compare candidates point for point. In some cases, we will actually benchmark individuals against specific attributes and qualities to see how they stack up. This does not mean the process is limited to what is on the paper, because the natural by-product of a good process will be information that colors outside the lines. But be sure that you have a process based on equal information when evaluating candidates.

Evaluate the data gathered from testing, profiling, and references and combine that information with your gut instinct and the opinion of other team members to make a decision about whom to hire. If everything seems right and your gut instinct says no, chances are you don't want to make that hire.

Step 6: Prepare and Make the Offer

Before a firm engages a hire or soon afterward, we recommend having the position documentation and offer ready. Make a formal offer to the selected candidate, along with an offer letter, a job description, a compensation package, a confidentiality agreement, and, where appropriate, a noncompete clause for professional staff. Many firms tell us they don't need nondisclosure agreements (agreements that prohibit employees from taking firm information, which is different from a noncompete clause), yet we know of two instances within the past year of firms engaged in litigation over departing employees who took confidential firm information with them to use to solicit client business from their former firm. In these cases, the firms are not preparing for when things go right—they are preparing for when they go wrong.

It seems many advisors don't develop proactive hiring processes because these require an investment of time and thought. We would argue that firms consider the cost of hiring the wrong candidate or one who is marginally acceptable but never truly fulfills the position to its full potential. Both can be disappointing and diluting to the business. In short, the cost of hiring the wrong person or the not-quite-right person can easily add up to far more than the cost of taking the time and making the commitment to follow a dedicated process to hire the right person.

CHAPTER 20

Tapping into Training

Most firms subject new hires to trial by fire. They in essence say, "Welcome, have a seat, and good luck." As a result, many new hires report that they experience disorder, lack of clarity, and confusion during this time. They work through it eventually, but a period of confusion is hardly a good way to introduce a new hire to your organization.

In this area of human capital research alone, there is no material difference in the performance of top advisory firms relative to the balance of the advisory community (Figure 20.1). In short, few firms, even the best ones, engage in thoughtful training. This suggests that our profession can do more and do better when it comes to preparing team members to succeed in the roles that they fill. Considering the time and thought required to design, develop, and deploy formalized training programs, it's no surprise that the advisory profession doesn't have a mature model for training.

On-Boarding

A process for on-boarding and training that helps integrate new team members should improve their performance, productivity, and contribution to the firm. Conversely, neglecting new hires will delay their learning curve and encourage mistakes, interruptions in service, and a potentially uncomfortable relationship between the team and the new hire.

An on-boarding process is an opportunity to meet with the new hire in the first week to explain the history of the firm and its vision, values, and goals and to set the expectation for the role and the relationship going forward. It's best to immerse people early and often in the firm's culture. Explain how the goals of the individual position intersect with the larger goals and vision of the firm. All of this will help the new hire get excited about and invested in the firm and his or her contribution to it.

FIGURE 20.1 Percentage of Firms That Use Various Training Methods

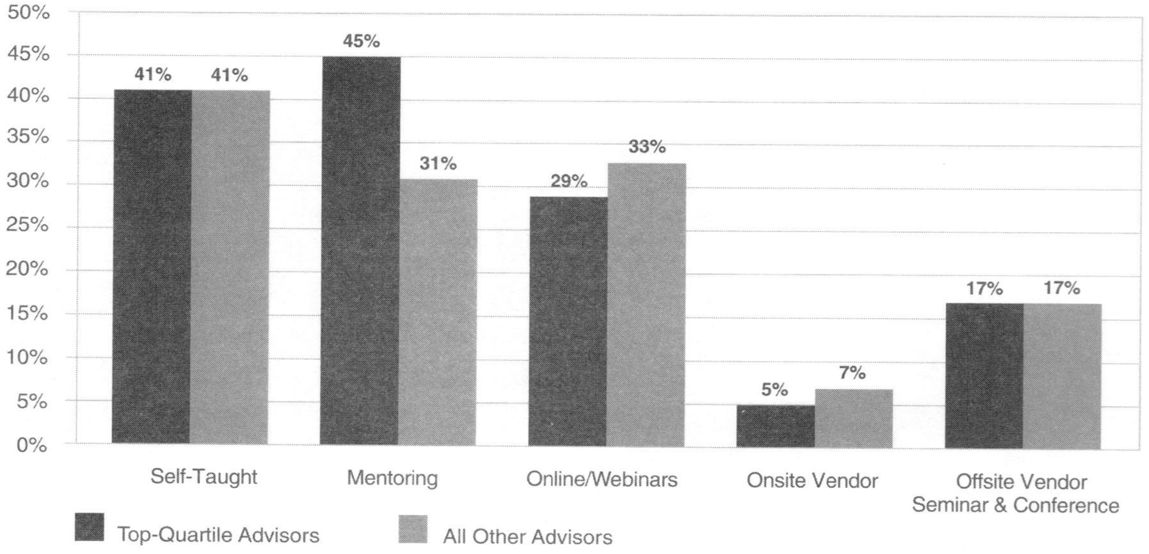

Self-Taught — Top-Quartile Advisors: 41%, All Other Advisors: 41%

Mentoring — Top-Quartile Advisors: 45%, All Other Advisors: 31%

Online/Webinars — Top-Quartile Advisors: 29%, All Other Advisors: 33%

Onsite Vendor — Top-Quartile Advisors: 5%, All Other Advisors: 7%

Offsite Vendor Seminar & Conference — Top-Quartile Advisors: 17%, All Other Advisors: 17%

■ Top-Quartile Advisors   ▢ All Other Advisors

During the first week of on-boarding, we recommend that firms get new employees grounded across three key areas:

1. Introduce them to firm people and systems.
2. Integrate them into their position by providing an overview of their job description and the training program so they are familiar with their duties and how they will fully integrate into the position over time.
3. Start gaining their investment by introducing the goals, philosophy, culture, and team.

What most people view as a series of unimportant tasks can be key in establishing the new relationship. For example, meet with the new person weekly for the first month to see how he or she is doing. You may want to assign the new hire a peer buddy who can answer his or her questions, and make sure the individual goes to lunch with each person in the firm (depending on its size) to build relationships early on. These are more opportunities to engage new hires in the cultural side of the business.

Training

Following the initial on-boarding period, we transition into training. Although this is an area that rarely gets adequate attention, we find that most of our advisor clients agree that training is important; they just don't want to be the ones to do it.

Depending on the firm's situation, size, and staffing model, it may well be that the owner or the partners are not best suited to train new staff members. That said, it is unlikely that they are going to escape any involvement in training new advisors to the firm.

To make the training process as efficient and effective as possible, for the sake of everyone involved, we recommend the following:

- Designate a training manager or team. If your firm has a dedicated manager or staff position that is best suited to oversee training, designate this person. If not, you may want to designate yourself.
- Develop a formalized training program that includes:
  - *General firm orientation.* Training managers should give new hires a tour of the office, introduce them to the team, and get them comfortable with the facilities and basic work functions, such as answering the phone, locating files, and so on.
  - *Position-specific training.* The better a firm defines the duties of a position, the easier it is to build a training program that covers all of the bases. For example, to train a new client service assistant whose duties include

scheduling client appointments, preparing new account paperwork, and preparing for client meetings, these duties can easily be broken down into a training program, with procedures for each step. The training program should designate a "key trainer" for each duty. A training manager will oversee training and may well conduct much of it, but in many cases, others in the firm may be best suited to train on a particular activity or duty. Of course, this all depends on the size of your firm.

- *Complexity, competency, and timetables.* With a clear list of the hire's duties, the trainer can evaluate the complexity (degree of difficulty) of those duties and the competency of the hire (introduction, proficiency, or mastery) and establish a timetable for meeting minimum standards on the road to mastering the job.

Think of the training program as a map: it lays out specific activities for the new hire to cover, learn, and accomplish. We recommend that advisors develop organized training programs that map out what someone is to learn in the introductory/orientation period (the first few days or week), the first 30 days, the first 60 days, and the first 90 days. Some positions—such as advisors, technical specialists, and/or managers—may extend the learning period over 6 to 12 months, given that some skills and abilities may take that long to learn and be tested in the day-to-day work environment.

Training time periods and content will vary by firm and by position, but the idea is to create a clear road map for what new hires need to learn, who will teach them, and how they are progressing along the way.

The training program agenda for an administrative assistant during a day in the orientation period might look something like the following:

Human Resources (1 hour) with John
Complete personnel forms.
Complete broker/dealer forms.
Review employee manual.
Review job description.

Your Desk/Communications (2 hours) with Martha
Organize your workspace.
Set up your inboxes.
Learn telephone answering, checking voicemail, setting up night ring.
Learn telephone conferencing, transferring, voicemail setup.
Learn how to use the fax machine/copy machine.
Learn mailing procedures (postage, outgoing mail, mail distribution, FedEx).
Take CRM tutorial.
Tour facilities.
Visit police department for fingerprinting.

Organizational Overview (3 hours) with Susan
Complete broker-dealer online registration process.
Understand the role of the broker-dealer.
Learn firm philosophy.
Get an overview of client meetings.
Learn about action plan meetings (introduction).
Get an introduction to compliance.

The first 90 days may go like something like this: After 30 days (the "intro-duction" period), the new hire should be familiar with his or her job require-ments and should be starting to manage responsibilities successfully. At 60 days, evaluate the employee for "job competence." The new employee should demon-strate a decent control over his or her job functions. If not, this is an opportunity to get questions and confusion out on the table, to keep reinforcing a common language about the job and the firm. The trainer evaluates the new hire at 90 days to determine proficiency with regard to job responsibilities.

Consistently use a clear and basic rating system. In the following example, the training process is measured by three competency levels: introduction (the hire is shown and understands how to perform the task), competency (the hire demonstrates the ability to perform the duty effectively), and mastery (the hire demonstrates excellence in execution of the duty).

We recommend that someone above the training manager, such as a profes-sional manager, a partner, or an owner, review the training schedule with the training manager and the trainee at the evaluation intervals. They should meet with the individual separately, to provide a forum for open and honest dialogue about how things are progressing and what hurdles may be surfacing.

Of all the things advisors enjoy doing, we suspect that the previously men-tioned activities don't make the list. This is probably because (1) these tasks involve work they don't want to do, (2) they don't have or haven't delegated a manager or another staff member to do the tasks, and (3) whenever someone new comes in, there's generally a lot of work for the new person to do, so taking time for training seems counterproductive. Yet it's an investment that can yield big dividends.

CHAPTER 21

Job Descriptions and Performance Reviews

Beyond attracting clients, how advisors engage their people in delivering on their duties and responsibilities may be crucial to their firms' success and the ability to sustain and scale it. Yet effectively managing people and their performance to tap their full potential requires knowledge, skill, and a commitment from the top down.

Overall, a greater number of top-performing firms establish job descriptions and conduct performance reviews for team members in their firms (Figures 21.1, 21.2, 21.3, and 21.4) than other firms. While the differences between top firms and others aren't huge, our Best Practices Study Series shows that such incremental differences seemingly drive exponentially better performance.

- Eighty-five percent of top-performing firms establish job descriptions for team members in their firms, compared with 67 percent of other advisory firms.
- Seventy-two percent of top-quartile firms review job descriptions outside of hiring and promotion, as part of the continual process of managing people, compared with only 63 percent for other advisory firms. And 83 percent of top performers conduct staff performance reviews, compared to only 61 percent of typical firms.
- Sixty-three percent of top-performing firms conduct performance reviews annually, 15 percent semiannually, and 10 percent quarterly. Fifty-three percent of top advisory firms conduct advisor performance reviews, while less than a third of the other firms do so.

So far, there are few discernible industry standards for managing advisors or for measuring advisor performance beyond production-related goals. Given the pending transition of many advisors and the likely increase in the demand for

177

FIGURE 21.1 Percentage of Participants Who Have Established Job Descriptions

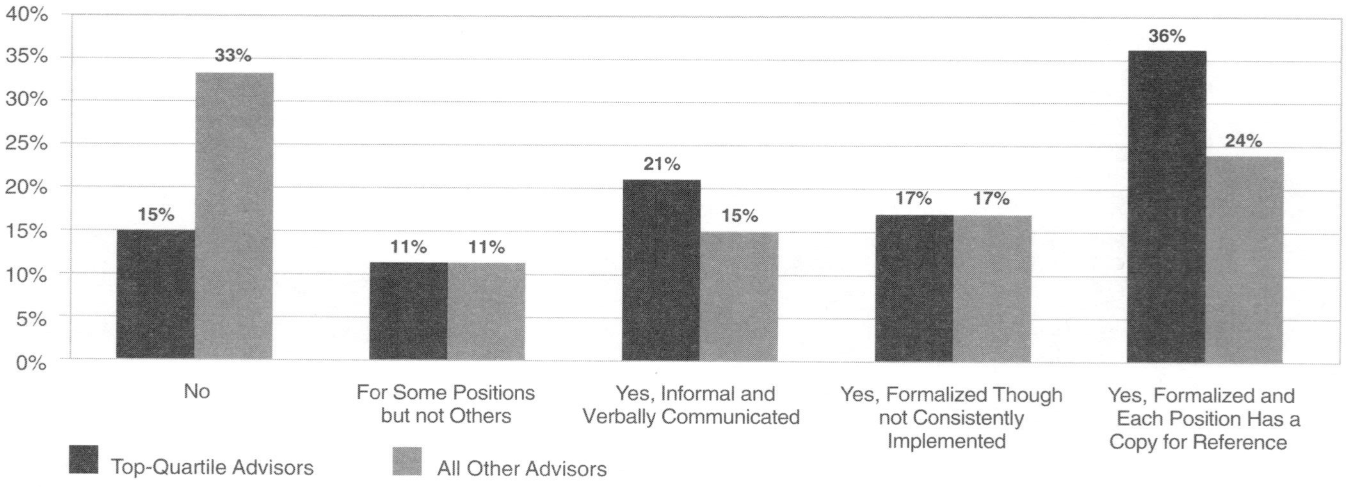

Top-Quartile Advisors

All Other Advisors

	No	For Some Positions but not Others	Yes, Informal and Verbally Communicated	Yes, Formalized Though not Consistently Implemented	Yes, Formalized and Each Position Has a Copy for Reference
Top-Quartile Advisors	15%	11%	21%	17%	36%
All Other Advisors	33%	11%	15%	17%	24%

FIGURE 21.2 Review Frequency of Job Descriptions

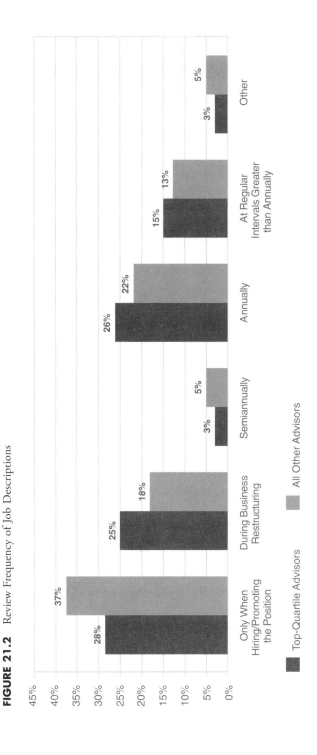

179

FIGURE 21.3   Percentage of Firms That Conduct Staff Performance Reviews

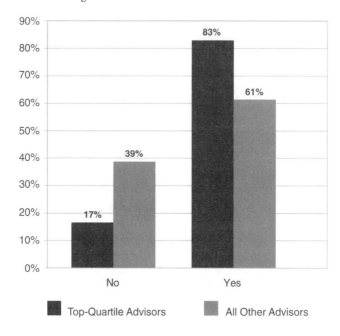

advice during the decades ahead, there's a compelling need to more effectively train and manage the next generation of advisors.

Aiming at Outcomes

The best-practices standard is to establish formal job descriptions for all team members to ensure that they clearly understand their roles and responsibilities. Yet even top firms fall into the trap of developing job descriptions that are little more than a list of activities and duties. Although this helps everyone understand the tasks and activities associated with a job, it doesn't define the desired outcome of a position and the purpose and function or its role within the organization.

Job descriptions should capture the fact that people are doing more than tasks; they are completing those tasks to add some value to the role, the organization, and the clients. It helps to translate job descriptions into actionable tools that create a common language of shared expectations to drive and measure performance.

Here are a few ways we help clients create job descriptions that are based on the desired outcome:

- *Create outcome statements for job descriptions.* Every position in your firm should have a clearly defined outcome statement to transform it into a per-

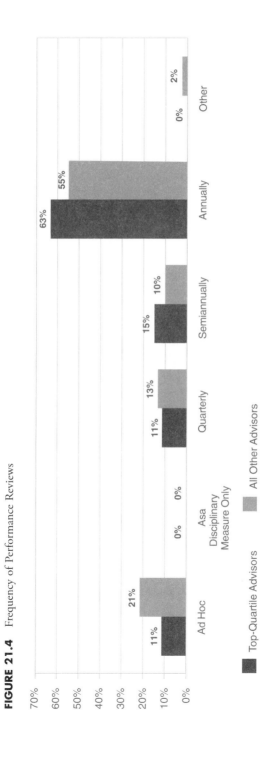

FIGURE 21.4 Frequency of Performance Reviews

181

formance tool. For example, client service assistants don't merely process paperwork and schedule appointments; they are key contacts between clients and the firm, who ensure a high-quality client experience. They also support advisors and other team members so that these people can focus in their advisory role on adding value to the client.

The outcome for a client service position could be to help the firm's advisors by effectively and efficiently providing service support and exemplary client service, thus enabling advisors to focus on revenue-producing activities. In this way, the measurement for doing a "good job" changes from completing tasks to supporting the desired outcome and the firm's goals.

- *Involve team members in the creation of job descriptions.* Involving team members in the development of job descriptions lets them own their positions and can lead to greater engagement, investment, and performance. Teams that feel invested and recognized are more likely to be satisfied, supported, and successful.
- *Create growth opportunity within a job description.* In the process of reviewing and developing job descriptions, help team members see how they can go above and beyond their basic duties to increase their contribution and compensation. Typical advisory firms raise this prospect only during promotions or at hiring, but 72 percent of top performers review job descriptions at other times as well. This suggests that the top advisory firms are slightly more likely to view job descriptions as part of a continual process of managing people, rather than as a one-time event.

If team members know about opportunities for growth in advance, they'll be more motivated and invested in sharing responsibility for their own growth and hence that of the firm. This adds to the common language where advisors and their teams share clear expectations about positions and pathways as tools to drive individual and firm growth.

The Importance of Feedback

The data for performance reviews in the previous figures show that top-performing firms do performance reviews more often than other firms. Job descriptions should form the basis of ongoing job performance reviews. Owners and employees need a mechanism to provide "objective" feedback to gauge the employee's effectiveness relative to the goals and desired performance of the employee and the firm.

This information comes from revenue and client feedback, readily available to owners/advisors. However, many nonowner advisors and staff members do not have access and remain in the dark. Not knowing how they are doing makes it more difficult for them to contribute in a meaningful way. Our consulting experience has shown us that the vast majority of team members want and need better feedback on a regular basis. Feedback shows them where they can improve and gives them recognition for their accomplishments.

It's no secret most advisors and team members dread performance reviews and for myriad reasons. Performance reviews can be time consuming and involve conflict and confrontation. As a group, advisors like to be liked and appreciated, and when given or giving criticism, no matter how constructive, they risk losing their likability. Moreover, it's uncomfortable to act like a team member one minute and then suddenly transform into a judgmental manager at the performance review. You work with these people every day, and suddenly you're standing back and, for all practical purposes, criticizing them. Once the review is over, you need them to get back on the same side of the table with you and support the team.

For their part, although team members sincerely want feedback, they may suspect that the manager is just humoring them with some compliments only to soften the criticism. As a result, the point of the review tends to become how much of a raise they will or won't get. All in all, these attitudes are not conducive to productive conversations about the individual's role within the team.

Given these dynamics, it's hardly surprising that most people think performance reviews don't work. But it doesn't have to be that way. After all, the concept and the desired outcome of performance reviews are to measure progress toward the goals of the position and the firm.

The Right Mind-Set

Most advisory firm owners have strengths that include revenue-producing and client-management abilities, which actually fund their employees' paychecks. Yet staff members typically have abilities that involve process, execution, and detail work that enables advisors to generate that revenue. In an ideal form, this is a very symbiotic relationship that relies on mutual need and benefit. Therefore, it calls for a dialogue—not a lecture.

This should be the mindset you cultivate to prepare for and execute a performance review. You want to share expectations for the job, the firm, and the future. After all, the potential benefits are all positive:

- Having an objective review of individual performance is crucial to understand how the team is functioning and therefore gauge the well-being of the firm.
- There is better management of employee and firm expectations.
- The performance review can get employees committed to and invested in the profitability of the firm if it's clear that how they execute is just as important

to the firm's growth as what the advisor does. Again, this is establishing a common language that evens the playing field.

It's up to managers to ensure that the performance review is a meaningful practice that engages all participants to make a lasting difference. Here are some best practices for a mutually beneficial performance review process:

- *Include a self-assessment.* Review processes should start with a self-assessment that allows team members to consider their own performance before hearing it from someone else. One challenge advisors raise when taking this approach is that some team members rate themselves differently (often higher) than a manager might. This suggests that the individual and the firm are not using the same standards of evaluation. It's the firm's responsibility to define these standards and educate individuals on the meaning and the reasons for those standards.
- *Include a firm assessment.* Allow your team to share how the firm and/or the manager is contributing to their ability to perform well, or not, and to the firm overall. The idea of soliciting team input on key areas, such as leadership, achieving goals, compensation of team members, creating a positive culture, following business practices, and so on, is a significant shift for many advisors, but it is one of the most productive steps they can take to communicate that everyone can contribute to the success of the firm.

  It's easy for advisors to get defensive when team members give managers low grades. It's best to say you appreciate the feedback and need time to digest it. Then you'll share with the team what, if anything, you want to do. Advisors should assess if there's merit in the criticism and determine lessons. If you respond to employees' constructive criticism, they will be even more on board.
- *Include a professional development plan.* In each performance review, think about personal attributes (is the person positive and resourceful, a team player?), position attributes (does the person have the skills and abilities to excel in the job?), and professional development (how is this person going to develop professionally?). By defining professional development goals and going over them in future reviews, both the firm and the individual can measure the commitment to development and progress.
- *Include a career ladder and a compensation review.* Performance reviews should measure more than short-term performance; they should also measure how people are progressing in their professional development and how they are advancing in their career and compensation track. By reviewing an individual's position and pay relative to his or her career path, the compensation review can shift from "how much are you going to give me?" to one in which the employee is required to demonstrate "how much he or she earned" based on predetermined standards for the job. Perhaps more than anything else, we have seen the development of career ladders, and their inclusion in all discussions

related to compensation transform the way firms and their teams work together. They create a clear and common language, as well as a compensation strategy based on shared responsibility, one in which both parties must contribute in order for pay to increase.

How Much Is Enough?

More frequent reviews can help reinforce and deepen positive behaviors and address and reduce negative ones. Of course, they also mean more paperwork and time costs for advisors/managers. Yet more frequent reviews can be less comprehensive and time consuming. Quarterly reviews can be highly effective at integrating performance feedback into a firm's operating rhythm and culture; however, we find that for most firms this is too often. In our experience, semi-annual reviews are a healthy compromise, with one of those reviews partly dedicated to compensation. Our best-practices recommendation is that all firms conduct performance reviews at least annually.

Don't wait until it's time for performance reviews to provide feedback. Some performance review feedback—"good team player" or "needs to improve attention to detail"—is too generic to act on, so share specific feedback as events happen. "I was really impressed by the way you identified [Sara's] need for help and pitched in. That shows real teamwork."

It also helps to share client feedback, positive and negative, directly with your staff when you receive it, such as an error caught by a client. By the same token, nothing is more uplifting than passing on praise from a client. The more specific and "real time," the more meaningful the feedback will be. The more often you give—and solicit—feedback, the more comfortable and productive your annual, semiannual, or quarterly performance reviews will be.

Advising Advisors

To date, the industry seems to have focused on staff performance reviews. Only half of top performers conduct advisor performance reviews, compared with a mere third of other firms. This isn't surprising. Owners/advisors tend to hire additional advisors and expect them to train and manage themselves, much as the owners themselves have done. In addition, the traditional measure of advisor performance has been production alone. Yet the feedback indicates that owners/advisors want to improve performance and productivity of nonowner advisors, helping them to succeed.

This is an important trend when you consider that many founders will soon be transitioning their firms to the next generation. The lack of training and advisor performance reviews raises the question whether these advisors will be prepared to take over. There's clearly a need to expedite the learning curve to ensure that the next generation of advisors can meet, and hopefully exceed, the performance level set by the current generation.

Advisor performance should include such measures as technical ability across a wide array of subject areas; qualitative abilities, such as delivery of advice and relationship management; business management; and business development skills beyond the delivery of client advice.

Just a few of the more common measures we have seen:

- Measurement against benchmarks and goals metrics (revenue per advisor, assets per advisor, clients per advisor, etc.).
- Measurement against production goals (new assets per advisor, closing ratio, etc.).
- Client satisfaction rating based on client surveys.
- Technical competency based on case studies and client work performed.

Given that advisor hires tend to be the most costly and—when successful— have the greatest return on investment, it seems logical that advisory firms would invest more time and effort into managing these hires and maximizing their performance.

CHAPTER 22

Climbing the Ladder

Advisors get frustrated when team members don't care as much or work as hard as they do. Yet advisors do not realize that it's hard for people to stay motivated if they don't see any reward for working harder, better, or faster.

Advisors can stay motivated because when they work harder, it's clear how that contributes to their income. If they want to make more money, they go out and get new clients. For staff, however, hard work and firm revenue growth do not necessarily correlate to increased compensation. As a result, growth is often a firm-driven directive, rather than an objective in which team members have a common interest.

As we mentioned earlier, we often meet with staff members to get their views of the firm, their positions, and their ideas of ways the firm can help them be more successful. The three most common answers we receive are:

1. Tell me the vision and the goals. (Why am I really here—what are we trying to achieve?)
2. Give me a job description. (Be clear in my responsibilities and contribution.)
3. How can I grow and get ahead? (How do I advance my role and pay?)

This often comes as a shock to the principals, who may have been working with these people for years: "How can Susan need a job description for the job she's been doing for two years?" They don't realize that Susan, like most of the quality employees that firms so clearly want to hire and retain, wants to know where she stands and what she can do to advance her career with some degree of predictability.

Hundreds of staff interviews over the years have shown us that team members want clarity about how to advance their contribution, their compensation, and their careers. Unfortunately, few firms have provided them with formalized career paths. Yet this is a best practice. Our "Best Practices: Human Capital 2010" study showed that 60 percent of top performers have some form of career advancement in place, compared with only 34 percent of other firms.

In this disconnect resides significant untapped potential for firms to better harness their human capital: to actively engage their teams in sharing their passion and pursuit for growth and greatness.

Clear and Common Language

Once again, it boils down to a common language: I do X, I expect Y. Without a career path that defines this common language, we've seen many firms suffer when team members lose that motivation because they can't see how their contribution to the firm is making a contribution to their own situation.

This is not just about giving out more money. If you give people a bonus because the firm made more money this year, it's really a gift. There is no discernible way for them to connect their work with the bonus, and there is uncertainty about the behavior being rewarded.

Annual raises not linked to advancement in responsibility or contribution frequently lead employees to expect a raise simply because they've been in their chairs for another year. Advisors who provide raises this way—beyond cost-of-living increases—can't quantify whether they're getting any real benefit in return for the increase in pay.

Instead, firms should provide raises when there is a tangible reason and a measurable benefit for doing so. Clearly defined career paths or "ladders" create a much-needed common language about advancement that allows firms to correlate increases in compensation to increases in commitment and contribution. We sometimes call career ladders the less-detailed cousin of the job description. Job descriptions provide team members with defined outcomes, roles, and responsibilities that clarify required contribution, while career ladders define how greater contributions lead to increased responsibility and compensation.

A Shift from Expected to Earned

Career ladders create an environment in which individuals share responsibility for advancing their compensation and careers—based on increased contribution—rather than simply expecting the firm to give it to them. As a result, performance reviews become less focused on "what you did" and "how much you get" and more focused on evaluating how individuals actively contributed to their own growth and how doing so advanced the firm.

This more collective view, based on common goals that clearly attach individual performance to firm benefit, is a game changer. Creating that link shifts responsibility for growth and advancement from being solely firm driven to being a shared responsibility of each and every member of a team.

A firm that we have been working with had issues with turnover, morale, and performance. When we conducted staff interviews, we found that employees lacked a clear vision of what the firm was seeking to achieve, felt that management ranged from absent to too strict, and had no idea how their contributions would benefit anyone besides the firm owners.

Our game plan included a thorough reengineering of the firm's human capital program, following the practices outlined in this book. When we finally launched the new compensation plan and career ladders, progress was swift. With these tools in place, team members and the firm had a clear and common language from which to discuss performance, professional development, and advancement in career and compensation.

One employee in particular exemplified how career ladders can make a difference. Although very capable, she had a negative attitude that affected the entire firm. When we talked with her, we found out she had once been motivated, but was now dissatisfied, and her performance had declined. She felt she was worth more and approached every performance review thinking, "Just tell me how much of a raise I get so we can move on." This was problematic because she was actually quite well paid for her work, particularly under the circumstances. The firm kept giving her annual raises, even though neither she nor the advisors felt good about them. She felt the raises were insufficient, and the advisors felt they were unearned. Introduction of career ladders changed the situation. The firm held a meeting with her, and reviewed the career ladder and where she was on it, highlighting what she needed to do to advance her position and pay. They then outlined a simple plan for the coming year that would support her in fulfilling these criteria. During the next few months, her performance and attitude improved significantly, and when it was raise time, because she had actually earned the increase, everyone felt good about it.

Of course, some employees also fail to meet the raise criteria. But when that happens, there's a lot less friction, because the career ladder provides an objective set of criteria to meet, and everyone knows the score before the review. The dynamic has shifted from "pay raise not given" to "pay raise not earned."

Career ladders create an environment of "shared responsibility," where employee and firm both contribute to advancements in position and pay. This is far more productive than being frustrated because employees feel entitled to raises they haven't earned or feel the firm doesn't reward them enough. Career ladders establish objective, measureable criteria for everyone involved.

Hire, Train, and Leave

A recent investigation into the "hire, train, and leave" phenomenon by New Planner Recruiting revealed that career ladders principles are now in practice in firms across the country. The study examined how the phenomenon affects the likelihood that new planners will continue their careers with their current firms. The results showed that new planners who have a clear career path are significantly more likely to stay with their current firms.

Of the New Planner participants surveyed who felt their careers were turning out exactly as they expected, 100 percent indicated they would be with their current firms in five years. This number drops to 41 percent for participants who rated their careers as being somewhat like what they expected. For participants who stated that their careers have been somewhat opposite of what they expected, only 18 percent indicated they expect to stay with their current firms.

Regardless of the reasons, the results are clear. Team members—new planners, in this example—value clearly defined expectations, roles, and advancement paths.

Blazing Career Paths

When developing career paths, here are some best practices to consider:

- *Create position and firm advancement paths.* Internal organizational growth goes beyond a single position, often defined by the firm's organizational structure and opportunity. For example, an administrative assistant may become a client relationship manager, then become a paraplanner, and eventually be made a junior advisor. Such growth paths can extend beyond individual positions across the firm.
- *Tie contribution to compensation.* Career ladders align individual interests with firm interests by demonstrating how a greater contribution to the firm results in increased compensation, assigning value and measurability to the raise.
- *Be clear about transitions.* Most firms struggle with the transition stage, where a team member changes positions or levels on the ladder. Best practices involve clarifying not only the requirements for advancement but also how to advance. The trigger date for transition to the next rung should include mastery of level 1 duties and the ability to successfully complete level 2 duties.

A career ladder applies a salary range to the job title that an employee has and to the titles to which the employee can advance. In the following example, the employee starts out as an office manager. His salary will increase within a certain range as he takes on more responsibilities within the office manager position, as depicted in Figure 22.1.

As he masters those duties, he adds more responsibilities beyond the office manager role. Once he meets his tenure and growth criteria, he can move to level 2 and become a business manager. His growth in responsibility results in greater contributions to the firm, and when he meets the criteria for advancement, his compensation advances with his responsibilities.

FIGURE 22.1 Career Ladder—Office Manager/Business Manager

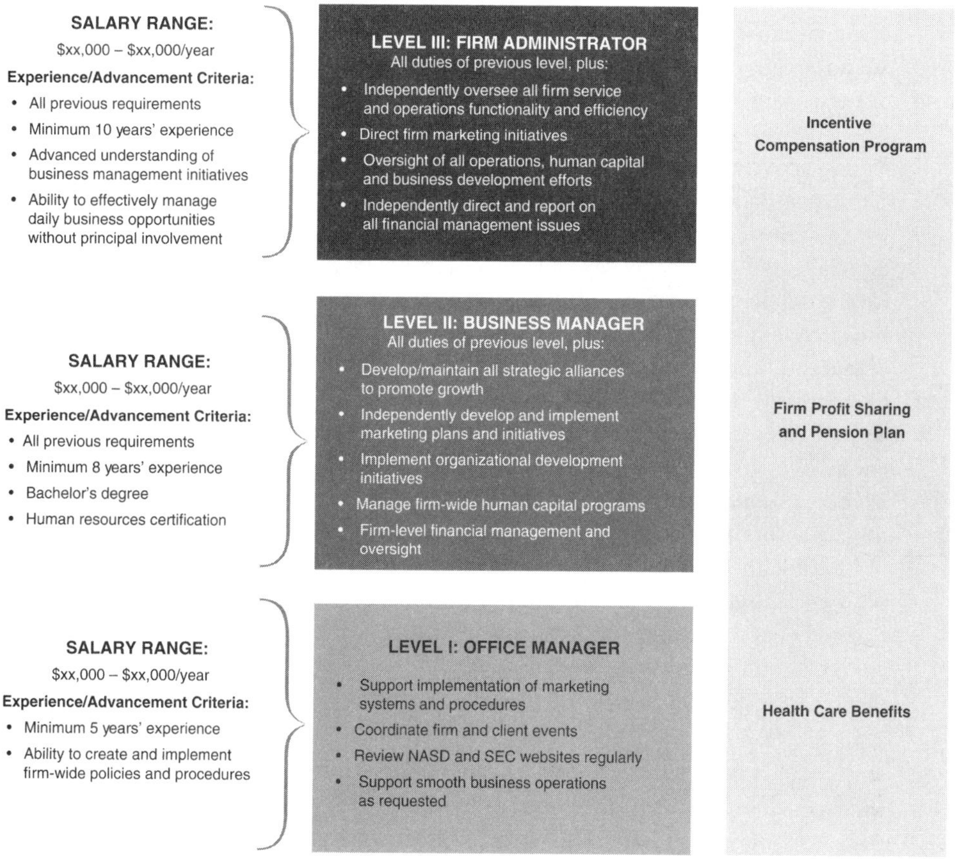

SALARY RANGE:
$xx,000 – $xx,000/year

Experience/Advancement Criteria:
- All previous requirements
- Minimum 10 years' experience
- Advanced understanding of business management initiatives
- Ability to effectively manage daily business opportunities without principal involvement

LEVEL III: FIRM ADMINISTRATOR
All duties of previous level, plus:
- Independently oversee all firm service and operations functionality and efficiency
- Direct firm marketing initiatives
- Oversight of all operations, human capital and business development efforts
- Independently direct and report on all financial management issues

Incentive Compensation Program

SALARY RANGE:
$xx,000 – $xx,000/year

Experience/Advancement Criteria:
- All previous requirements
- Minimum 8 years' experience
- Bachelor's degree
- Human resources certification

LEVEL II: BUSINESS MANAGER
All duties of previous level, plus:
- Develop/maintain all strategic alliances to promote growth
- Independently develop and implement marketing plans and initiatives
- Implement organizational development initiatives
- Manage firm-wide human capital programs
- Firm-level financial management and oversight

Firm Profit Sharing and Pension Plan

SALARY RANGE:
$xx,000 – $xx,000/year

Experience/Advancement Criteria:
- Minimum 5 years' experience
- Ability to create and implement firm-wide policies and procedures

LEVEL I: OFFICE MANAGER
- Support implementation of marketing systems and procedures
- Coordinate firm and client events
- Review NASD and SEC websites regularly
- Support smooth business operations as requested

Health Care Benefits

There is clear definition at each career ladder level, with responsibilities, professional development, and experience made known to the employee. If he doesn't meet those requirements, he can't blame the firm for not raising his pay. If he does, he is helping the firm meet its goals and there is alignment for both employee and business.

Career paths can exist at any level position. For example, a receptionist who is new and has limited experience is not as valuable to a firm as a receptionist with five years' experience, who is still not as valuable as a receptionist with experience in a financial planning firm.

Of course, in market downturns, revenues drop and firms may not be able to provide raises. Yet the fact that the career ladder is there tells the team member that that's a temporary detour off the career path.

A career path also supports team members: it says we want you to grow and contribute more to the firm, and when you do, we're happy to pay you more. The firm can directly measure the value it receives for the raise. Increases in pay are no longer contentious (an employee wants more, the advisor feels put out) or mysterious (we had more money, so we gave everyone a raise). With a career ladder–driven forum, performance reviews focus more on evaluating how individuals actively contribute to their growth and advance the firm.

Career ladders can also be a big draw in a highly competitive job market, where trained planners from upcoming generations are highly sought after, especially by Boomer advisors looking to slow down or transition their businesses (nearly 33 percent of firms plan to transition during the next 7 to 10 years). A prospective hire who sees that working in a firm has a path leading from paraplanner to junior advisor to senior advisor and eventually to partner is far more likely to take a job and deliver above and beyond the call of duty on a regular basis. Career ladders in this way discourage the "hire, train, and leave phenomenon." We have spoken with many young planners who take jobs because the advisors promise them the keys to the kingdom, but it never happens. Invariably, these advisors are surprised when their chosen heirs up and leave.

Although many firms have yet to adopt career paths, our experience has been that those that do become far more attractive to employees. Firms that have taken the time, trouble, and expense of creating formalized job descriptions, compensation plans, and career ladders appear to be professional and clearly demonstrate commitment to their team members.

CHAPTER 23

The Role and Value of Compensation Planning

Compensation represents the most significant cost of doing business for the majority of advisory firms. Yet compensation is more than a line item in the profit-and-loss (P&L) statement. Compensation is the single biggest investment most advisors will make in leveraging their time, servicing their clients, and ensuring the ongoing success of their businesses.

In its purest form, compensation is a means for motivating employees. Firms want to motivate people to join their firms, to show up and fulfill a set of duties each day, to service their clients, and, ultimately, to invest in and contribute to the overall success of the business.

It seems that firms are willing to invest in paying people but are less inclined to invest in building a framework that establishes a strategy and a structure for *how* they pay people. Fewer than half of all firms in our "Best Practices: Business Performance" study had a compensation plan in place, formal or otherwise. It seems that despite the fact that firms invest more in their people's pay than in anything else, they choose to do so by default, rather than by design.

Our research did note that even though most firms lack a compensation plan, top-performing firms invest more in their teams than other firms do:

- Top performers spend more than twice the amount on a per-staff-member basis than other firms.
- On average, top-quartile advisors earn 33 percent more than other advisors, and lead/senior advisors earn more than twice as much as their junior counterparts do.
- More than 80 percent of top-performing firms invest in benefits for their team, while less than 50 percent of other firms provide benefits.
- Fifty percent more top advisory firms provide incentive compensation than their counterparts do.

Given the data, it is not difficult to construe that compensation is a key contributor to a firm's ability to recruit, retain, and reward talent effectively. What is less obvious is the compensation's contribution to a firm's ability to align individual success with the success of the firm. Understanding that compensation, together with culture, drives behavior is the fundamental basis for designing a plan that motivates team members, enhances performance, and clearly contributes to firm growth and success.

Developing an effective compensation plan extends well beyond defining an amount to be deposited into a payroll account. It requires advisory firms to consider how the contribution to the payroll account can yield a real return by making a material difference in the quality of a firm's staff, service offering, and long-term performance.

The Wrong Way

The first step in any discussion of how to design a firm compensation plan is arguably to understand the mistakes that are consistent across almost all types and models of advisory firms when it comes to the compensation planning:

- There is a lack of alignment between business strategy, culture, and compensation philosophy (or, in most cases, a lack of these things altogether).
- Subjective evaluations or feelings determine compensation, rather than objective measures.
- Compensation reinforces the wrong behaviors and/or fails to reward the right ones.
- Plans borrowed from other firms may be inappropriate or ill fitting.
- Plans reward potential instead of performance.
- Plans are either too simple or too complicated.

One particularly ambitious and fast-growing advisory firm we consulted with expected much from its staff, including the investment of long hours and tolerance of a chaotic culture driven solely by growth at the expense of everything else. After several years of high staff turnover, the principal asked us for help. We interviewed every member of the team to understand the firm's difficulties in retaining top talent. In one particularly noteworthy interview, a newer advisor to the firm summed the situation up succinctly: "If they want the Goldman way, they need to show me the Goldman pay." It seemed that the firm expected unquestionable commitment, deep intensity and drive, long hours, and the highest level of performance, but with an average compensation package. This firm faced challenges of culture and compensation, but the underlying problem was that it lacked alignment between its business strategy, culture, and compensation philosophy.

Some firms will offer a key hire a percentage of firm revenue when the firm is small to secure good talent when funds are low and upside high, yet the owners/advisors regret it later when the firm grows beyond the point where the key team member is making far more than his contribution would warrant. At some point, compensation outstrips contribution, no matter the level of client service and performance. The firm pays for performance unrelated to the value received. In this situation, firms inevitably find themselves feeling locked into pay practices that they not only resent but cannot afford. One firm owner called us when he could no longer financially sustain the $180,000 salary of the director of insurance (a glorified title for a highly experienced processor) in a firm with revenue of just under $1 million. Although we certainly wouldn't recommend the pay practice used in this case, we realize that advisors act with the best of intentions, and in this case, the firm did get a highly experienced employee at a formative stage when the contribution outweighed the pay.

The owner failed to consider the long-term impact of that compensation. Certainly, if the owner felt the position was so valuable in the early days that he was willing to share upside with a key hire in order to secure a higher level of talent and contribution, one could argue that this was the right decision at the time. However, he needed to establish a pay cap model, whereby base compensation and incentive pay would better reflect the firm's circumstances.

A Culture of Compensation

Given the competing demands for their time, financial advisors often fail to take time to develop a strong culture around compensation and compensation practices that reinforce the firm's culture. We find the reasons for this to be relatively straightforward:

- Many advisors are conflict averse and uncomfortable in conversations related to people, pay, and performance.
- Advisors expect people to be naturally motivated to succeed, contribute, and grow, just as they are.
- They expect people to work hard and have faith that their contribution will be fairly rewarded, without needing details on how this will come to pass.
- Few advisors understand and capitalize on the connection between culture, contribution, and compensation.

A Well-Developed Plan

Advisory firm owners and partners often overlook the fact that the way they increase their income and improve their situation is largely within their control and thus requires no real clarification. Again, advisors simply bring in new business if they want to increase their earnings. For the vast majority of advisors, this single-handedly drives their behavior. How easy would compensation planning be if the formula for financial gains was just as clear to everyone else in a firm? Unfortunately, for most advisory firm owners and their employees, this level of clarity is rare indeed.

A simple definition of compensation might read as follows: Pay provided in exchange for work performed. Although we are fans of simplicity, a broader view of compensation planning is necessary. An effective compensation plan should allow every member of a team to clearly understand how he or she can contribute and earn more by helping the firm do the same.

Thus, best-practice plans recognize the role and value of compensation planning in deepening the culture of their firm, developing the potential of every team member, and driving improved business performance and growth.

In this sense, compensation plans are valuable tools that add to the common language between the individual and the firm. An effective compensation plan clearly establishes:

- The firm's philosophy about pay and performance and what it values.
- The behaviors and outcomes the firm wishes to reinforce and reward.
- How people earn their pay and what they can contribute to earn more pay.
- The short- and long-term impacts for both individuals and the firm.

With these ground rules firmly in place, advisory firms can develop a compensation plan that defines the why, what, and how of pay. The firm's interests and goals are well defined. Individual and team performance contributes to advancing not just the business but also personal interests and goals, and there is alignment between individual and firm success. Such plans communicate reciprocity, making sure every member of a team feels "when I win, the firm wins, and when the firm wins, I win."

An effective compensation plan can be much more than a mechanism for pay. It can be an important recruiting and retention tool and a reward system that reinforces the right behaviors and outcomes.

From Philosophical to Practical

Observe certain fundamentals when developing your compensation plan. You should recognize the role of strategy, philosophy, behavior, and attractiveness, regardless of plan design.

Strategy

An effective plan will clearly support a firm's business strategy and drive the desired outcomes. One advisory firm's business strategy centered on a defined niche market, yet it compensated its advisors for any client brought into the firm. Strategic alignment suggests that you not only say what you mean but that you also mean what you say, enough to align your compensation practices with your strategic objectives.

Philosophy

A compensation philosophy establishes the intent, objectives, and priorities that will guide the design and management of a firm's reward system. When asked about his pay philosophy, one advisor said that he paid people just enough to keep them from leaving. That is a philosophy, only not one we recommend.

Another, more enlightened advisor's philosophy included "top pay for top performance." The resulting plan paid competitive base wages, while providing the opportunity for individuals to earn up to 125 percent of the top-end compensation based on a comparable benchmark for their position (as determined by a blending of industry compensation studies). Note that there were incredibly high bars set to achieve this level of pay, and four years out of five the total pay doesn't reach this level. Yet we would be remiss if we did not point out that few firms ever experience the level of investment, contribution, and motivation exhibited by the staff in this firm.

Values

Every firm has a distinct set of values driving behavior. The more aligned a compensation plan is with these values, the more effective it will be in attracting people who share them and in garnering the commitment and contribution of those who stay. One firm that retained us to review its compensation practices cited "winning and competitiveness" as a firm value. However, the firm had no culture, goals, or compensation incentives to reward people for exhibiting this value. Quite the opposite, the firm paid discretionary bonuses at year-end based on the owners' subjective view of each individual's performance. The owners said they valued winning, but their pay practices suggested that what they really valued was someone's ability to stay around for another year.

Behavior

Qualitative behaviors, such as teamwork and integrity, are really values. More tangible behaviors, however, such as client service, revenue production, and professional development, have their rightful place in a firm's compensation plan. Unless a plan encourages the behaviors the firm wants to promote and reward, people wind up getting paid purely on performance, with no regard for and, in some cases, despite their behavior. We've experienced firsthand the disconnect that occurs when a new advisor with unrivaled acquisition skills is also aggressive, obnoxious, and rude to staff and openly dismissive of clients.

In a more positive example, we redesigned the compensation plan for a large firm that was having difficulty managing the pay and advancement expectations of its younger advisors, who felt their pay should be more in line with that of seasoned advisors who had demonstrated rainmaking ability. They had no proven rainmaking ability of their own but thought that was the easy part that anyone could do. They felt they were doing all of the heavy lifting so that the partners could go out and do the easy work of bringing in clients. In other words, they wanted to be paid based on their future potential, rather than on their current performance. Needless to say, this created a lot of friction between the two groups.

We redesigned the advisor component of the compensation plan to create an incentive pool for junior advisors. The incentives were earned by completing specific types and volumes of rainmaking activity, such as reviewing client files to identify opportunities, reaching out to and meeting with other professionals, attending professional and community events, giving presentations, and calling clients to inquire about their satisfaction and seek referrals. If these activities resulted in new revenue, an additional incentive was paid. Incentives increased accordingly for exceeding the revenue target. For example, the incentive pool paid 125 percent if they delivered 125 percent of revenue goal.

Two positive outcomes resulted from the redesign. First, these younger advisors gained invaluable experience testing their hands at what they had perceived as "easy" rainmaking, which they soon realized wasn't so easy after all. As a result, they gained a new level of respect and appreciation for the rainmaking ability of the partners. The second was the insight gained concerning where the junior advisors' talents lay. Some junior advisors showed a talent for rainmaking, whereas others lacked either the natural aptitude or the personal passion for it. This was extremely valuable information, which allowed the firm to develop different career paths that would enable each type of advisor to advance his or her compensation in different ways.

Attractiveness

No matter a plan's design, if it isn't attractive to those it seeks to reward, it won't be effective. Such plans need to account for market wages, competition for talent, the caliber and quality of people it seeks to attract, and so on. The compensation plan has to be attractive to the firm as well, both now and in the future. With the overpaid director of insurance, the pay was very attractive for the individual but not for the firm; it seemed unfair and was financially unsustainable. The firm created an environment in which employees could earn well above market wages, with pay conditions tied to the firm's financial performance. Without this, it would be unable to meet its compensation commitment. To be truly effective, to promote the growth of both people and profits, a compensation plan has to support a firm's philosophical framework within the limits of its financial resources and goals.

CHAPTER 24

Components of Compensation

Compensation planning is an opportunity to help develop the potential of every team member as well as the performance and growth of the firm. In designing the more practical components of the plan, you should address compensation philosophy, values, behaviors, and attractiveness. These include:

- Base pay
- Benefits and perks
- Bonuses and incentives: individual, team, and firm
- Profit sharing
- Equity participation

Base Pay

Base pay is compensation received by employees in exchange for work performed, driven by fair market compensation for the duties assigned. It can be in the form of fixed pay (base salary or hourly wages), variable pay (commissions), or a combination of the two. Base wages apply to full- and part-time employees, owners, and nonowners.

Typically, the greater the risk taken by the individual, the greater his or her percentage of variable pay and the resulting upside. The less risk taken, the greater the percentage of fixed pay in overall compensation. Revenue generators tend to have a high degree of compensation risk and thus higher variable pay to provide upside potential commensurate with their risk. Revenue supporters tend to have a low degree of risk and thus limited or no variable pay, given the stability of their work and related performance.

Base pay generally makes up most of the total compensation. This component should compensate team members for satisfactorily performing the roles and responsibilities expected of their position. It can be a fixed salary or offer a salary range that is competitive with comparable positions, helping to attract and retain quality employees. The firm's financial ability to pay also determines compensation.

Many firms create compensation parameters around a person, generally at the time of hire, or base their salary on what the person made at his or her last job. This leads to a chaotic mosaic of different salaries that don't adhere to any standard. It's better to define compensation for a position based on fair market value, competitive circumstances, firm philosophy, culture, and caliber of talent desired.

Establishing the range of base pay for positions can be challenging. As firms consider appropriate base pay for each position, they can benefit from considering how they can provide base pay:

- *Fixed pay.* Pay for the job, based on going market rates, paid in the form of a base salary.
- *Commission pay.* Pay for the job, paid on a variable basis, such as a percentage of revenue generated or managed.
- *Draw.* Pay for the job, paid on a calculation and drawn against anticipated compensation. Typically, it is calculated and paid as a percentage of the prior year's compensation. For example, advisors and/or revenue generators may take a base draw of 50 percent of the prior year's compensation to provide reliable pay to cover their basic living needs while they work toward earning variable pay.

Base pay and sometimes incentive pay compensate the majority of positions in advisory firms. As we discussed in Chapter 22, "Climbing the Ladder," base pay should reflect a pay range for a position, allowing for increased pay with increased experience and contribution. Factors that play a role in establishing base pay include:

- The duties and responsibilities performed.
- Experience and tenure.
- Compensation benchmarks for advisory firms.
- Local marketplace (the demands for talent and the market rate for pay).
- Professional market demand (the demand for talent and the market rate pay for advisory firms).
- Education, credentials, licenses, and designations.
- Firm size (large advisory firms tend to pay more than smaller ones do, increasing competition for talent in their marketplaces).

All of the variables can make it difficult to confidently set compensation ranges. We recommend that advisors review compensation benchmarks published in industry studies, explore the compensation of their key competitors, and consider market conditions, job demands, and the competition for talent. For example, what your firm expects of an operations manager (long hours, demanding environment) may well differ from what another firm in your area expects (standard hours, blissful workplace). For example, some advisory firms reside in small to midsize towns where major corporations are dominant employers, providing reasonable hours, attractive pay, and deep corporate benefits, thus making for fierce competition. These factors, together with a good dose of common sense, can help firms establish relevant base pay for their situation, location, needs, and goals.

The growing trend is for advisors, both owner and nonowner, to receive some portion of their compensation as base salary. Firms that pay revenue generators a set percentage of the new revenue secured will foster a mentality that favors the individual over the firm.

Benefits and Perks

Base compensation includes benefits such as health insurance, 401(k) plans, life insurance, disability, fitness club memberships, and educational reimbursement. More than ever, firms must also factor in the role of benefits when considering compensation, particularly given the competition for talent, coupled with skyrocketing health care costs, both of which are likely to continue into the future. Noncash perks count, too. These include massages, lunches, parties, trips, and additional time off, for example. Note that benefits and perks say as much about values and culture as the compensation plan itself does.

Providing relevant, adequate, and appropriate base compensation is the foundation for an effective firm compensation plan. Building on that foundation is essential for creating alignment between the firm and team interests and harnessing the power of human capital.

Bonuses and Incentives

Bonus, or incentive, pay is the amount above and beyond base salary, determined by meeting certain performance targets or expectations. It applies to activities above and beyond those that are accomplished by the individual, the firm, or both. It is not base pay. The discussion of such pay mechanisms should begin with a review of the various forms:

- *Bonus pay, discretionary.* Determined at the sole discretion of the firm and not based on any measurable expectation or agreement.
  - *Example:* These include holiday or year-end bonuses paid at the discretion of the firm and not tied to any measurable criteria.

- *Advantages:* Discretionary pay provides firm owners with complete flexibility and latitude in determining amounts paid and avoids requirements to measure performance or commitments to pay.
- *Disadvantages:* Because there is no link between performance and pay, discretionary bonuses often dilute any ability to drive desired behaviors and outcomes. When firms pay such bonuses at regular intervals (e.g., at year-end), they tend to become an expected form of compensation.
- *Bonus pay, nondiscretionary.* Bonuses are nondiscretionary if the firm contracts, agrees, or promises to pay a bonus to an employee.
  - *Example:* Individuals who refer a new hire or a new client to the firm receive referral bonuses.
  - *Advantages:* These bonuses allow firms to simply and easily pay for desired behaviors and outcomes.
  - *Disadvantages:* They lack the ability to align behavior and performance on an ongoing basis because they are focused on a specific event or transaction, rather than being a time-driven view of performance.
- *Short-term incentives.* Short-term incentives are performance driven, reflecting an amount earned over and above base pay when an individual, a team, or a business achieves certain performance targets or goals. They link performance to pay, based on measurable expectations within a short time horizon (usually a year).
  - *Examples:* This could be compensation paid to an advisor for hitting new-client goals, to a service team for meeting client satisfaction survey targets, or to a chief operating officer when firm productivity and profitability metrics improve by a targeted amount.
  - *Advantages:* Specific performance behavior is linked to outcome; governed by specific and measurable criteria, they allow firms to reward performance with pay and clarify value received.
  - *Disadvantages:* They require that firms define and measure criteria to achieve bonuses, which can be challenging for firms that aren't clear on what targets, behaviors, or criteria they want to meet; they create a need for measurement and management of performance related to incentive pay.
- *Long-term incentives.* Long-term incentives are performance-driven awards that pay long-term noncash compensation, typically with the goal of securing the employment and/or performance of a key employee. Common forms include phantom stock, deferred compensation plans, and employee stock ownership plans (ESOPs).

There is no incentive value until a triggering event occurs, with owners using these incentives to guard against loss of ownership control and/or income dilution. In these cases, short-term incentives may be a better option, as we generally find that key employees prefer actual equity to proxy equity and that owners who harbor these fears need to thoughtfully consider what they are trying to achieve and how they can best achieve it. In one client firm, the two partners have devised a deferred compensation plan for the junior partners. The challenge is that the work they are doing to grow the firm and take over partner duties is occurring in the here and now, while the benefits they are to receive (control and value) won't be realized until more than a decade in the future, assuming everything goes smoothly. This makes the incentives less motivating.

Profit Sharing

Profit sharing differs from incentive compensation in that it distributes profits for the collective performance of the organization, without calling out any specific person or performance measure. There may be a formal distribution plan, as a documented component of the firm compensation plan. There may also be an informal plan, based on a discretionary decision by firm owners at fiscal year-end after all other firm compensation and expenses have been paid.

Some firms worry about sharing firm profitability openly because of its use as a means to encourage productivity, efficiency, and cost savings. They're concerned that employees could use that information to take issue with their own level of compensation. Or employees could challenge decisions made by owners to invest in hires, growth, or other improvements because their profit sharing will be negatively affected (we often find that the person is the issue, not the transparency). By contrast, other firms feel it's productive to openly share expenses (with compensation reported only in the aggregate) and profitability.

They feel that it helps to invest their team in maximizing the use of resources with the goal of improving the current year's profitability while also fueling the growth that will help ensure future profitability. In the case of one team, when capacity was becoming constrained, the partners held a meeting to discuss the need for a new hire. It was the team, not the partners, who suggested the firm invest in a technology solution and use contractors to implement the new system. This would incur a one-time expense versus the annual expense of a new hire.

Equity as Compensation

A growing number of firms are using equity compensation for recruiting, retention, and retirement/succession planning objectives.

Equity plans are long term: Align them with and tie them to long-term business behaviors. Do not consider it a quick fix for an employee problem or a quick way to attract someone who comes along. We also often see firms grant equity as a retention tool to individuals who have been well paid all along. In effect, these firms are really just rewarding people for staying. Given that it takes years for owners to build equity in their firms, we believe it should take considerable time for those following in their footsteps to earn it.

Equity is often provided (in various forms to be discussed further) to accomplish key business objectives:

- *Recruiting.* As Baby Boomers drive demands for advisory services, and as more firms look to growth and/or transition, the competition for advisor and key employee talent is increasing. As a result, a growing number of advisory firm owners are putting equity on the table to attract top talent.
- *Retention.* It is equally important to be able to retain employees because firms make a significant investment in recruiting, training, and educating them. Retention is particularly crucial in the current environment, where there is an increasing scarcity of highly trained individuals with the specialized knowledge and skill sets advisory firms need. Retaining qualified talent is becoming a greater priority in all firms, particularly those with an eye toward growth, building value, and transition.
- *Succession planning.* Involves transitioning equity in the businesses to a successor gradually over time or after a set period. The equity transfer is to retain the successor, while also transitioning the firm and ideally ownership responsibilities as time horizons or thresholds are met.
- *Scale.* This is becoming more important, particularly to the contingent of fast-growing advisory firms that need talent to drive and support growth in the business. While interested in building long-term value, these firms are motivated to scale up their business by adding advisors and key employees who can significantly drive growth.

There are many ways to accomplish transfers of equity. Following are the most common methods:

- *Stock options.* Awarding stock options is the most commonly used form of long-term performance incentive. The grant awards are designed to incentivize key employees to perform because they have a long-term stake in the future of the business through eventual stock ownership. There are two types of stock options:
  1. *Nonqualified stock options (NSOs).* NSOs provide the option for an employee to purchase firm stock at a future date at the stock's fair market value at the time of the grant. This way, individuals can acquire shares of a company's stock at either a discounted price or at market value. NSOs are subject to ordinary income tax on the difference between the grant price and the exercise price. NSOs are simpler and more common than ISOs.
  2. *Incentive stock options (ISOs).* ISOs are similar to NSOs, but they have a more favorable tax treatment. When they're exercised, any income received

is treated as a capital gain, instead of as ordinary income. To qualify for this tax treatment, a formal plan must be in place and approved by a firm's board, the exercise price must equal the strike price, the plan must be offered only to employees, and there is a maximum dollar grant of $100,000 per year. ISOs may be subject to the alternative minimum tax, and the firm is not entitled to any deduction. ISOs require the holder to take on more risk by having to hold onto the stock for a longer period of time.

- *Phantom stock.* This is an employee benefit plan that gives selected employees many of the benefits of stock ownership without actually giving them any stock. Rather than getting actual stock, the employee receives pretend stock that follows the price movement of the company's actual stock, paying out any resulting profits.
- *Performance shares.* These are shares of company stock given to employees if certain company-wide performance criteria are met. With performance shares, the employee receives the shares as compensation for meeting targets, as opposed to stock-option plans, where employees receive stock options as part of their compensation package.
- *Restricted stock.* This is nontransferable stock awarded to an employee with specific restrictions; typically, a certain length of time has to pass or a goal has to be achieved before the stock can be sold. This period is the vesting period. Restrictions can be listed during a period of time or can lapse gradually.
- *Stock appreciation rights (SARs).* These are a right to receive payment equal to the appreciation in the company's stock over a specified period. Like stock options, SARs benefit the holder with an increase in stock price; the difference is that the employee is not required to pay the exercise price but rather simply receives the amount of the increase in cash or stock. For example, an employee receives 100 SARs. The firm grows and the stock price increases $100 per share during the next five years. As a result, the employee would receive $10,000 (100 SARs × $100 = $10,000), paid either in cash or converted to equity. Preset targets determine when and how SARs vest.
- *Stock purchase plan.* Employees have the opportunity to purchase company shares at a discount to fair market or book value. These shares may be part of a nonvoting class of shares.

Before transitioning equity, through a sale, a grant, or a performance-driven model, firm owners should ask themselves a series of important questions:

- *Do I want to share equity or management and/or ownership control?* Voting or nonvoting stock allows different levels of control beyond equity distributions. There are several ways to share equity without sharing voting rights or management/ownership control. So owners should ask themselves what goals they want to accomplish.

- *What are the criteria required for equity and/or partnership?* In many cases, equity is shared (whether bought or granted) based on an advisor's producing revenue for the business. Yet over the years, we've seen many firms share equity based on someone's rainmaking ability or because he or she brought in client revenue, only to soon learn that while the person met the firm's revenue criteria for ownership or partnership, he or she didn't meet any of the other criteria. That's usually because the firms hadn't set any other criteria and had no standard to measure against.

  In one case, for example, an advisor left a firm and a large book of business behind but was able to bring a small group of clients and his rainmaking ability with him. The new firm devised an equity-sharing model that would grant him an interest in the firm equal to the percentage of total revenue he held at a set point in time. The advisor met his revenue expectations and ended up owning 20 percent of the firm. However, within a year the partners realized they didn't really care for this person and, after calling on us for help, had to endure the unpleasant process of unadmitting a partner from the firm. This is one area where firm values can be useful. We recommend that firms establish criteria for sharing equity and/or admitting partners. Alongside quantitative criteria, such as revenue, consider qualitative criteria, such as adherence to firm values, management responsibilities, attitude towards mentorship and development, and community involvement.

- *What impact will the equity sharing/selling have on the business?* Will it dilute the value of other owners' stakes? Will it impede a firm's ability to sell? Will the firm share anything beyond equity, such as management responsibility and voting rights?

- *What does the firm expect of equity holders/partners, now and in the future?* Granting equity/partnership based on current performance can work just fine. It is the future performance and behavior of those allowed into the equity pool that often creates challenges down the road.

- *How will the firm define the value of ownership?* Will the firm impose its own valuation standard in a partnership agreement, make reference to an outside professional such as a certified public accountant (CPA), or conduct or call for an independent valuation to determine value?

- *What is the percentage and form of shared ownership?* Aside from how much equity a firm is willing to share, it should consider the question of ownership control. How will the partnership make decisions? If the firm consists of a founder with a 97 percent interest and a successor with a 3 percent interest that will grow over time, the management and decision-making model should be different from that of a seven-partner firm with an executive committee whose members all hold equal voting rights.

- *How will equity affect compensation?* An effective compensation plan should address professional labor compensation (pay for being an advisor/owner) and equity (profit) distributions (the owner's return on risk).

Bringing It All Together

Following are some further thoughts on compensation plan design and pay practices for firms to consider before they engage in the design of a formalized compensation plan.

Simple, Not Simplistic

The clearer and simpler the compensation plan is, the more likely it is to be an effective catalyst for performance. One firm approached us for help in redesigning its compensation plan after spending three years dealing with a plan that was so complicated it required five tabs on an Excel spreadsheet to calculate.

The firm paid incentives earned in year one over a five-year period, which required a formula that accounted for the preceding five years in addition to the current one and was composed of no less than six independent variables, each with its own weighting system. The firm was required to engage in a more complex budgeting process each year: it had to calculate participants' anticipated earnings and include estimations about achievement percentages and weightings. It also required the firm to calculate and have funds on hand to pay for the prior five year's performance.

A good plan will be at least moderately simple, without being simplistic. We ultimately believe that a great compensation plan allows someone to calculate his or her pay, within a reasonable estimate, on a piece of paper. If members of your firm cannot calculate their potential compensation with relative ease, no amount of compensation is likely to motivate them. Moreover, make sure that the linkage between the performance and the pay is clear and within the control of the recipient.

Pay for Performance, Not for Time

We often remind clients that owners want to pay for performance, not for requests or the passage of time. Advisory firm owners will feel good about raises or incentive pay when they can correlate the increased cost with an increased contribution that will deliver an increased return. We have also done enough compensation consulting to recognize that the way most firms increase base pay compensation follows a simple formula:

- Someone asked for a raise.
- Some period of time has passed, typically a year.
- The employee is performing well, so a raise must be in order.
- The firm did well this year, so raises must be in order (or the contrary).

The challenge with the basis for such raises is that they in no way correlate to increased contribution or performance. Over time, this means that compensation costs continue to increase, independent of contribution and performance. Beyond traditional cost-of-living raises, which typically range from 2 to 3 percent and which firms typically provide at one- to three-year intervals, base pay increases should sync up with increases in contribution. In one firm, a "good" employee who performed consistently from year to year received a 5 percent raise every year, accruing to a 25 percent increase over five years, even though her contribution remained essentially the same.

The Gap between Performance and Pay

The shorter the time between performance (behavior) and pay (reward), the more motivating the plan and the pay are likely to be. For example, an employee refers a new client to the firm and receives a bonus three months later. The delay between behavior and compensation dilutes the impact of the reward. If the behavior is ongoing, the payout should be ongoing as well. If an advisor receives incentive pay for acquiring new clients, the payout should take place quarterly. If a staff member meets a performance target in the first quarter of the year but doesn't receive the incentive payment until year-end (when total pay is calculated), there exists too much distance between behavior and reward. As a result, the "incentive" is less likely to drive the desired behavior in the future.

Insight on Incentives

Firms often fail to distinguish between individual, team/group, and firm incentive pay when calculating short-term incentive pay. One of those three elements, generally, determines the incentive pay. The challenge with this model is that it tends to force firms and their employees to gravitate to one of two operating attitudes.

The "I" attitude prevails when advisors pay people exclusively for their individual performance. For many firms, this creates an environment where advisors care only about their own performance. This attitude may advance certain goals, such as revenue growth, but it can gravely endanger firms in other important ways. It can encourage an advisor to take care of his own clients without regard for other clients of the firm, or he may not feel he has to adhere to firm standards of practice because there is no financial incentive to do so. In one firm, the advisors refused to follow the review process or even enter notes in the firm's Customer Relationship Management (CRM) database. Why? Because the owners paid the advisors exclusively on the assets they retained.

The "we" mentality takes hold when the incentive pay focus is so broadly inclusive of the group or the firm that no one individual can truly discern his or her individual contribution in achieving the collective goal. We-based incentive plans avoid an I-based environment. In one large firm with four nonowner advisors, the founder redesigned the compensation to include incentives paid equally to all advisors, based on the firm's hitting its asset and revenue performance targets. This incentive structure would certainly avoid the mentality that focuses on the individual at the expense of the team. Yet it stifled individual performance as everyone received equal pay regardless of his or her individual contribution. After 18 months, we redesigned the plan to inspire a combination of individual, team, and firm performance.

Tips on Transparency

Because benefits and other types of noncash compensation may be part of base pay and are a part of everyday life, team members often take them for granted and forget their value over time. What's more, team members rarely understand that the total cost of compensation can be significantly more than their take-home pay, further diluting their perception of value and making it increasingly difficult for firms to keep up with expectations.

We suggest providing team members with transparency regarding the total cost of their compensation. You can provide a simple, one-page annual compensation summary that outlines the cost of base, incentive, and performance compensation, together with the costs of benefits, licenses, vacations, and any other forms of noncash compensation. Also included could be the added costs, such as Social Security taxes paid by the firm. When you add it all up, the numbers tell a much more expensive story than what team members see on their pay stubs.

Although it's not appropriate to share the amount of individual team members' compensation across a firm, some firms find it beneficial to share the percentage of total revenue spent on compensation to help teams understand its true cost. We find that this level of transparency helps firms have more open, productive conversations around the contributions required to support growth in compensation.

Designing Advisor Compensation

New business development should be a component of variable pay if rainmaking is a desired behavior for an advisor. As we said earlier, we don't recommend making 100 percent of an advisor's pay discretionary because that encourages the "me-over-we" behavior.

Relationship management and referrals should be a portion of compensation if these are desired behaviors. Interestingly, most firms compensate service advisors based on assets managed and do not use performance-based standards, such as meeting service delivery standards, client satisfaction, or referrals generated, as a function of pay.

How can you change compensation structures to account for the three advisor roles critical to initiating, managing, sustaining, and servicing client relationships? Advisors who find clients and develop new referral sources from square one are, of course, quite valuable, and their compensation should reflect this. Because rainmakers tend to be founders, conventions for compensating nonfounder rainmakers tend to be wide open to definition.

Two methodologies are emerging. One centers on aligning the risk-reward relationships via an incentive compensation model—the greater the risk, the greater the reward. This approach generally provides a small base salary—perhaps as low as $60,000—with incentive compensation that is virtually unlimited and tied directly to performance. The more new clients the advisor finds, the greater the income increases.

The second emerging methodology is a higher base compensation, often required to retain quality rainmakers, topped by an opportunity for incentive compensation. Here, base salary is a more significant component of total pay. Less compensation is at risk, but there is a new assets under management (AUM) or client revenue minimum required. The base salary is higher, but so are the expectations.

In both cases, we encourage firms to include nonfinancial criteria as part of the compensation plan to promote alignment of values, behavior, and outcomes among firm advisors. This helps to avoid the situation where advisors produce revenue but are unsuccessful in other aspects of their relationship with a firm.

Nonrainmaking or client service/relationship advisors could have their incentive compensation based on other factors, such as growth in assets or revenue managed, implementation of service-model standards, continuing education/ professional development, and community involvement. They are all client- and firm-building activities that don't directly create new business but play an important role in the success of the firm.

Many firms pay service advisors for client retention. This approach may unintentionally pay for behavior that service advisors are not directly driving, given that our research (and others) shows that most firms have a 95+ percent retention rate. Without specific qualifications, any incentive based on retaining/ servicing clients may not be rewarding the right behavior. If an advisor is not servicing clients in line with firm standards, the clients may still stay, in which case the firm is paying for the clients' behavior, not for the advisors' actions. Retaining and servicing clients are still important and can be a component of compensation, because they are highly valued behaviors, but be clear on the circumstances and the reasons for including such criteria in an advisor's or a staff member's compensation plan.

We recommend that our advisory firm clients find the underlying behavior they wish to motivate, not only the outcome. Using the client retention example, we've seen many firms where there was no formal service model, and nonowner advisors served their client base as they saw fit. Their retention rates were good, but that didn't mean the advisors were fulfilling the firm's potential to serve those clients better, generate referrals, and increase share of wallet. For this reason, in one case, the firm added a requirement to eligibility for incentive compensation that firm advisors service clients in line with firm standards, demonstrate a consistent referral generation process, and realize a percentage of growth from client contributions.

Whether the advisor is a pure rainmaker or fulfilling a hybrid role, it's essential that new revenue generated exceeds compensation paid; otherwise, the rainmaking compensation is a drain on the firm's performance and value.

Where senior advisors want to scale back their hours or prepare for retirement, the business strategy, of course, is to develop rainmaking skills in those who will be taking over. In many cases, recruiting individuals with these skills already in place is prohibitively expensive. Those with records of landing new business are scarce, and, if you can find them, they command astronomical sums. So most firms need to develop these skills from within, and nothing encourages the behaviors necessary for learning and change like effectively targeted incentive compensation.

Understanding that compensation, together with culture, drives behavior is the fundamental basis for designing a plan that accomplishes your goals. In the next chapter, we'll guide you through the process—from defining your vision to launching and managing your plan.

CHAPTER 25

Creating a Compensation Plan, Step by Step

A well-designed compensation plan serves to create clear alignment between individual behavior and firm performance. It links individual success with firm success, aligns compensation practices with business strategy, and does all of these things while ensuring that individuals are paid fairly for their roles in the growth, development, and performance of a firm. In doing so, such plans can transform pay into a performance catalyst.

Institutionalizing Employee Compensation Practices

Every facet of a firm's compensation plan, from how it defines and updates base salary ranges to the form and function of incentives, profit sharing, and equity, should be formalized, that is, clearly defined, documented, and driven by specific and measurable goals and criteria.

Although the design of a firm's compensation plan is a robust and comprehensive process that should be personalized to each firm, any plan design process should include the following steps:

- *Step 1: Define and/or review the firm's vision and goals, as well as the compensation philosophy.* Know and keep in mind what strategy, objectives, behaviors, and outcomes you want to drive at a firm, team/group, and individual level. Beginning with the end in mind is the best way to make sure your compensation plan delivers on your hopes and expectations.
- *Step 2: Establish base salary ranges and criteria for advancement.* Start by doing compensation research on competitive pay ranges for each position. As noted earlier, we recommend breaking the overall range into set levels. For example, if the overall range for a position is $40,000–$70,000, reflecting growth from

215

entry level to seasoned performer, you might break this range into three levels of $40,000–$50,000, $50,000–$60,000, and $60,000–$70,000 to reflect the relative contribution at each level. In addition, we often set similar ranges for incentive compensation. In this example, the incentive pool for this position might be set at 5 percent in the first level, 10 percent in the second level, and 15 percent in the third. Each position should have a defined career ladder to clearly set out the ranges, responsibilities, and criteria for advancement at each level.

- *Step 3: Define specific compensation components and amounts by position.* Determine what compensation components will be included in your plan. Base pay is in every plan. While every firm is different, we often design plans with a tiered model: base pay, individual incentive pay, team incentive and/or profit sharing, and, where applicable, equity participation. This combination of individual and team/firm incentive helps promote feelings of independence and interdependence, and firms can achieve an effective balance between individual performance and firm commitment.

  In this step, you would also determine whether any bonuses would be included in the plan. Many firms include referral bonuses, paid when a team member refers a new hire or client to the firm.

  Remember, the role of individual incentives is to drive position-specific behaviors and performance. The role of team/firm incentives is to get individuals to work together to achieve a team/firm goal or objective. The role of firm performance is to promote firm success, and the role of profit sharing is to encourage profitability.

  The position best drives the role of incentive compensation, the performance goals, and the portion of total compensation the incentive will make up. Typically, the greater the impact and/or reward, the higher the incentive pay. For example, pay for revenue generation ordinarily has a high degree of variable/incentive pay, and revenue managers (service advisors/relationship managers) normally have a lower degree of variable/incentive pay. A role that directly affects firm management or revenue performance, such as a chief operating officer or a business development officer, tends to warrant much higher incentive pay than that of a portfolio administrator or a planning assistant—not because one position is more important than the other but because one has the ability to affect performance more than the other does.

  The percentage of variable or incentive pay should correspond to the business impact delivered by the position and the risk taken. For example, 5 to 10 percent of the pay for administrative positions may be incentive based, 5 to 15 percent for technical specialists, 10 to 20 percent for managers, 20 to 30 percent for non-revenue-producing advisors, and 50 percent or more for revenue-generating advisors.

- *Step 4: Define the performance criteria or measures that drive the incentives.* Firms most commonly use performance measures focused on either top-line measures, such as assets under management (AUM) and revenue, or bottom-line measures, such as profitability. As firms begin to recognize the true cost of compensation and appreciate the relationship between pay and performance, more firms are making a point to include measures that recognize how the top line becomes the bottom line. The role of performance measures varies by position. The trend of compensating the advisor based on production is changing. Establishing clear performance measures allows a firm to focus on improved performance in a set area or areas. Using benchmarks to align compensation with key performance measures is an emerging best practice in top firms. Although every firm should define the performance measures that are most relevant and impactful to them, following are some examples of performance measures that extend beyond the basics:

- *Growth in year-over-year revenue.* In one very growth-oriented firm, at year-end the partners calculate that year's annual revenue growth, establishing that dollar amount as the growth baseline for the coming year's incentive pool. For example, if the firm grew from $1 million to $1.2 million in revenue in a given year, the following year's incentive pool would be $200,000. When the firm's growth in the following year reached $100,000, the pool was funded 50 percent. Likewise, if the firm exceeded its growth target by 125 percent, the incentive pool funded at 125 percent.
- *Improved productivity measures.* One firm focused on containing expenses and increasing productivity through better use of its people, processes, and technology. It established key productivity measures based on benchmarking process (e.g., clients per advisor, profit per client) and paid incentives for meeting target improvements.
- *Specific behaviors.* One of our clients was having trouble getting its service advisors to educate clients on referrals in order to receive more of them. They reduced base pay by a set amount (within reason), and increased incentive pay equal to three times the amount of the base pay withdrawn. The new incentive pay was tied to both referral behavior (e.g., documentation that the discussion on which they were trained was in fact occurring in client meetings) and to results (actual referrals received). The referral behavior pay replaced the base pay reduction so that, if an advisor made the effort to engage in referral compensation discussions in all client meetings, his or her compensation would be whole. This motivated the advisors to have the referral conversations, and the result (not surprisingly) was an increase in referrals—and even more money for the firm and the advisors.
- *Important business priorities and projects.* Every firm has a wish list of extra projects it would like done, but people are so busy doing their jobs they don't have the time to make changes that allow them to do their work better. Many of our clients include bonus projects in their compensation plans to reward the above-and-beyond effort required to get them done. Firms should not pay for what is already in the job description.

Although it would be nice if individuals understood these projects in the normal course of business, if it's important to get them done, we recommend allocating bonus pools or incentive pay for their successful completion. One client had put in a new CRM system, to much fanfare. Yet business-as-usual soon consumed everyone's attention, and nearly a year later the firm had not tapped into much of the system's productivity-boosting functionality. To address this and to ensure that the firm realized benefits, they created a bonus pool and identified a set of actions for which the firm would pay. It allocated a set amount to each, based on the time required and the degree of difficulty. Six months and just a few thousand dollars later, more than 60 percent of the list was complete.

- *Accountability and support.* We realize that this may seem counterintuitive, but even successful advisors can benefit from accountability and support to perform their best. Sometimes a little help, driven by a bit of additional pay, will do the trick. In one firm, our client was a great rainmaker who simply struggled to find the time to get people on the phone and in meetings out of the office. It was unlikely that without accountability and support he would change his behavior, but he didn't have the cash flow to hire another staff member. So we suggested he seek the aid of his assistant, spurring her on with a special incentive plan.

He instituted a marketing bonus that paid her an additional $1,000 per quarter for scheduling a set number of calls and meetings with top clients and their professionals. The firm produced a list of all of these individuals and, based on the total number, established a set number of calls and meetings the advisor wanted to hold each month, given the time he wanted to allocate to such activities. The assistant earned a quarterly bonus simply for going down the list, sending letters, and making appointment calls. The advisor became an avid and active rainmaker once his role focused on "showing up," and the assistant earned an extra $4,000. The firm won because the advisor regularly engaged in more revenue-generating behavior at a bargain-basement price.

This is but a small sample of some of the creative ways we have helped firms develop bonus and incentive plans to tap into the true power of incentive compensation.

- *Calculate opportunity and costs.* Make sure the plan meets the attractiveness factor, with the total position pay being attractive to the individual and to the firm (now and in the future). We model out compensation opportunities and costs, calculating the minimum and maximum pay for each position when accounting for total compensation paid (all forms). We also calculate the minimum and maximum compensation costs incurred by the firm in any given year. We then calculate the projected costs as the firm grows to make sure future revenue and earnings goals align with the compensation so that the plan doesn't break down in the future.

Nonetheless, all plans require ongoing review and adjustments, but you want to avoid relaunching a plan every two years because of a failure to consider all of the costs and impacts at the time of design.

If the position earned all base pay, bonuses, and incentives assigned, add the total potential pay available. Evaluate this compensation relative to the firm's philosophy, financial health, market conditions, and so on.

Next, measure total compensation, all types and for all positions, against your economic model (as discussed in Chapter 7, "Building a Business Blueprint") to make sure that the percentage of revenue consumed by total compensation costs does not exceed the percentage budgeted. If your economic model goal had 20 percent of the revenue allocated to indirect staffing and your plan consumes 24 percent of the revenue, you will want to modify your plan to stay in line with the budget. In a firm where this was the case, we simply increased the revenue targets required to trigger the incentive plan, so that if the plan were fully funded, it would consume no more than the 20 percent of the revenue allocated.

- *Step 5: Launch and manage the compensation plan.* Once a thoughtful firm compensation plan design is complete, it's time to introduce it to the team. To help maximize the understanding of, and investment in, a plan, we recommend that firms include the following to prepare for a plan launch:
  - *Firm compensation plan document.* This document follows the principles and the process outlined throughout this chapter, including the firm's vision and values (the why), the compensation philosophy and practices (the how), and the compensation plan design (the what).
  - *Firm compensation plan presentation deck*: Passing out a multipage document rich with details is a sure way not to have a positive dialogue about the plan design. Instead, we recommend distributing a copy of the plan at the launch meeting, with a summary presentation (PowerPoint works great) of the plan fundamentals—that is, a brief overview of why the plan was designed, what it seeks to accomplish strategically (alignment, the environment of shared success, top pay for top performance, etc.) and tactically (if you do X, you get Y), together with an overview of how the plan will be managed.
  - *Position-based compensation summary.* Following the plan launch, we recommend that firms meet with team members individually to answer questions and educate them on how the plan will affect them personally. We found that preparing a pay summary showing total compensation paid and total compensation potential can be helpful in highlighting the total cost of compensation. Firms should examine compensation summaries with the employee at review time, and/or adjust it to ensure that employees are aware of their total compensation outlay.
  - *Support documents.* These include the individuals' job descriptions and career ladders. Incorporate the support documents into the performance

FIGURE 25.1 Frequency of Staff Member Compensation Reviews

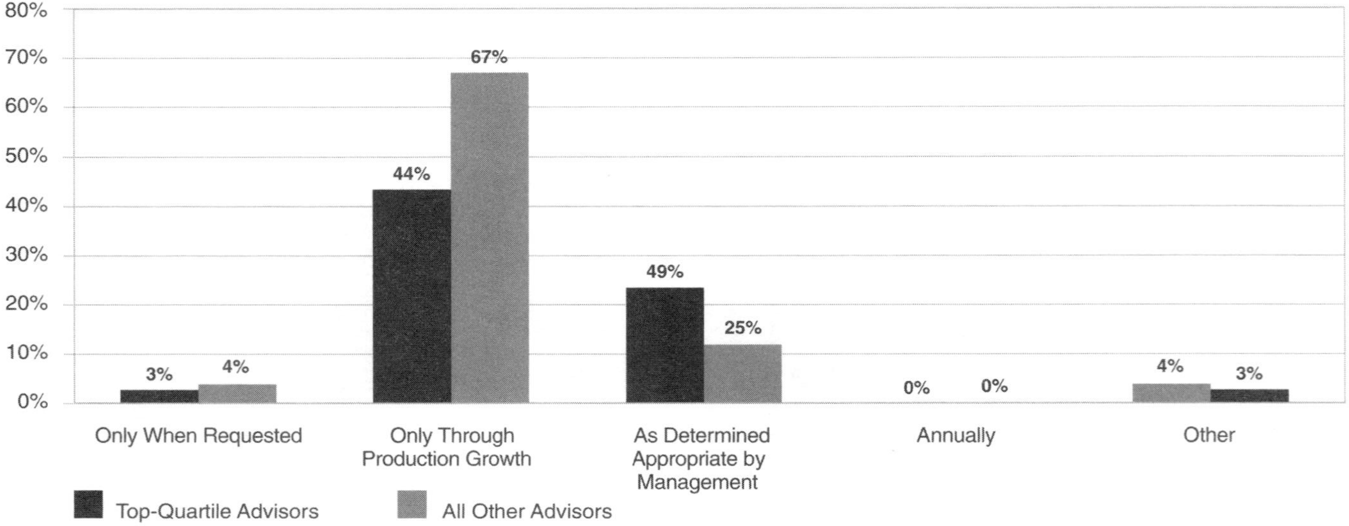

Legend:
- Top-Quartile Advisors
- All Other Advisors

Categories (x-axis):
- Only When Requested: Top-Quartile Advisors 3%, All Other Advisors 4%
- Only Through Production Growth: Top-Quartile Advisors 44%, All Other Advisors 67%
- As Determined Appropriate by Management: Top-Quartile Advisors 49%, All Other Advisors 25%
- Annually: Top-Quartile Advisors 0%, All Other Advisors 0%
- Other: Top-Quartile Advisors 3%, All Other Advisors 4%

discussion and outline requirements for contribution, advancement, responsibilities, and long-term pay prospects.

- *Following the plan launch, it is critical to implement a compensation review process.* When it comes to reviewing staff compensation for promotion and increases, our best-practice study revealed that compensation increases in top-performing firms tend to be management driven (though not process driven), while others focus more heavily on production growth, probably because that drives the cash flow that provides for compensation increases.

Surprisingly, no significant percentage of participants selected "annually" as the frequency for staff compensation reviews. One explanation is that the category "as determined appropriate by management" typically drives the review schedule, which may or may not be annual.

Best-practice firms recognize and respect the role of the compensation review, ensuring that they maintain clear and consistent communication with their teams on matters of performance and pay. Firms should conduct annual compensation reviews at a minimum, and plan on paying bonuses and incentive compensation two to four times per year to close the gap between time of behavior and receipt of reward.

CHAPTER 26

Owner Compensation

Defining a firm compensation strategy should extend beyond institutionalizing employee compensation and also put in place formalized compensation practices for owners. Even firms with well-defined compensation plans neglect owner compensation until payment of all other expenses. Owners may face significant challenges to business growth and management by relying on this compensation practice.

Without a formalized ownership compensation plan, owners, much like employees, can become accustomed to the discretionary compensation that comes in successful years and, as a result, can find themselves unprepared in less-than-ideal years. Although ownership compensation planning cannot completely eliminate the financial risks that come with owning a firm, it can help owners plan for and mitigate such risks.

The ownership compensation plan for each firm should vary, but the following best practices provide a guideline for what to consider when designing a plan that fits the needs and goals of your firm:

- *Avoid "do what I say, not what I do."* A successful ownership compensation plan sets a strong example for the entire firm and helps reinforce at the highest level the link between performance and compensation. A formal ownership plan should include the same type of components expected of team members, such as formal job descriptions, clearly defined performance objectives, and formal evaluations that determine the overall performance and contribution of the owner. By establishing this standard, an ownership plan demonstrates the firm's values and measures and rewards the performance of all team members—even owners.
- *Align owner compensation to the firm's compensation, philosophies, and values.* Just as we described in the section that focused on designing a firm compensation plan, owner compensation should align with the firm's compensation philosophies and values and should promote and reward the desired behaviors and

223

attributes in those holding ownership. Setting these standards allows the firm to hold not only employees but also owners accountable and to reward their contribution to the firm's success.

- *Make it a part of formal business planning.* With a formal ownership compensation plan, a firm can adequately conduct business planning. These plans should put in place a system that determines compensation for ownership roles, profits distributed to reward ownership risk and contribution, and profits retained by the firm. Including owner compensation as a part of business planning provides firm owners with a clear understanding of their compensation, the upside, and the potential financial risks involved in ownership.

- *Keep it simple, not simplistic.* As with employee compensation planning, the ownership compensation planning should be simple without being simplistic. If you need a PhD in mathematics to determine the outcome, then the plan will be ineffective. However, if it's too simple—profits distributed solely on the basis of ownership percentage—firms with multiple owners may find that friction emerges at profit distribution time.

- *Separate compensation for role and ownership contribution.* There should be a clear distinction between compensation for the role an owner is performing, such as senior advisor, CEO, or chief operating officer, and compensation provided for the financial risks and contributions that come with being an owner. This becomes increasingly important as firms grow and add owners. The skill sets of owners often vary, and each owner's contribution to the firm and the risk he or she takes can vary significantly. As firms grow and, as often happens, contributions become disproportionate while pay does not, tension among owners frequently arises.

- *Consider the long-term goals of the firm.* A good plan thinks about tomorrow, as much as it considers today. Many firms assign equal compensation and weighting to the ownership structure, assuming that partners contribute equally to the success and development of the firm. This type of ownership structure often works in the short term but can cause significant issues in the long term: it becomes particularly evident as firms consider bringing in new owners or plan for the transition of ownership for exiting or nonworking partners. A formal ownership plan sets standards for the contribution and the commitment required to receive compensation for the role the owner plays in the firm, while also accounting for the financial risk and liability that come with ownership.

- *Follow the "bigger pie" rule.* In designing ownership compensation plans, we often come across one or two owners who are not able to look beyond what they are giving up in ownership compensation today, even though this will ultimately contribute to the increased growth, success, and productivity of the firm. Often, these owners feel that they are getting a smaller piece of the proverbial pie. While in some cases this may be true, the more likely scenario is that the change will result in a smaller piece of a larger and more profitable pie. Our best advice is to remember that in order to gain something, you may need to give something up.

Striking a Balance

The most common issue we have seen is that often ownership plans are determined early on in the development of the firm, with little consideration given to the future needs and growth of the firm. As firms grow, the potential for ownership responsibilities to become specialized and for ownership to extend beyond the founding partners becomes increasingly probable. As firms increase in complexity, there is often little consideration to how the firm will handle this from an ownership and compensation perspective.

One particular example comes to mind when facing this type of challenge. We were working with a firm that had a long-established ownership compensation plan that provided each owner with equal base compensation and equity percentages. This plan worked well in the early stages of the firm's growth. Yet as the firm grew, the partners' natural abilities set in, and they gravitated toward specialized roles. Although each role was valuable to the organization, contributions to the growth of the firm became disproportionate and caused tension among the partners. While two owners worked 60-plus-hour weeks and took only 2 weeks' vacation a year, another partner worked a 40-hour week and took a month of vacation each year. Friction stemmed from both sides; although the partners had similar philosophies and goals for the firm early on, this changed over time, and each partner valued differently the contributions the others made.

The challenge they faced in redefining how the firm structured owner compensation was twofold. First, they each had to acknowledge that the contributions they were now making to the firm's success were not equal and that although each had contributed equally at the onset, this was no longer the case. Second, they had to acknowledge that their system of anticipated equality was no longer a viable model under which they could work successfully.

In this example, during this time frame, the firm was also bringing additional partners into the organization. Fortunately, this second round of ownership planning allowed them to address the differences among the roles each partner had in the firm and account separately for their contributions as owners.

A best-practice owner compensation plan has three levels of compensation: base compensation, incentive compensation, and profit distribution.

The base compensation component should be based on the primary role performed by the owner and should align with industry standards for the role. If one owner performs the role of advisor, while another acts as the firm's chief investment officer, the compensation for each position should align with the industry standard for each position. This compensation should be accounted for preprofit, which also provides a framework for establishing free cash flow to ensure appropriate financial management and valuation.

In many cases, we set aside an incentive compensation pool. Firm profits fund the pool to reward *role* performance and contribution, and distribution to owners is based on predetermined criteria. These criteria may vary, based on role, responsibilities, and contribution. For example, in a "partner-in-charge" model, where each owner takes on responsibility for an operating function within the firm (such as marketing, technology, or operations), the criteria for each role may vary. In a managing-partner model, the additional responsibilities, and resulting criteria, taken on by the managing partner weight differently than other partners' contributions. Ultimately, how a firm defines and divides partnership responsibilities and desired ownership traits (such as rainmaking, operational, or human resource management) will help establish criteria for measuring performance.

As you define these criteria, they should be clearly stated and measurable. In the example provided earlier, we helped the firm define criteria for key attributes desired in owner performance. Then, we helped create measurable targets that determined the compensation they received for achieving each criterion. In this example, the firm weighted the traditional owner skill sets such as rainmaking, client management, and operations management. Weighting and distribution of available compensation focused on each partner's contribution and achievement of agreed-upon goals.

The final component, profit distribution, pays out to partners based on the equity structure of the firm.

A formal ownership compensation plan with multiple levels extending beyond equity percentage allows firms to recognize, respect, and reward the fact that, as firms grow, each owner/partner makes different contributions and, thus, should be compensated accordingly. How a firm determines allocation across each level is the most common question. Depicted in Figure 26.1, this distribution model shows how expenses and profits flow, allowing the firm to define the distribution of each component of its owner compensation plan:

- *Base compensation—direct owner compensation.* Distributes 40 percent of firm revenue as base compensation to firm owners for professional labor.
- *Profit-based incentive compensation—owner incentive pool.* Allocates 38 percent of firm profits to an incentive pool divided among firm owners based on predefined performance criteria.
- *Profit distribution—owner equity pool.* Distributes 25 percent of operating profits based on the ownership percentages of each partner.

With the owner compensation plan, the firm also chose to retain 38 percent of firm profits as "retained earnings" until such time as it held six months of firm expenses. They intended to use the retained earnings as a way to cover

FIGURE 26.1   Example of Owner Compensation Flow

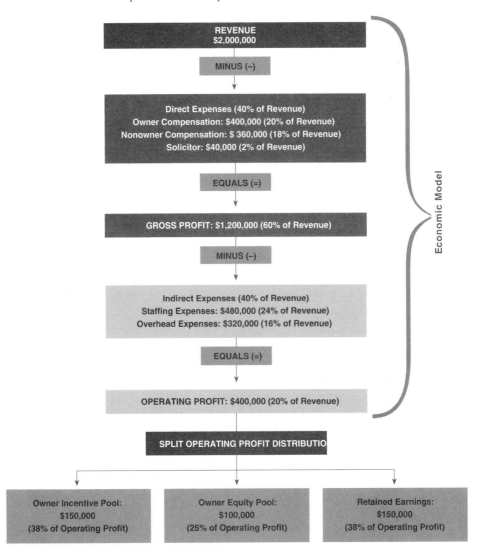

revenue decline or make significant capital investments in the firm. As the firm met this goal, it redirected this percentage to the profit-based incentive and profit distribution equity pools of its owner compensation plan.

Steps to Developing Ownership Compensation Plans

While similar to the design of firm compensation plans, the process of designing ownership compensation plans reflects the additional details, deliberation and decisions required of such a plan.

- *Step 1: Review the firm's vision, goals, and compensation philosophy.* Just as it should be an integral part of employee compensation planning, take into consideration the vision, goals, strategy, objectives, and outcomes at the firm level when designing your ownership compensation plan.
- *Step 2: Establish base compensation ranges and criteria for advancement.* Your compensation philosophies regarding employee compensation should extend to compensation designed for the role performed by each partner. Compensation for each role should be in line with industry standards and should allow partners the room to grow. For example, if a younger owner grows as an advisor and takes on additional rainmaking or client management responsibilities, his or her compensation should reflect these changes as they grow.
- *Step 3: Define performance and ownership criteria that drive incentives.* Although this will vary for each firm, include in your plan performance and ownership contributions that the firm wants to reward. For example, if the firm wants to double in size over the next three years, then contributions toward this aim weight differently than other goals of the firm. Whatever the defined criteria, there needs to be agreement by all owners and, most importantly, no guarantee of these incentives. Make the criteria measurable and evaluate ownership performance in each area.
- *Step 4. Define the balance between ownership incentive, profit distribution, and retained earnings.* As a part of financial and business planning, firm partners need to review and agree on profit allocation in the ownership incentive pool, profit distributions, and retained profits. This includes careful consideration and agreement on financial risk for ownership, contributions, and profits retained for a future safety net. Settle on a starting point and run various models in order to determine the implications of the designed plan.
- *Step 5: Calculate the short-term and long-term implications.* Test any financial model for viability prior to implementation. You should also go a step further to ensure that the plan is attractive to the individual and the firm, now and in the future. The rule of simple, but not simplistic, applies here. If the plan requires complex calculations to be calculated and seems to be too difficult to manage, it probably is. Whatever the plan design, test plan viability and ensure

that all partners understand the short- and long-term impact on firm success and individual compensation.

- *Step 6: Implement the plan and set a schedule for review.* Once you have a fully designed plan, determine a schedule for implementation and stick to it. In addition, we recommend that firms allow for flexibility in the review and development of their ownership compensation plans. When designing long-term plans, plan for owner contribution as well as the inevitable realities of new owners entering the firm and departure of current owners. Review owner compensation plans to ensure that they promote the vision, goals, and long-term success of the firm. How often you choose to review and/or revise your plan will vary. Do not use this frequent review to completely revise your plan; instead, make minor adjustments to profit distributions in each category or take into account the transition of ownership.

The True Cost of Compensation

Compensation represents much more than a paycheck for individuals and a line item on a firm's profit-and-loss statement—it represents an exchange of contributions and rewards between an individual and a firm. This exchange is about much more than money—it represents a relationship that, in its best form, contributes to the sustained satisfaction and success of everyone involved.

PART IV

Optimizing Operations

CHAPTER 27

Operations Optimization

When we think of the operations of advisory firms, two things come to mind: their delivery of services to clients and the practices and processes by which they deliver these services. Both are important, and neither is easy. As firms seek to give greater value to clients and make their firms more productive and profitable, the discussion of operations takes center stage.

Many advisors started their practices intending to serve clients well and hopefully earn a good living in the process. And most do. Challenges enter the picture when the practices grow or someone makes the decision to transform the practice into a full-fledged business. In either direction, the need to standardize, systematize, and scale operations to deliver high-quality services consistently, reliably, and profitably replaces small business simplicity.

As firms grow, they eventually outstrip the owner's ability, with limited resources, to market for new clients, cater to existing clients, and manage business operations. Owners frequently lament that there just isn't enough time to do everything. At some point, they hire staff to support them in these duties, only to realize they have added another responsibility to their list: managing the staff.

The solution is for advisory firms to optimize their operations so they can deliver a high-quality client experience as efficiently and effectively as possible. There is a difference between efficient and effective. We've seen many advisory firms effectively deliver quality services to their clients; they're just not very efficient. By the same token, a firm can operate very efficiently without delivering sufficient quality to clients or achieving the intended result. Either way, business performance, productivity, and profitability can suffer, diluting income and value for the owners.

Operating Models Drive Delivery

Operational stresses and strains are an inevitable result of doing business. These show up in firms in any of the following ways:

- The firm reacts to clients, rather than reaching out to them proactively.
- The quality of services and deliverables is inconsistent.
- There are constant interruptions—from clients, staff, and anyone else in the vicinity.
- Staff requires frequent instruction and direction to complete tasks.
- Last-minute fire drills are regular occurrences. By 10 A.M., the day's to-do list has been set aside for more pressing matters.
- Nothing goes as smoothly as it should. There exists insufficient time to do what's needed, much less make forward progress.
- Processes never go the same way twice.
- There is a lack of confidence in the outcome if the owner/advisor is not directly involved.
- The owner/advisor spends time on administrative, service, and operational work.
- High stress and low productivity characterizes the workplace environment.

There are many reasons for these challenges, but they boil down to one of three basic operating styles:

1. *Client driven.* Clients steer the ship. They call and come in, and whatever results from the interaction is the direction pursued by the advisor and his or her staff, regardless of the cost or imposition.
2. *People driven.* Employees define, drive, and deliver the work flow, with their experience and knowledge of what should happen, when, and how. Should those with the knowledge depart, they take it with them, leaving the business to start from scratch.
3. *Process driven:* Process defines and drives the work flow, with technology and/or staff delivering the services. Business practices have clear definition and are intentionally designed, well documented, and well managed. These practices drive client services and internal business activities.

In an era of market volatility—with limited time and compressed margins—staff members do more in less time. Thus, a process-driven model helps firms achieve three important business objectives: they can reliably deliver a consistent, high-quality client experience; master the efficient use of people, process, and technology; and maximize results, while managing costs.

When we talk with owners about what they want from operations, they consistently say the following:

- To shift from chaos and confusion to order and organization.
- To have a predictable, proactive client process.
- To spend their time on what they enjoy and do best, and delegate the rest.
- To deliver incredible value to clients, while growing revenue, income, and profits.

- To see repeatable, reliable results without their direct involvement.
- To be able to grow the business without growing all of the headaches.

Institutionalizing the Business

Optimizing operations is about developing an operations infrastructure that allows for all of the above. It enables firms to deliver their service in an efficient and effective manner, while also creating a high-quality experience for the client. This requires firms to identify, recognize, and develop these essential components: strategy, people, training, management, selection, process, and technology.

Strategy

As we discussed at length in the business planning section, the clearer a firm's vision and business strategy, the better it can build its business practices in alignment with and in support of them.

Recently, we consulted with a firm whose business strategy was simply to grow. The firm had a unique niche, serving executives in a certain industry, and as a result continuously brought on more clients than the staff could possibly support. They hired people as fast as they could and lost them almost as quickly. The partners realized this but chose to do nothing about it. As a result, their key staff member of 10 years who handled all of the client service, staff, and operations management finally had enough and walked out. When a firm lacks a clear strategy and fails to build its business to support that strategy, there are real risks.

The firm grew, but at what price? It had sacrificed the staff's personal satisfaction and its professional standards—not to mention that its profitability was in the single digits.

People

This refers to the individuals who perform the work that is required to deliver services to clients and run the business. How firms leverage their people has an enormous impact on operational performance and productivity. When staff members are clear about their roles and responsibilities and are given the proper training, their empowerment drives the process. Delegating to them is key to optimizing performance.

Training

Many firms that lack standardized processes have not effectively defined or communicated to staff members the outcomes the firm wants to achieve or how to achieve them. They provide sparse, if not downright cryptic, instructions; leave little time to discuss or review the work product; change their methods without notification; and all the while expect the staff to complete each task to their utmost satisfaction.

Management

Few firms have dedicated professional management, and fewer still have dedicated operations management. Owner/advisors often lack the time, talent, or temperament to evaluate operations and develop effective solutions, as well as train and support the team on how to execute and oversee operations, processes, and staff. As firms grow, it makes sense to hire an operations manager to establish standards and execute them with discipline.

Selection

Firms need to hire the right people to perform operations work. Everyone has a particular strength, but some are hardwired toward analytical thinking. They maintain a sharp attention to detail and perform best with established standards and systems. Others go with the flow; they often interact well with clients and deliver services with a personalized touch. Having the right person in the right role is essential to performance in all areas.

It's people who foster the relationships by delivering services and advice, while process and technology are tools that leverage their time and talent.

Process

Process organizes a collection of related, structured activities into a series of steps of routine performance that achieves a predictable, desired outcome.

Many firms lack processes because defining, drafting, and documenting every step in a business routine is no small task, and most advisors don't find the work very entertaining. Yet crafting processes is critical to attracting, retaining, and servicing clients, as well as ensuring that staff can support these tasks with the highest degree of quality.

At a recent event we conducted on optimizing business operations, we started the day with an exercise to highlight the value of process. We broke attendees into four groups and gave each group a bag that contained a jigsaw puzzle. Each group had 10 minutes to assemble its puzzle, with the first group to finish being the winner. The winning group assembled its puzzle in 3 minutes, the next group in 6 minutes, and the remaining two groups did not finish in the time allotted.

What we didn't tell the groups at the outset was that the contents of their bags were different. The winning group's bag contained the puzzle as well as a photo of the puzzle assembled. Each piece featured in the picture was numbered, and on the back of each puzzle piece was a corresponding number. To assemble the puzzle, all the group had to do was look at the puzzle, identify which numbered piece went where, and put it in place. The group that required 6 minutes to assemble the puzzle also had the puzzle pieces and a picture of the assembled puzzle. Yet there were no numbers on the puzzle pieces or the picture. The third group received a bag with puzzle pieces, but nothing else. The fourth group received a bag with most, but not all, of the puzzle pieces.

The exercise demonstrated that by defining and documenting the details of what and how to do things, their teams could complete work more easily and effectively in far less time.

Technology

Technology tools—including financial planning software, performance reporting tools, CRM software and paperless office systems—support key business functions.

No twenty-first-century conversation on enhancing operational performance is complete without a discussion of technology. Two technology trends emerge across our profession. First, more and better technology exists today than at any other time in the history of the advisory profession. Custodians, broker-dealers, transition assistance management programs (TAMPs), and third-party providers are continually bringing a broader and better set of capabilities to the table. Although the big problem for firms using these technologies has been lack of integration, that is beginning to change for the better. The second trend is that only the smallest minority of advisory firms actually use technology to their best advantage.

We have seen too many firms buy technology only to ignore all but its most basic functionality. For example, most firms rely on their CRMs for basic blocking and tackling, such as scheduling and maintaining client information. Yet CRMs can utterly transform a firm's operations if used to their full capacity. Once you design and integrate processes into a CRM, it can create and automate an entire process. The technology automatically sequences and triggers the events that need to take place.

Fortunately, more firms are using CRM software. We believe no firm should be without it. Which software is best depends on each firm's situation, needs, goals, and budgets, but Junxure, Redtail, and Salesforce seem to be the most popular in the advisory profession. The Financial Planning Association did a series of studies on technology with Actifi, Inc., which provides valuable insight. You can find these studies at fpanet.org. In addition, David Drucker and Joel

Bruckenstein, through their newsletter *Technology Tools for Today*, have resources available to help advisors make the selection. Jennifer Goldman of Virtual Solutions is a technology consultant who specializes in helping financial advisors evaluate, select, and implement software. Julie Littlechild of Advisor Impact has developed a technology-based client feedback (survey) service that automates the development of customized client surveys and generates materials to support advisors using what they learn in meaningful ways.

Financial planning software is another technology that is different in each advisory firm. Drucker and Bruckenstein are both experts on evaluating this technology and an excellent resource for advisors.

In one client firm, a highly personalized financial planning process required the development of proprietary Excel spreadsheets to achieve the desired analysis. This took an incredible amount of time. When we suggested that commercially available software might meet the advisors' needs more efficiently, they said their needs were too specialized.

We then discussed what they stood to gain by using commercially available software. The list of potential benefits included staff appreciation and productivity (the staff found the spreadsheets burdensome and time consuming, and thus hated them), fast turnarounds, improved accuracy, and valuable time savings. Would they, we asked, be willing to use software to prepare for the next plan review meeting to see whether the outcome (as experienced by the client) was materially different enough to justify the current solution? To their credit, they agreed to the experiment. Suffice it to say that the clients failed to notice any differences. They focused more on the meeting discussions, the relationship, and the advice given—not the data points and format. Even the partners had to conclude that the client meeting was as successful as any they'd conducted using their own spreadsheets.

The overarching point is that while more and more firms recognize the value of investing in technology, few firms truly take advantage of its full potential. Firms that are ready to optimize their operations should start by leveraging technology to the utmost.

Insights on Institutionalization

Institutionalization is the combination of people, process, and technology to create formalized business systems that promote a firm's ability to deliver a predictable result in a sustainable fashion, independent of any individual or group of individuals.

Institutionalization provides clarity, consistency, and control over business operations. A new level of consistency emerges when all firm members are clear on how a series of specific steps combines to drive a specific outcome. Such clear execution provides firms with a highly desirable asset: control.

The ability to develop a level of control over business operations is the result of three interconnected elements: standardization, systematization, and scalability.

Standardization

Advisors at multiadvisor firms worry that standardization will impede each person's ability to do things his or her own way. It's true that standardizing will limit each advisor's ability to build his or her own unique processes within the business. That said, a better question is: how does what these advisors stand to gain from standardization compare with what they give up? They stand to gain quite a lot.

Financial planning and wealth management involve a set of standardized steps: gather and organize client information, analyze options, make recommendations, implement a plan, monitor, and review. Although each advisor approaches these steps differently, the underlying work is similar. The differentiator is the personalization provided by each advisor, not the actual steps themselves.

Standardization requires that advisors give up their own preference-based process for a firm process. The real sacrifice isn't in the approach; it's in the advisors' acceptance that their way may not be the best way for the firm. They therefore have to defer individual interests to those of the group. If each advisor can accept that the result will be only 80 percent of what he or she wants, and that the advisor will need to be able to live with the remaining 20 percent, the benefits of standardization usually outweigh this cost.

If every advisor in a firm follows the same approach, using people, process, and technology consistently, the inevitable result is greater efficiency and productivity. There are other benefits. By following the same process, the whole firm gains greater redundancy and reliability, as well as far greater scalability. Operational consistency leads to clear increases in quality and performance.

Advisors also frequently say that they provide personalized solutions to clients, and you just can't automate that level of customization and service. On the contrary, systematizing the client engagement process frees advisors up to lavish more time and attention on clients—and that's the personal part.

We worked with firms who cater to ultra-high-net-worth clients and still found that most of the work can be standardized and systematized. In one situation, the firm had to help the client transfer an airplane into his living trust as part of his estate plan. This was indeed a one-off situation they had not seen before. But as the staff figured out how to do this, they documented the process and stored the necessary forms and materials. If that situation ever arises again, they will be ready—no additional research required. This extreme example highlights how even the most unusual client request or need converts to a routine business process. Determine easily documented, repetitive tasks—developing financial plans, building portfolios, executing trades, rebalancing, and so on—and create processes for them so your advisors spend their time engaged in more valuable activities.

The real secret of standardization is that a consistent, repeatable process is more likely to add value to a client's experience and a firm's performance than is a specialized approach; using one best method leads to greater control and more time saved. This allows advisors to provide a personalized experience in what really matters: the advice given and the relationship maintained.

Systematization

Systematizing the firm requires advisors to look objectively at their mechanisms (people, processes, technology), which support operations; figure out what's missing; and develop a plan to bridge the gap. Systematizing your business means defining a logical sequence of events that fits together to form a system for each key business function. Each of these independent systems works together as a whole to deliver a firm's offering successfully.

Business systems in advisory firms include compliance, marketing, client service, investment management, financial planning, and many more. Each contains one or more processes that define the series of steps necessary to produce an outcome.

To begin the systematization process, we take an inventory of a firm's key business systems and develop a business systems model document that defines the business systems that exist or need to exist within each area of the business. Each system has a space in the document for the firm to designate the system owner, the target date for completion, and the completion status. This model lets firms establish the systems required to support each area of the business, designate an owner, and engage a plan to complete the systematization process. An annual review of the firm's systems ensures that they remain up to date.

Scalability

Scalability is the system's ability to expand to accommodate that growth, preferably in an orderly and organized manner. In the case of advisory firms, it refers to the capability of a firm's systems to increase total throughput under increased volume while managing expenses.

Despite the market volatility of the past decade, advisory firms have grown at a healthy rate since the opening of the twenty-first century. With the first Baby Boomers entering retirement and more to follow every day, the need for financial advice during the next decade is likely to outpace advisory firms' ability to provide it. Firms that can scale up their business operations will be best able to expand and accommodate that growth, positioning them to lead the industry.

Benchmarking Operational Performance

How do you effectively measure and monitor operational performance? Once you implement improvements, how do you discern value yield? Although each firm's level of comfort and ability to engage in operational performance analysis will vary, we recommend that advisors determine the benchmarks or methods they will use to measure performance.

As discussed in the chapters on financial management and benchmarking, the key performance metrics provided by the benchmarking process are readily accessible and easy to measure. Don't focus on all of them at once. Instead, identify a subset of four to six that have the most impact. We suggest that firms conduct their benchmarking exercise before making any changes or improvements, in order to establish a meaningful baseline against which to measure improvements and ongoing performance.

As each system within a business is developed, identify which measures will gauge performance. For example, good measures to start with are advisor and staff hours spent on financial plans, the number of days to process and fund new accounts, the number of outbound calls to clients each year, and the amount of advisor and staff time spent doing preparation work.

That said, don't be afraid to think outside the box. Candidly speaking, many of the improvements we regularly institute in our clients' practices start out as nothing more than an idea that might solve a problem. In one firm where costly trade errors happened routinely, we designed a system for trade execution and identified measures the firm could monitor to ensure that the improvements paid off. These included the total number of trade errors and the percentage of trade errors relative to the number of trades executed. We then established a historical average for the cost of these trade errors. To invest the team in improving its performance as well, the firm created a bonus pool for the operations team, equal to the cost of the trade errors for the prior year. In any quarter that no trade errors occurred, a percentage of the bonus pool was paid to the staff who executed the trades, and the balance at year-end if the dollar amount of trade errors stayed at a predefined level (to ensure that any costly trade errors late in the year were accounted for).

You might wonder what the partners initially thought when we presented the idea: why would we pay people to do their jobs the right way? The partners figured that because people are human, mistakes happen, and despite all of the frustration and attempts to make it otherwise, the errors would still occur. We disagreed. The idea was to help motivate the team to adopt new behavior, not create an easy annual bonus pool with incentives paid at the start of the year—a better application of the expenditure than merely covering trade error costs. The worst-case scenario was that nothing would change, so the firm literally had nothing to lose—they already spent the money. The result was a near zero trade-error rate, with bonuses being paid out in three quarters. The trade error measurements improved dramatically. The team members felt better about their work, and the owners felt better about their team. With everyone now clearly aware that performance could be better, and that errors were avoidable, the team was set to maintain the standard in years that followed. Moreover, firm expenses fell and profits rose—not significantly, but imagine if a firm can repeat similar results in 20 small ways each year.

When you consider that every inefficient or ineffective process potentially dilutes performance by 1 percent, 5 percent, or maybe even 10 percent or more, it doesn't take long for the benefits to add up.

The Cost of Complacency

Although most advisors recognize that optimizing their operations would benefit them and often complain about the symptoms of poor operational performance, few of them are taking steps to remedy the situation.

They say that their time is better spent meeting with clients, not building processes. Their staff already knows what to do, so how will putting it on paper change anything? And, as we said earlier, the advisors believe that "my way" is better than one standardized way and that their clients are so unique, they couldn't possibly systematize something so personal.

To provide advisors with a broader view, we ask whether they spend enough time with their top clients. (No.) We ask whether they feel their firms are a reflection of order and organization or of chaos and confusion. (The latter.) We ask whether their staffs truly leverage the advisors' time and talent or consume it by requiring constant supervision and interaction. (The latter.) We ask whether they are driving the firm, or whether it is driving them. (The latter.) We ask them whether they would be proud or embarrassed to have their peers and their clients silently observe how their business runs for a few days. (Embarrassed.) You get the point.

The entire goal of operations optimization is to deliver the same, or more, services to clients but to do so better, faster, and smarter. The by-product for advisors is increased job satisfaction and financial success. What these firms are really saying is that they *don't know how* to improve their business operations or where to start. Yet if learning to standardize and systematize business processes saved time for each person in the firm, what would the value of that time be worth? Optimizing your operational performance frees up your time, and time is a firm's greatest revenue-producing asset.

The Power of Process

Perhaps what is most interesting about the process experience is that, ultimately, it becomes second nature to everyone in the firm and, as a result, is easy to execute. It actually takes more effort not to follow the process. No matter where you are in your operational development, or what way is right for you, you can standardize, systematize, and scale your business to improve your operational performance and deliver optimal outcomes for your clients and for your business.

CHAPTER 28

Client-Facing Processes

The average advisor does not anticipate a discussion of marketing when steeped in a discussion of optimizing operations. Yet the way advisors think about and engage in marketing in their practices can have a huge impact—if they are ready to change the way they think about client service and marketing.

We've described how systems and standardizing processes can improve performance and free up time. Similarly, when advisors want to drive systematic growth in their firms, they can do so also through systematic processes to market to, attract, and acquire new clients.

The Client Experience

Most firms we know are highly focused on delivering great service to their clients. The challenge with this approach is that it focuses on just one aspect of a broader concept: the client experience. Great service is a must, for certain, but the client experience extends broadly to each and every interaction a prospect or a client has with your firm.

According to a McKinsey & Company survey, more than half of consumers switch their primary financial advisor after the age of 40, and of those, half make the move before retirement. The reason for the switch doesn't appear to be investment performance, so what is it?

Our theory is that the clients who seek another advisor as they age (after working with one for years) are looking for more as they face major milestones in their lives. In short, the lack of a defined client experience creates a vacuum, leaving room for what we call the "un-experience." No intentional planning goes into the experience a client (or a potential client) has with a firm, leaving the client feeling ho-hum about the advisor. This is a lost opportunity for advisors.

Frequently, we see talented and committed advisors, rich with investment and planning expertise, provide good service but fail to build deeply committed client relationships. We're not implying that these firms do not have good client relationships, but rather that they are missing out on an opportunity to develop better, deeper relationships by crafting a significant client experience, so clients will choose not to leave.

View the client experience as a holistic, integrated approach to engagement and interaction with both prospects and clients alike. This approach highlights how a firm engages and interacts with prospects and clients at every step in the relationship, from initial inquiry to ongoing relationship management. The goal is to create a predictable, consistent, high-quality experience through consistent delivery by way of day-to-day business operations.

Building an ideal client experience, as with building any system, requires you to evaluate every step, from the initial telephone conversation to your letters and e-mails, the office facilities, the amenities for clients, the agendas for client meetings, and so on. The goal is to assume nothing and question all things from the perspective of how a client will see, touch, hear, and feel it.

In one firm that focused on high-net-worth women with $2 million or more in investable assets, we noticed during our initial business review that the conference room had cracked paint and a small hole in the wall, and the conference table was a bit past its prime. When we pointed this out, the owners realized that the office environment didn't reflect their clientele or create a positive client experience. In another firm, once we completed the brand development (see Chapter 12 on branding), we had the entire staff leave the office and walk through, one by one, as if they were clients, and write down their observations. A team of 10 generated more than 58 observations, which resulted in six distinct areas where the firm's offices didn't align with the brand or the client experience it should evoke.

Defining your client experience is essentially an extension of operations optimization. To do it well, a firm must identify all of the business systems that make up or contribute to the client experience, then review those processes through the lens of not only what is operationally efficient but also what will create the client experience the firm wishes to deliver.

Here are a few everyday examples of how firms can be more efficient and effective as businesses and improve the overall client experience:

- *Situation:* The firm sends a letter confirming a prospect's initial appointment. The letter arrives in a standard letter-size envelope via general mail. The letter denotes the date and time of appointment, asks prospect to bring information to meeting, and indicates that the firm looks forward to the meeting.
  - *Experience shift:* Envision this same action through the lens of the "best possible" experience for both the firm and the prospect. These days, not much comes in the mail in a letter-size envelope except junk mail and

notices from government agencies that people don't want to receive. *You aren't trying to confirm an appointment; you are trying to create an impression.* Given that the recipient's financial future is at stake, the initial interaction should suggest that this is a very important, high-priority process.

The letter-size envelope doesn't convey that message, so we suggest sending this communication via FedEx standard overnight. This costs a bit more than the postal service, but it also communicates the important message that the prospects are well worth it. When someone receives regular mail and a FedEx envelope (or an equivalent service), the FedEx envelope gets opened first every time. It tells the recipient that this package is important, so important that we overnighted it to you. It will get the prospect's immediate attention, and he or she will get the message that the meeting with the firm is important. The FedEx envelope also tells the prospect that the firm delivers on its commitments. That's because the prospect expected a FedEx envelope the next day with important information about the meeting—an expectation created during the appointment-setting phone call. On that call, the firm's representative also shared that she would follow up in a few days to confirm receipt and to answer any questions the recipient may have as he or she prepares for the meeting. When you set an expectation from moment one and deliver on it quickly and professionally, you make an important impression and enhance the client experience.

- *Situation:* Clients are inundated with paperwork when opening or transferring accounts. Everyone, except the client, knows this will happen. Nobody likes it, particularly the client.
  - *Experience shift:* Set an expectation and then provide a solution. Explain the inundation of paperwork to come and allay their fears. All they need to do is place all of the incoming paperwork in a folder (which you have provided) and bring it with them for their 60-day review meeting, where you will identify items to keep, items of importance, and items to be discarded. You can either return the organized paperwork to the client or post it to his or her online file cabinets. If you use online file cabinets with clients, this is a good time to physically log in and get the clients comfortable with using the tool.

Is either of the above examples a major component of the client experience? Probably not, but they are steps routinely overlooked. Returning client calls on time is also a part of a positive client experience, but this act or other similar courtesies do not make for a pleasant client experience on their own. Firms can benefit greatly from viewing their process through both an operational behind-the-scenes lens and the onstage client-experience lens.

We recommend using one simple standard in developing your ideal client experience: question everything. Evaluate everything, from your initial phone conversation to your correspondence. This includes your office facilities, the client amenities, the service protocol, the meeting materials and agenda items, and so on. One client firm decided they wanted prospects and clients to feel more comfortable in meetings, so we repurposed the smaller of its two conference rooms into a living room setup. Those coming in for meetings could sit in the other conference room or the living room. They overwhelmingly chose the living room. This is a great example of how questioning everything from the client's point of view can change his or her experience.

Each of your business processes touches clients in some manner and, ultimately, becomes part of the client experience. Given that this book isn't thick enough to cover all of them, we want to address two of the main systems that drive the client experience: the prospect process and the new client process.

The Prospect Process

Conversations about prospects and prospecting often turn into discussions about services, fees and pricing, and how hard it is to get a meeting. These are important, but they sometimes miss the mark. When advisors complain about fee pressures or negotiating fees with clients, we often remind them that fees are only an issue in the absence of value. In the book *Clued In*, by Lewis P. Carbone, Carbone highlights the value of experience by noting that coffee, as a commodity, costs roughly 25 cents a pound. As a product in the grocery store, it costs $2.50 to $6.99 per pound. At a regular café, it's $1.25 a cup, and at a Starbucks, it's $2.50 to $4.50 per beverage. How is it that coffee—a commodity in every sense of the word—became a highly leveraged and profitable product? Carbone's answer: Starbucks doesn't sell coffee, they sell a coffee experience.[1]

You are not talking to potential clients about their investments or assets or planning needs. You're talking to them about their financial future, their ability to feel safe and secure, to retire comfortably, to make the most of their wealth, or whatever it is that has driven them to contact you. Few firms craft the prospect process intentionally; rather, it just sort of evolves over the years.

Although the process each prospect goes through will vary slightly, as a rule each case is strikingly similar: The phone rings or an e-mail is received, an advisor talks with the prospect about his or her interests and needs, an appointment is set, a letter is sent, an initial meeting is held, more meetings are held, and the potential client says yes or no.

These steps seem relatively simple and straightforward, so we can appreciate why advisors might question why They need a process in the first place. Yet once you view the process—informal though it is—through the client-experience lens, a different story emerges.

A firm focused on delivering a more deliberate client experience would recognize the incoming call inquiry as the first opportunity to craft the prospect experience—in this case, by making sure to focus the discussion on the firm's brand promise (the outcome it delivers) and on how the advisor can work with the caller to deliver it. For example, a phone call, with client experience in mind, could include the points made in the following script (not intended to be read to a prospect) as part of a discussion with the prospect:

It was very thoughtful of [client] to mention us to you and I'm glad you called. We'd be happy to arrange a meeting, but first I'd like to share a little bit about our firm and approach to help you understand not just how we will work with you, but why. These days, financial planning can mean just about anything, from selling stocks to insurance products. For us, it's all about simplifying your financial life so that you can feel in control and can more easily define and reach your life goals. Our priority is to help you secure your financial future, while doing all we can to simplify your life along the way. As part of our process, we work very closely with you to learn your financial goals and what is most important to you. We then design and implement a financial plan that will help you and your family achieve your goals. Although this process never really ends, we begin by scheduling two hours for you to meet with [advisor name]. During this time, he will learn about you, discuss your options, and make sure you have a real understanding of what planning can do for you.

To make sure your time with [advisor] focuses on your personal situation, please provide us with some information on your situation prior to your meeting. We encourage you to complete the Planning Questionnaire and send it to us before your appointment. It will take a few minutes to get ready, but we'll provide you with a red folder to compile your paperwork, and when you come in, we'll sort, copy, and organize it while you meet with me/the advisor.

During that meeting, [advisor name] will discuss your personal situation, your planning options, and ways that we can help you face your financial future with confidence. If we feel we can add value to your life through the planning process, and you would like us to, we will have you sign an engagement agreement. From here, we will complete a financial planning and investment analysis and then meet with you again in two to three weeks to review our recommendations with you. We'll answer any questions you have and make sure you're comfortable with the plan. After this, we'll work with you and your other professionals [if appropriate] to implement the recommendations we've made. We will meet with you again in 90 days to review your accounts and answer any questions you have. From here, we will meet with you on an ongoing basis to review the things that matter to your financial future: your life, your finances, your goals, and various aspects of your financial plan and investments. We will continue that process to make sure that your planning keeps up with your life, and that you feel confident knowing you have a trusted advisor with you every step of the way.

Our goal is to ensure that by the time you leave our office, you've started down the road of feeling in control of your financial future. If you would like to move forward, our next available meeting is . . .

This scenario goes well beyond the initial discussion and scheduling of a meeting. This step sets the expectation for the entire process going forward, so that the firm can deliver as promised. Prospects know what the puzzle looks like put together. They know they're going to provide documents, then come to a two-hour meeting, after which they're going to make a decision. They know if they say yes, they're coming back in two weeks, and they know what to expect after that.

This process isn't an exact fit for everyone. Every firm is unique in its value proposition, service offering, and process. Yet every firm can build a process that questions—and successfully answers—how to best interact and engage with prospects, crafting the best possible experience every step along the way.

The secret is to define a powerful, unique, and emotion-based prospect/client experience and then make sure to follow that through in the "backstage" processes you build. For example, a client gets an e-mail reminder for an upcoming meeting with an agenda. Someone from your staff calls to make sure the client is happy with the agenda and to ask whether he or she has something to add. After the review meeting, the client receives a personal phone call, in which someone from your firm says, "It was great to see you again for your annual review. There were some follow-up items in your meeting with [advisor's name]. I would love to review those with you quickly and then send a confirmation letter so that you're clear on what our next steps are. I'll follow up again in 90 days to report on our progress and check in on yours."

How would you feel, as the client receiving that call? No doubt, pretty special, and certainly more special than if you had not received the call. Additionally, the client is likely to deepen his or her view that the firm is highly professional, helpful, and competent as staff members follow through on their commitments.

Executing on the Prospect Process

How you execute on the prospect process can make or break the experience. How prepared are you for the meeting, whether it's a discovery meeting, a presentation, or a review? Do you take 10 minutes before that meeting to review the client's file and get in the zone? Are you fully prepared to be present for the meeting? While various people greet the prospect, prepare his or her documents for the advisor, and handle the phone calls, your seamless system of service and your preparedness all convey an impressive experience to the client.

Your CRM system is the central hub of prospect and client processes. Your business process "planes" take off and land in your CRM, capturing important client data in the process. But your team has to be completely on board as well. Ideally, the team members will help you develop the prospect process. This not only helps ensure the best process and experience possible but also helps the team understand the process that prospects go through and conveys how crucial each person's role is to a successful result. The receptionist may be simply answering the phone, but the clarity and friendliness of her voice and the welcoming slogan she uses to align with the firm's brand are the client's first introduction to the process.

When you intentionally evaluate your prospect process through the lens of making every step in that process the best experience it can be (for the firm and the client), you'll realize the opportunities in often overlooked everyday details of doing business.

Although every firm's process is different, we've found that most follow similar steps. These should include, but certainly are not limited to:

- Prospect inquires about firm (you called the prospect or he or she called you).
- Add the prospect to the CRM.
- Update the prospect tracking form.
- Open the prospect intake form and use it to gather prospect information.
- Review the interest points with the prospect.
- Gain the necessary background as to why he or she is seeking advice now.
- Explore the prospect's situation, needs, goals, and finances, to determine whether he or she is a fit for the firm.
- If the prospect is not a fit, provide options that are best for him or her (e.g., referral to a more suitable advisor). If the prospect is a fit, proceed with the process.
- Gather the basic information, name, address, and so on. Inquire how the prospect came to your firm.
- If a referral, note the source and complete the appropriate referral process.
- If not a referral, note the source.
- If the prospect wishes to move forward, set an initial meeting.
- Set expectations for the meeting prep and the meeting.
- The team prepares for the initial meeting.
- The firm holds the initial meeting with the prospect, culminating in yes, no, or maybe from the prospect.
- If yes, send a welcome letter and proceed with the new client process.
- If no, send a thank-you-for-consideration letter.
- If maybe: Send a thank-you-for-consideration letter and initiate follow-up process.

Regardless of the details, you can effectively develop a prospect process to follow consistently by using:

- A prospect flow diagram
- A prospect checklist
- Process materials
- CRM integration

Prospect Flow Diagram

Figure 28.1 is an example of a prospect flow diagram. It may appear complicated at first glance, but arrows direct you from step to step. Similarly, the diagram you create for your firm should provide a visual map of the prospect process flow so that the team can quickly and easily understand the major steps.

Keep the diagram simple and limit it to the prospect movement through the process and any other necessary major steps required. For example, one step will indicate that the firm meets with the prospect. The diagram does not need to cover what happens in the meeting, only that there is a meeting and what the flow choices are after the meeting: yes, no, or maybe. The diagram then shows the flow of activity if the prospect says yes to proceed, no to proceed, or maybe (indicating that he or she needs to think about it). There is no mystery or magic to a prospect flow diagram, and you can easily create it with programs such as PowerPoint, Visio, and mind-mapping software.

Process Checklist

The process checklist documents each and every step in the process, in detail, defining what happens, when it happens, how it happens, and who is responsible for making it happen. Each step should also reference any needed forms or materials to complete that step in the process. The trick here is a painstaking level of detail. It's worth the work, since this is the document that will drive the consistent delivery of your prospect experience.

Once you have your process steps defined (the what), the next step is to define how each step in the process happens, who completes it and when it is completed, and how it triggers the next step—best done in the form of a process checklist.

Process Materials

Every process requires documentation, such as forms, materials, packages, and presentations. Support the process with necessary forms keyed to points of execution (per your checklist). The first is a conversation with the prospect. How does

FIGURE 28.1 Process Flow Diagram

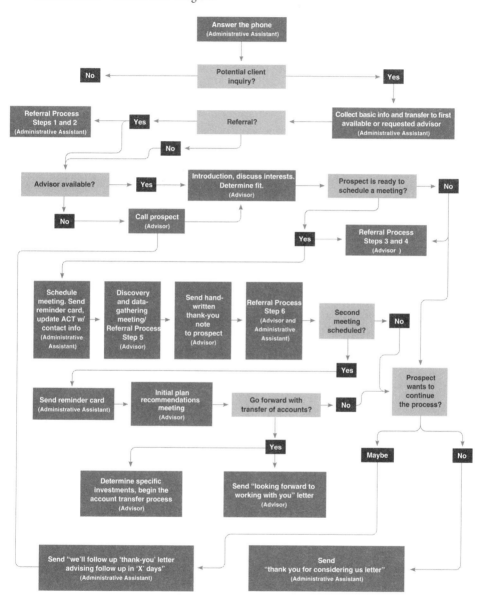

the firm ensure a consistent, high-quality conversation that covers all of the information needed for a good call and to make sure the firm and the prospect are right for each other and ready to continue the process? We recommend a prospect intake form to ensure a consistent framework for the prospect call and to gather all of the necessary information.

The person conducting the initial call simply inputs the information into the form (preferably directly into a CRM program, but that's a bit more advanced) and passes it to the next person in the process chain. The form documents the appropriate next steps so that everyone knows what these are. For example, if the prospect was not a good fit, the form would note that and the resulting action item (referral elsewhere, etc.). If the prospect wants to think about it, there is a place to note that and indicate the appropriate next step, which should also be a defined part of the process so that the response can be consistent as well.

Continuing the example where the prospect says she wants to think about it and get back to the advisor, the advisor has the option of agreeing and moving on or of setting some expectation for engagement. The advisor might say that she understands, as this is an important decision, and that she will have some information sent out overnight to help the prospect better understand financial planning, her options, and how the firm may be able to help. The advisor may then say something like, "Would it be all right if I called you back in a week to answer any questions you have and see if you would like to schedule a meeting to learn more?"

If the prospect says no, the advisor knows she is not ready and there's no need to follow up, and the advisor checks that box on the form. If the prospect says yes, then the advisor knows to check another box. Per the process, checking this box results in overnighting a predetermined package of materials and a follow-up call's being set for one week out. If the prospect requests a different time frame, the advisor writes in an alternative follow-up date. And by using the form, the advisor ensures follow-up by sending the package and scheduling phone calls.

The form then passes to the next person in the process for handling. Many advisors choose to note the firm's key prospect messaging points on the form to make sure that the discussion of how the firm adds value is consistent, regardless of who is holding it. At first, our client advisors find this very calculated and unnatural. But we're not proposing that you "read" the bullet points as they are; rather, that they serve as a gentle reminder of the talking points the firm decided to share with prospects to ensure the best possible call, for the prospects and the firm.

Everyone's style is different, so not every advisor or staff member will communicate the points in the same way. Yet we will often draft a prospect dialogue script that lays out an example of how the conversation might go. (We've included a script example earlier in this chapter.) No one should read the script—that would make for a horrible prospect experience. It simply serves as an example of how one might weave the talking points into the conversation. For seasoned advisors seeking to transition this duty to staff members or younger advisors, this is an invaluable aid.

Some firms use e-mail to send materials to prospects. While this works, we are still fans of preparing printed materials with a strong, tangible brand and getting them into the hands of prospects. This helps set the right tone and establish appropriate expectations. Marketing materials printed on a prospect's home or work computer never look the same as professionally printed materials.

Other documentation typically includes a call script of what the staff members will say (generally) when they reach out to prospects following delivery of the meeting package (Did you receive it? Let's take a few minutes to walk through it together. Do you have any questions?). A meeting agenda is another piece of helpful documentation to establish a framework for the initial meeting.

CRM Integration

Integrating a firm's processes into its CRM technology is the second major operational game changer (institutionalizing processes for entry in the CRM is the first). With a process checklist and materials in place, firms can fully integrate their step-by-step prospect process into their CRM program, defining each step, its timing, and the relationships between steps.

A way to ensure consistent implementation of the process is to use the CRM for every defined step. Program the CRM to task a staff member with sending the prospect package on a predetermined date. Because the firm indicated it would follow up with the prospect in a few days to see whether he or she had any questions, an activity would show up automatically on the appropriate staff person's calendar for, say, three days later. When that activity completes in the system, the CRM triggers the next activity called for in the process.

The New-Client Process

Once a prospect has agreed to move forward with the firm, the prospect process transitions into the new-client process. Again, the goal is to have a clearly defined process that can be consistently delivered and that also creates a high-quality and remarkable experience.

The new-client process picks up with signing the engagement agreement. This involves an account initiation, account follow-up, new-client welcome, and transition review. Whether this happens today, tomorrow, within one week, or in 30 days, it should be clear who does each step, by when, and whether there are materials needed.

We recommend sending a welcome package with a cover letter welcoming the client to the firm and introducing the team. One of our advisor clients drafted a letter from the president that welcomed each new client to the firm and provided his contact information should the client at any point want to share praise or problems. The package included a nicely designed "meet the team" page with a headshot of each person on the team, his or her role, when to contact the person, and how to reach him or her. A staff person follows up after the package is sent to confirm it was received, walk through the "meet the team," review whom to call when (which helps ensure that the advisors don't get service questions), and thank the client for his or her trust in choosing the firm.

If the client was referred by one of the advisors with whom the firm already had a relationship (the client's certified public accountant [CPA] or estate attorney, for example), the firm would—with the client's permission—send a modified version of the welcome package to the client's other professionals. The package contains a similar welcome letter, sharing that the firm has just retained the client and that it believes firmly in the team approach and so wants to make an introduction and welcome the professional. The letter goes on to say the goal of working together is to ensure the best possible outcome for the client. Being the marketing fans that we are, the letter, of course, indicates that the firm would like to meet in person to walk the professional through the process his or her client has been through, what process the client will experience going forward, and the firm's process for working collaboratively with other members of the client's professional team.

There generally is positive reception of the package sent, often leading to new referral relationships. This is likely because we doubt that any of the professional's other clients' financial advisors demonstrate such professionalism, care, and competency in handling their clients' affairs. It's fair to say that this process has brought our clients many a new referral relationship at the expense of another advisor, one who didn't understand the power of experience and process.

The steps to evaluating and developing a new-client process are identical to those for the prospect process: Create a flow diagram, build a checklist that details how each step in the process takes place, develop the materials needed to execute the process, and, ideally, integrate it into the firm's CRM software.

Client Review Process

All advisors should meet with their clients at periodic intervals, and we'll talk more about what service levels are appropriate in the chapters that follow. First, let's look at the client review process from the standpoint of building a process-based experience. Usually, advisors will meet with clients at least once a year, so we will use that example, and focus on how to make the steps in a normal process a better overall experience.

Scheduling the Meeting

A meeting will need to be scheduled. Firms take a number of approaches that cover the range of extremes, from calling clients, leaving a message, and waiting for them to call back, to scheduling next year's review meeting at the end of this year's. Still other firms schedule a review meeting every quarter, and others schedule all review meetings during certain months of the year. No one size fits all. We do recommend, though, that the firm make clear to clients the details of when you will meet. If you're going to meet with the client twice per year, every six months, then communicating that information should be a step in the new-client process (as described earlier), so that the firm can deliver on the experience promised.

Reach out to clients a minimum of 30 days in advance, giving them adequate notice. It also ensures that the meeting is held in the month desired. Have established meeting times in the calendar so the staff is aware of the exact number of meetings per week and the appropriate time slots for those meetings. We've had clients complain more than once that the staff scheduled too many meetings in a week. Developing a standard for meetings and creating a process to ensure adherence helps the staff with scheduling the calendar.

Usually, we have advisors calculate the number of meetings they can comfortably hold in a week, determine the times they want to have them, and share that information with the staff. Using the CRM, the staff blocks the meeting times in the calendar. When the week's meetings are full, the staff simply goes to the following week. In many of our client firms, there is a report generated that shows the client meetings to be scheduled in any given month. This allows the firm to manage capacity closely.

Send an e-mail to the client when it's time to schedule the next review. Indicate that someone from your staff will reach out within the next few days to schedule the appointment. Automate and manage the process via your CRM software, identifying the client due for review, handling staff notification, and placement of the call "to do" on your assistant's calendar.

Following the e-mail, we suggest that a staff person contact the client to schedule the call, using a basic script or talking points that follow the firm's review call standards.

Meeting Prep

Start preparing for the meeting at the time it's scheduled. Usually, firms conduct a review of the client's financial planning situation and investment portfolios and prepare related materials for review in the client meeting. We recommend a prepared written agenda.

Regardless of the steps, the review process should detail all of the work to be completed and should allow ample time for a job well done. Perhaps the greatest frustration advisors have in the client management process is preparing and following up on client meetings. Often, the advisor doesn't have what he needs or asked for, or he believes he doesn't, and/or he is asking for new materials or edits to materials just before the meeting. We have found, in many cases, that the time when an advisor is most attuned to preparing for a client meeting is about an hour beforehand.

This is not an ideal process. It leaves the staff unsure of the materials the advisors need and leads to last-minute confusion and unhappiness for both advisors and staff. The remedy for this is a clearly defined process that both advisor and staff have agreed to and adhere to, spelling out what materials are to be prepared, when they are to be ready for advisor review, when the advisor is to review them and return them by, and when materials are ready for the client meeting.

We recommend that client materials be ready in final form at least two to three days prior to the client meeting. This allows everyone time to do his or her work, with a little bit of wiggle room. Given that unpredictable things happen—people get sick, markets make major moves in a day—it's best to allow a bit of leeway.

We also suggest that every client meeting have an agenda to demonstrate that the firm is clear on its goals and objectives for the meeting, has done its homework, and is ready for the meeting. We recommend that the agenda start with the client's goals (in a section at the top), then follow with key questions related to the client's situation (in the next section). One of our advisor clients starts every meeting agenda with the question, "What's changed since we last met?" He makes the first order of business knowing what's going on in his client's life. He would say that this is the best part of his meeting, because he gets to focus on what's happening in their lives, instead of in their investment accounts. This way, he always knows what's going on for clients, and he can make sure that any work the firm does reflects this understanding. The agenda also lists tactical items for discussion, such as investment reviews and planning issues, among others.

Every meeting will, to some degree, cover the technical information but the agenda will depend on the firm's service model. For example, in the meeting, some advisors do a brief review of every aspect of planning to cover all of the bases. Others have a more extensive process, in which every client is on a review cycle, and the topics for the meetings will alternate over time to allow the firm to do a deeper review and/or discussion of each area. Our experience has been that the all-at-once review is more appropriate for small and midsize clients and that the piece-at-a-time approach works well for larger clients with more sophisticated needs.

Once an agenda is prepared, we recommend sending it to the client a week or two in advance of the meeting so that he or she knows what to expect. This is an opportunity to ask whether there's anything else the client would like to discuss in the meeting or whether any significant changes have taken place since the last meeting.

In one of our client firms, the firm sent the agenda, as described previously. The client responded that her mother was ill and required transfer to a long-term care facility. As a result, the advisor was able to review the client's planning situation with this in mind. He had his staff pull information on the average cost of care facilities so that he could run a view of the plan showing the client how the cost of her mother's care might affect her near-term cash flow and long-term financial plan. He could do this because he knew the client well: The client explained that she and her mother enjoyed a wonderful relationship, that her mother made many sacrifices to ensure meeting her daughter's needs, and that the mother had no financial resources. He also had the staff research facilities in the area and put together a summary of facilities, ratings, proximity from the client's home, and average costs. In total, this work took less than two hours, but imagine the result! When the client came in for her review meeting, not only did they discuss this major life change, but the firm had also prepared information that would help the client make better choices based on what had happened.

Another advisor we know learned that a client couple had just returned from Paris and loved the city, particularly its food. So the advisor had the staff pick up a French cookbook at the local bookstore and gave it to them as a gift during their meeting. These are just a few examples of how systematizing the process allows advisors to personalize the experience.

Postmeeting Follow-Up

It's a good idea to provide clients with a summary of the meeting discussions, the action items that resulted, and who will do what by when. Some firms do this in a written letter, others in an e-mail. The form is less important than the function. Send a summary within three business days of the meeting—anything longer seems as if you're dragging your feet. A well-defined process provides you the time to draft the summary, and you schedule the delivery date at the time you schedule the meeting. We also like to have a staff member call the client after the summary is delivered to make sure he or she felt good about the meeting, to confirm that the client received the summary—and particularly to review any action items the client needs to complete. All of the action items from the meeting should have a due date, even if it's arbitrary (because you can't schedule an action without a date), and should be calendared in the same three-day window, for the firm and the clients. If a client is supposed to engage in some action, calendar that action on the date due, so that the firm can check in, answer questions, and offer help, if need be.

Between Meetings

Best-practice firms communicate with their clients between meetings. Automate this process and it won't take much time. We recommend making touch-base calls on a set schedule between review meetings, depending on the size of the client. These calls are simply to reach out and see how the client is doing. This is particularly important because the number one complaint clients make about their advisors is that they don't call. You don't score any points if the client has to call you to ask about the follow-up from last week's meeting. Yet you do get credit when you call a month later and say, "I know it's only been a month or so since we met, and our next review meeting is not for another few months, but I just wanted to check in and see how things are going, if you have any questions following our meeting, or if there's anything you'd like to talk about."

A reasonable person will not complain about such a call from an advisor, and will most likely be very appreciative. These calls usually take only five minutes, and most of the time they go to voicemail, which is perfectly acceptable, because the client will call you back only if there's something to discuss. Yet you will still get credit for reaching out.

In one client firm, we devised what we call BWC (because we care) calls. The staff calls top clients every other month and smaller clients every six months, just to ask how things are going, whether they have any questions, or if there is anything they would like to discuss with the advisor. If the client says yes, the staff schedules a 30-minute call between the client and the advisor and enters notes about the upcoming call in the CRM. The staff schedules the call during the appropriate calendar time block. Thus, the advisor enters the call focused and prepared to discuss the client's issues. Such processes save the advisor an incredible amount of time and keep him abreast of any changes in his client's life.

Making It Your Own

These are the client systems that are most crucial to the overall client experience, but, as we've noted, there are many others. For example, we've developed processes for clients that cover every step imaginable, including, but by no means limited to:

- How to fill out new account forms.
- How to set up the conference room for a client meeting.
- How to manage a client event.
- What to do when a client has a baby or a grandbaby.
- What to do when a client has a child graduate from college.
- What to do when a client gets divorced.

- What to do when a client is about to retire.
- What to do when a client has moved.
- How (exactly) to schedule the owner's travel arrangements.
- How to schedule a meeting in the advisor's calendar.
- How to take and schedule return phone calls.

The point is that you can (and probably should) build a process for any activity or event that is recurring—even if it's not frequent—to ensure that the work is conducted the same way each time.

The main challenge is that while processes themselves don't take that much time, defining the details of who does what, when and how, and drafting the support materials does take time.

Yet the investment of time up front will pay off a hundredfold later. It could take 40 hours to draft a process that saves the firm many hours with each new client and, more important, crafts a superb prospect experience. That's a dividend that continues to pay well into the future.

CHAPTER 29

The Client Model

The longer an advisor is in business, the more clients they acquire and, as a result, the more staff, overhead, and time they require to appropriately service your customers. As the business becomes more complex, advisors think they can grow their way out of the problem, only to find that the problems grow, too. The more successful advisors become, the more demands they have to meet, and the more they have to drive revenue to keep it all going. Somewhere along the way, the pressure and frustration hits a boiling point, and advisors and their teams can end up feeling as if they're working harder just to keep pace.

We call this the "client complex" because the more clients a firm adds, the more complex the business becomes, and the more difficult it becomes to run the business, grow the business, and feel good about the business.

At some point in almost every practice's evolution, what is required to keep it all going becomes as large as, or larger than, the revenue that drives the business. As a result, firms struggle to grow, or to grow efficiently and profitably.

When the balance is out of alignment, the business continues but with less and less efficiency and effectiveness. This can result in symptoms such as increasing staff and overhead costs, struggles to serve consistently at the level desired, strained capacity, and diminishing profits. This lack of balance doesn't always prevent advisors from building a successful practice, though it regularly results in friction that slows a firm's development, impeding revenue and profitability growth.

Through an exercise we call the client model, it is possible for advisors to restore a healthy balance among their client relationships, the level and quality of services, and their profitability. The client model is a business system designed to help advisors evaluate the profitability of each client segment, evaluate service capacity, establish service standards, and ensure that fees and account minimums result in revenue and profitability in line with firm goals. A client model is composed of two key components:

1. *Client-base analysis.* This assesses a firm's clients, services, fees, capacity, and profitability. Firms define distinct client segments and identify the services appropriate to those segments.
2. *Service model.* This defines and formalizes what services a firm will deliver to each segment of its client base, the frequency of those services, who will deliver said services, and how they will do so.

Client-Base Analysis

Together, the client-base analysis and the service model make up a fully developed client model that provides advisory firms with key insights and information. The model can help the firm objectively determine how best to add value to clients while also adding value, in the form of profitability, to the firm.

The key factors involved are clients, revenue, time requirements, cost, and profits. The outcome provides firms with a sense of how they can effect changes to their client base and resulting business performance. It also tells them how they can better prepare for and manage growth, and provides a view into whether and when they need to add new staff and/or advisors.

In the majority of firms with which we've consulted on client model design, the initial analysis often reveals the following:

- Lack of profitability, driven by unprofitable client segments.
- High variability in the profitability of client segments.
- High percentage of small and/or unprofitable clients.
- Too much or too little capacity for advisors and staff.

The first step to developing a client model is to conduct a client-base analysis, defining distinct client segments. For example, a firm can define an "A" client as someone who generates $10,000 in revenue and receives two meetings per year, two phone calls, and an invitation to the annual client event. Yet this doesn't tell the firm (1) whether it can provide this service profitably; (2) the relationship of clients in this service tier to others (e.g., whether one group is more profitable than another); (3) what capacity the team has to provide these services now and as the firm grows; and (4) what will happen to revenue, costs, and profits as the client base grows.

Firms that seek to develop their own client model should consider the following steps:

1. *Segment the client base into revenue-based segments.* Create distinct client segments, such as A, B, and C, and establish revenue ranges for each tier.

    We typically recommend the following tier system to ensure that the revenue ranges within segments are not too broad given that all clients in that segment receive the same level of service. For example, $0–$5,000 might seem practical, but the reality is a client with $500 in ongoing revenue is unlikely to need or warrant the same level of service as a client with $1,500 or $4,500. As part of our Best Practices Study Series, and accounting for the fact that most firms have a wide range of clients, we have defined segmentation tiers as follows:

Tier 1: $20,000+
Tier 2: $10,000–$19,999
Tier 3: $5,000–$9,999
Tier 4: $2,500–$4,999
Tier 5: $1,000–$2,499
Tier 6: $0–$999

We recognize that the ranges across tiers are not consistent (the ranges are smaller in the lower tiers). Our experience shows that a majority of firms have many clients under $5,000 in revenue, with many of those under $2,500 and even $1,000. By creating smaller break points, the service model works within the revenue parameters provided by each tier. Additionally, we find the service needs of clients in the three segments under $5,000 (tiers 4, 5, and 6) tend to have greater disparity in the service needs than clients in tiers 1, 2, and 3.

2. *Calculate the average revenue per client for each segment.* Calculate by adding the total revenue for each segment, then dividing by the total number of clients within that segment. For example, if a firm has 50 clients in tier 3 and total revenue of $335,000 generated by the clients in this segment, the average revenue per client for tier 3 would be $6,700.

3. *Define the services that are or will be delivered to each segment.* For example, "A" clients receive two in-person meetings per year; "B" clients receive one. We discuss this in detail later in the chapter.

4. *Define who delivers the services and estimate the time required to perform each activity.* Be careful to account for all activities performed by both advisors and support staff. This should include preparing for client meetings, the meetings themselves, any follow-up work resulting from the meetings, as well as a host of other work we commonly find firms perform but fail to include in their estimates.

5. *Determine the average expense per client for each segment.* The simplest way to calculate this is to divide total overhead by total number of clients. For example, if a firm has 123 clients and total overhead expenses of $487,000, the average expense per client (for all segments) is $3,959.

Firms that want a more refined view of the cost structure than the averaging method above can use a fixed-cost plus variable-cost structure to account for the fact that advisor and staff time does not have the same cost and that some client segments require more time than others. Fixed costs are costs that do not change with the addition of clients (e.g., office space). Variable costs do change with the addition of clients (e.g., advisor and staff time). In this case, you would calculate the average costs (fixed + variable) for each segment separately.

Using the preceding tier 3 example, let's assume the advisor's total cost of compensation (including salary, incentives, bonuses, and benefits, but *not* including profit distributions as an owner) is $300,000 per year. His effective hourly rate is $144. If his two support staff earned a combined total compensation of $93,000, then the effective hourly rate for staff time would be $22.35 per hour (the combined salaries of $93,000 divided by 4,160 work hours, reflecting the total annual work hours of both staff). The service model in this example sets out that "A" clients require 8 hours of advisor time and 20 hours of staff time, and the fixed overhead cost per client (all overhead, excluding all compensation costs, divided by total number of clients) is $3,500. The formula for determining profitability for the tier 3 client segment using the fixed + variable method would be:

Average variable costs (advisor): $1,152 ($144 × 8 hours)
+ Average variable costs (staff): $447 ($22 × 20 hours)
+ Average fixed costs (overhead): 3,500
= Average expense per tier 3 client: $5,099

Run a profitability analysis on each client segment. Simply subtract the average expense per client from the average revenue per client.
Continuing the use of our tier 3 example:

Average revenue per client: $6,700
Average variable costs (advisor): $1,152 ($144 × 8 hours)
Average variable costs (staff): $447 ($22 × 20 hours)
Average fixed costs (overhead): $3,500
= Average tier 3 profit per client: $1,601

- Compare client segment performance and assess profitability across segments. Some clients, typically but not always smaller ones, will be less profitable than others. At this stage, the analysis will identify client segments that have lower profit per client than the other segments, no profit per client, or negative profit (or loss) per client. All three scenarios require attention in the steps that follow.
  - Set a profit-per-client goal for each segment. Firms can choose to set the profit per client the same across all client segments or to establish a different profit-per-client goal for each client segment. For example, if tier 1 clients generate $5,100 in profitability, tier 2 clients $2,890, tier 3 clients $1,601,

and tier 4 clients $287, a firm may decide to set a profit-per-client goal of $3,500 or better for all client segments. Or the firm may decide to reset the profit-per-client goal for each individual level, such as tier 1 $5,000, tier 2 $3,500, tier 3 $2,000, and tier 4 $1,000. In the latter scenario, working with tier 3 and tier 4 clients significantly dilutes profitability and warrants a consideration of how to address these clients.

- Identify potential changes that will drive improvement in the profit per client in order to achieve the goals over a set time period. Common changes made following this analysis include reducing and/or adjusting services for each segment, increasing average revenue—by increasing fees, increasing account minimums, or both—changing who delivers the service (from advisor to staff), and/or transitioning clients to a more junior or outside advisor.

The ultimate goal of the client-base analysis is to identify the profitability of each client segment, assess changes that can improve profitability to meet goals, and provide a lens through which advisory firms can assess whether the service model adds value to the clients and to the firm.

Done right, a client model will not only capture a firm's decisions but will also clearly show the impact of those decisions (on revenue, capacity, and profitability) in advance.

Building a Service Model

As noted at the beginning of this chapter, a service model defines, documents, and formalizes what services a firm will deliver to each segment of its client base, the frequency of those services, who will delivered the services, and how they will do so.

The client-base analysis is imperative. Without it, there is no way for a firm to determine the profitable delivery of the service model. These firms actually may be sacrificing profitability because they are not aware of the business and financial impact brought about through improper decision making. These effects can easily run into six figures annually. Given the ongoing nature of recurring revenue, the lifetime cost of such compromises can be high indeed.

With the information from the client-base analysis in hand, firms should next set out to formalize their service model. A formalized service model:

- Defines delivery of services to each segment of its client base.
- Defines service delivery frequency.
- Defines who will deliver each service.

A formalized service model will create a suite of services that serves each client segment *fairly* but not *equally*. Far too many firms provide the same service to all clients, which tends to be either whatever the clients ask for when they call or come in, or a level of service that is not appropriate to all clients.

Once done, the service model can be documented and formally distributed to the team or, preferably, integrated into a CRM system. The staff's job with the CRM is to run the process so that the advisors (the revenue generators) simply show up, do their work, and move on. We find it's a win-win-win: advisors get more time, the staff gets more consistency and control, and the clients get better and more proactive and predictable service.

To develop a formal service model, firms should list each client segment and itemize the services they plan to provide to each. The next step is to define the frequency of the service. Advisors should pay particular attention to identifying all of the services provided. One of the most effective ways we have found to ensure that all service activities are included is to break down the list by category. Following is a brief example of what a firm may decide, though it does not represent the format we would propose.

Review Meetings and Calls

- Client review meeting
  - "A" clients, two times per year (senior advisor): Every other quarter.
  - "B" clients, two times per year (service advisor): Every six months.
  - "C" clients, one time per year (service advisor): Annually, on anniversary date.
- Client review calls
  - "A" clients, two times per year (senior advisor): Every other quarter, alternating with client review meetings.
  - "B" clients, two times per year (service advisor): Every other quarter, alternating with client review meetings.
  - "C" clients, one time per year (service advisor): N/A.

Once the service model is developed, the first step is to determine the steps required to deliver the services. For example, a client review meeting requires scheduling a meeting with the client (staff), preparation for the meeting (staff), review of meeting preparation (advisor), the review meeting (advisor or advisor and staff depending on firm), follow-up actions/work (staff), review of follow-up actions/work (advisor).

The second step is to systematize the service model with the development of a client process. As discussed in Chapter 28, "Client-Facing Processes," we have our advisory firm clients map out each step of the process and define who does what, when they do it, how they do it, and what tools (CRM, financial planning software, etc.) and materials (checklists, dialogue scripts, form letters, agendas, etc.) they will need to do so.

Challenges with the Client Model

In our work helping firms develop client models, we have found that putting the information on a piece of paper is one thing and putting the idea into practice is yet another. So, here we share some of the implementation issues our clients have faced and how we have addressed them:

* *Exceptions to client segments.* There may be legitimate exceptions to segments based purely on revenue per client. A tier 2 client with $10,000 in revenue who is taking distributions and whose account is never going to grow may not need the same level of support as a tier 2 client with $10,000 in revenue and who will be adding $250,000 over the next three years. Often, top clients are very successful, and thus very busy, and prefer not to meet as per the frequency dictated by their firm's service model or may prefer to have most of their reviews by phone. If you have a "C" client who will roll over $1.5 million from his company retirement plan in three years, you might want to meet with him more frequently over the coming years, given that it will help to ensure that he becomes an "A" client.

   The best solution we have found to this issue is to create separate revenue segments and service tiers. *Revenue segments* categorize clients based on the revenue they generate. The services provided to this segment are the *service tier*.

   By design, an "A" client revenue segment is automatically assigned to the "A" client service tier. But that does not always have to be the case. We frequently create two categories in an advisory firm's CRM system: revenue segment and service tier. In the case of the "A" client with a potential $1.5 million rollover, the client would be assigned to the "C" client revenue segment but to the "A" client service tier. Instead, what most firms do is put the "C" client in the "A" segment, which also works but also erases the firm's ability to distinguish between revenue and services. The solution of creating two categories allows the firm to quickly identify the revenue segment while still providing the higher level of service that comes with the higher service tier.

   There are other examples of exceptions to client segments. For example, firms often put their best client referral sources in a higher client segment because they want to meet with them more frequently.

   In few cases have we found that more meetings result in more referrals, but we have found that more personal interaction does (quality over quantity, it seems). So, instead of conducting more (costly) meetings than the client really needs, we create a "referral source" service tier that spells out that clients in this category get access to other relationship-building activities, such as special events (to which they can bring potential future friends of the firm), personal phone calls, lunch with the advisor on the client's birthday, and so on.

Meeting with all clients on the same frequency schedule. Smaller clients don't need or want to pay for the same level of service and advice as larger clients. The general thinking among advisors seems to be that if one meeting is good, more is better. When considering the volume of work required for advisors to schedule, prepare for, conduct, and follow up on client meetings, this seems a high bar to set.

- *Lack of regular meeting schedules.* Many advisors simply schedule meetings as clients request them, or when they realize it's been a little too long since the last meeting. That's not proactive service in the spirit of the planning process. It seems that some advisors service their clients really well early on, but eventually leave it up to the clients to ask for a meeting. Often, it's because the firm is busy trying to find new clients and has no organized way to allot their time to existing clients. A service model solves this and does so in a way that is appropriate for each client segment.

- *Meeting with clients quarterly.* The genesis of quarterly meeting, whether advisors remember or recognize it, is the quarterly performance report. Except perhaps for the largest and most sophisticated clients, not many changes take place during the three months between quarterly meetings and, as a result, investment performance tends to be the focal point of the conversation. Performance reports are important, but ongoing quarterly reviews train clients to use investment performance as the measure of the relationship rather than their ability to achieve their long-term goals and objectives. Many advisors are inadvertently training their clients to do the very thing they don't want them to do.

  Moreover, quarterly meetings consume a lot of time and, at a certain point, advisors simply run out of it. One advisor with whom we worked met with all of his clients quarterly. Meetings—including preparation for and travel to the appointments—consumed much of his time, and he ended up doing the bulk of his work on evenings and weekends. We ultimately reduced his meeting schedule for all clients, even the largest ones. We also replaced a good number of in-person reviews with phone reviews, which tend to take less time. The advisor was concerned that clients would be offended and leave, but the majority of his clients were pleased (or at least not adversely affected) with this new arrangement, because it meant they didn't need to take time off work, arrange their schedules, and so on, to get to quarterly meetings. After two quarters, the advisor called to tell us he wondered why he had so much time on his hands these days and then realized it was because of the new service model. Now that he wasn't so overwhelmed with client meetings, we turned our attention to helping him develop a marketing plan. No doubt some advisors will shudder at the thought of a phone review, but some of the country's top firms engage in client review by phone quite successfully.

- *Dealing with unprofitable clients.* The vast majority of firms with whom we have completed a client model analysis during the past 16 years discover that a significant portion of their client base has little or negative profitability. These firms are subsidizing these relationships via reduced profitability, and the firm's larger, more profitable client relationships are footing the bill.

Advisors often get stuck on the fact that all clients generate revenue. We realize this cash flow helps keep the doors open and contributes to profits. Yet growth contributes to increased overhead, and if that growth isn't carefully managed, firms become unwieldy. Then advisors have no time to spare, staff is overwhelmed, and profit margins erode.

A better solution is to find ways to enhance the profitability of the underperforming clients and then seek out new, more attractive clients. Advisors either increase share of wallet, decrease services, or increase fees to accomplish this. Because most advisors are reluctant to pull any of these levers, firms often try to "grow" their way into a solution by taking on more clients. Then they wonder why the condition worsens. In reality, however, advisors are more likely to grow the middle and the bottom of the client base because these are the easiest clients to get. Yet these are the very clients who are causing the firm's performance drain. Firms do this, we believe, because they don't realize the opportunity cost of taking on and maintaining unprofitable or less profitable clients.

- *Having too many small clients.* Having a lot of small clients is the perfect reason to do a client model. It gives firms a mechanism to determine whether smaller clients are unprofitable and what impact that has on the business. Firms don't need to send their smaller clients packing; these clients can be as profitable as other client segments. The solution is the service model, allowing the smaller clients to fall into the client segment that is right for them, and that generates a level of profitability that meets the firm's goals. This isn't typically an issue, given that small clients generally have simple needs and often don't need the same level of support as clients with higher net worth and larger account sizes.

Sometimes profitability goals cannot be met, or the firm has made a decision to focus on a target client profile and adhere to higher minimums. In these cases, we would suggest (1) placing clients with smaller accounts in a lower service model that meets firm profit per client goals, (2) bringing in a new advisor to serve them, or (3) bundling the clients up and selling or revenue-sharing them with another advisor in the area who is beginning his or her career and eager for new clients.

Transitioning Clients

Given that client model conversations inevitably lead to discussions of client transitions, whether inside or outside the firm, we will address some of the common issues and concerns we have faced over the years.

We do not recommend that advisors draw a line in their client base and immediately terminate all client relationship below that line. Carefully weigh the situation and options against fairness to the client and the firm before making decisions. Additionally, no matter how profitable, jettisoning even 15 percent of firm revenue in a single swipe does not generally play out well. We prefer to plan, prepare for, and phase in these transitions over time.

We often hear from advisors that they simply cannot transition their clients to another advisor. After all, these are *relationships*, and they cannot bring themselves to let them go. Our first question is always to inquire as to when the firm last met with or spoke with the list of smaller clients identified for transition.

In all but a few instances, it has been an extended period of time since any quality engagement took place. It would seem that in some advisors' minds, when it comes to smaller clients, the relationships don't actually require meaningful interaction.

The reality is that advisors may well be doing their small clients a favor by transitioning them to an advisor who will actually pay them the attention they are due. Whether transitioning to an external advisor or an internal one, when advisors stop looking at the situation from their own perspective (often based more on fear than fact) and start looking at it from the clients' perspective (serving clients' needs first is one of the key tenets of quality advisors), they often come to realize that some of their clients can be better served by working with someone else. Following are some options to consider:

• *Bring in a new advisor to service the firm's smaller clients.* This can also serve to meet other firm needs and provide a potential succession plan. The first step is for advisors to determine the experience level they require. An advisor with limited experience tends to be more affordable, and you can better train them to your firm's processes than a more seasoned advisor. Keep in mind the severity of the learning curve when taking that avenue. An advisor with midlevel experience, say four to eight years, is seasoned enough to know the drill but not necessarily ready to fly on his or her own and may still be flexible enough to adapt to the firm's needs. The cost obviously would be higher. More experienced advisors who can step in and readily take over a client base are highly desirable, but firms will pay more and may have to work harder to integrate them successfully into the firm. At the high end of the market, veterans with years of experience may be better sale or merger candidates than service advisors. In some cases, however, an advisor in his or her 50s decides to be free of the responsibility of running a practice, and seeks to find a position that can draw on his or her expertise, pay at a desired level, and provide the freedom he or she seeks.

  The firm will benefit from being clear on what type and level of advisor will best suit their client and firm needs. As noted in the chapters on human capital, this process should begin with the design of a job description, career ladder, and compensation plan.

- *Bundle the transitioning clients and either sell them to another advisor or engage in a revenue-sharing arrangement in exchange for the client transitions.* This option is more than just hiring an advisor or simply granting the clients to an outside advisor. Locate a suitable candidate and then define, document, and manage the details carefully.

- *Refer clients to an outside advisor in whom you have confidence.* Advisors mention that no such relationship exists within their area. When we press on the issue and suggest that outside advisors don't need to be identical in their approach, but rather experienced, ethical, and oriented to the same type and quality of services, the pool tends to broaden. In one recent client meeting, it was determined that the firm needed to increase its minimums to reflect its target client profile. This required transitioning smaller clients to an outside advisor. We suggested bundling these clients and selling them, but our client didn't feel right about receiving any value for the relationships. Understanding his perspective, we pushed back on whether there was really no one in his area who was suitable, or, given the clients we were discussing (quite small), whether he was raising the bar too high. A few days later he called to tell us he had thought of a younger advisor whose experience he felt would be well suited to the clients in question.

- *Give clients the choice to engage with the firm under the new service model or to go elsewhere.* We never suggest that any advisor "fire" a client. In instances where this option is undeniably the right one for both the client and the firm, we prefer to apply an "options-based transitions" strategy. In this strategy, the advisor explains to clients that times have changed, the cost of doing business is more expensive, there's a lot more regulation, and so on. If necessary, the advisor can also note that he or she has been undercharging for services compared to industry standards for some time now and has been reluctant to increase fees given the advisor's high regard for the client relationship. At this point, the advisor presents the clients with clear options from which to choose:

  "We have made the decision to make adjustments to how we charge for our services to ensure that we can continue to provide a high level of service while maintaining a healthy business. We want to present you with options for how we can best serve you in the future. (1) We can increase your fees to our new fee schedule, (2) you can increase the assets in your accounts, (3) we can recommend another advisor in whom we have confidence who caters to clients in your situation, or (4) you can find another advisor on your own and we will do all we can to facilitate a smooth transition. Should you choose not to stay, I want you to know that I understand, and I won't take it personally, and I hope we can part as friends."

  When we suggest this approach to advisors for the first time, they often comment that they find it to be remarkably simple and surprisingly fair. It's important to be confident when having this talk. Advisors simply need to remember the courage they demonstrate when advising their clients to keep their money in the market when it is plummeting. We recognize that this is a difficult situation, but the first discussion is the hardest. It gets measurably easier after that, and, in the end, advisors report feeling very positive about the decisions and the results that follow.

We've talked with clients of ours who have had this conversation. On average, each client has perhaps one client who doesn't pick an option. In one case where an advisor sold a client an insurance policy some 17 years back, the client said to him, "You mean you're going to start charging me for advice after I bought that insurance policy from you?" The client was upset at having to pay for advice long provided for free. The advisor said, "Yes, that seems to be the case, and now we have a difference of opinion." The meeting soon ended after that exchange. The advisor shared with us that that was the depth of the interaction, and once it was over, he knew it was for the best.

The Opportunity Cost of Your Client Base

The opportunity cost is the revenue advisors give up by not sticking to their target client profile, account minimums, or fees. Here's how advisors can quickly calculate the opportunity cost of their decision to make exceptions:

- Identify the average revenue per client for your target client (the clients you would like to have). For example, $5,000 in revenue per client.
- Multiply the average revenue per target client, above, by the total number of all clients currently served by the firm. For example, if the firm has 150 clients, multiply 150 by $5,000 to reach $750,000, which is the firm's opportunity revenue, or the revenue the firm would generate if all of its clients were target clients (or paid the published fees, etc.)
- Subtract the current firm revenue from the opportunity revenue. For example, firm revenue is $550,000, subtracted from $750,000, which is $200,000.

    In this case, the opportunity cost is the $200,000 difference between actual firm revenue and total opportunity revenue.

In short, the opportunity cost is the amount of revenue a firm sacrifices by making exceptions. In the preceding example, the opportunity cost is $200,000. We also recommend that advisors run an analysis on the opportunity cost of reducing fees, calculated by determining what clients pay based on their agreed-upon fee schedule and comparing that to the revenue the firm would receive if all clients paid at the published fee schedule.

Knowing the opportunity cost accomplishes two important goals. First, it helps advisors understand the cost of their past client-base decisions, empowering them to improve client-base performance over time. Second, knowing the true cost of the alternative tends to increase advisor commitment to focusing growth on target clients.

A Catalyst for Change

A client model, including both the client-base analysis, the systematized service model that results, and the decisions and actions that follow, is a catalyst for dramatic change.

We believe that great client relationships should be reciprocal—that what is good for the client is good for the firm. We find that implementing the best practice strategies discussed in this chapter are first-rate game changers for our advisory firm clients. That said, transformation isn't easy and doesn't take place overnight. Such change takes thoughtful planning, a diligent approach, and a disciplined execution. However, the time and effort can yield results that fundamentally change the path and future of a firm for the better.

PART V

Building and Realizing Value

CHAPTER 30

Preparing for the Future

Advisors typically do not view succession planning and mergers and acquisitions as practice management services. Yet, over the years, we have helped many advisors to position themselves to maximize and monetize the value in their business when the time is right. To that end, we provide an overview of the strategies for valuing practices and transition options for advisors who are ready to move beyond building value to realizing it. Once an advisor determines he or she is ready to transition, the advisor must evaluate all options and decide which strategy is best suited to his or her needs and goals, including the search and selection process. Advisors must carefully design the rules of engagement and develop a plan to ensure successful integration post-transition.

While the technical components of a deal, such as valuation, are crucial, we encourage advisors not to overlook the full spectrum of issues to be faced when planning for a sale, merger, or acquisition. Fortunately, in recent years, we have seen a shift toward building value to prepare for such events, and more advisors are recognizing the value of proactively preparing for their transition.

Realizing value is an act all advisors will undergo at some point, whether by design or default, but understanding how to build value is just as important as the strategies for realizing it. The best practices contained in the previous sections do just that. They provide advisors who want to improve their business and in turn build business value with proven strategies they can apply to review, refine, and reengineer their firms. They can then monetize the business and realize value that rewards them for their efforts. We have seen firsthand how hard advisors work to help their clients realize their financial goals and dreams, and so we feel strongly that advisors should, through their work, have the opportunity to do the same.

Given the focus of the book, and the limitations of size and space, we do not explore and discuss the many qualitative issues that surround the building of value in preparation for sale, merger, or acquisition. These issues include, among many others, the emotional and financial readiness of the owner(s); the ability of owner(s) to share, transition, or cede control; and the role owner(s) want to play following the transaction. In the case of mergers, all of these issues and more apply, as well as integration issues and internal issues, such as how firms search for, select, hire, retain, and prepare the successor to take over while at the same time preparing the owner(s) to let go.

Key areas impacted by the transition transaction include financials, management, clients, operations, business development, and human capital. Any transaction type is about far more than the terms of the deal, and the effects ripple across every aspect of a firm. When firms recognize the effects and implications of transactions, both in the present and the future, the odds of success—and genuine satisfaction—are far higher.

Whether you are in the stage of building value for a transition that will not occur for many years, will occur in the next few years, or is happening now, the topics in the following chapters outline the fundamentals of valuations and transition options.

CHAPTER 31

The State of the Industry

To a large extent, the independent advisor industry started about 40 years ago, as the first entrepreneurial pioneers began setting up their own businesses to deliver financial advice without corporate ties or conflict. Although going independent had its advantages, advisors were largely on their own when it came to building effective businesses that had transferrable value. These early pioneers attempted to extract equity from their business and experienced declining assets. Their only succession option was phasing out.

Today, independent advisors have many more options for selling their businesses. They can sell internally by transferring the business to a junior advisor or a partner. This requires succession planning at least five years in advance; however, only 20 percent of advisors have a well-defined succession plan that is ready to implement. Advisors can also sell externally to another firm. We will explore both paths later in this section.

Other outlets have cropped up in the past 5 to 10 years, including strategically aligned broker-dealers and custodians. Often, broker-dealers will arrange a merger or a sale among advisors, rather than lose the assets of the selling firm as advisors start to retire. For example, some broker-dealers realized they had a potential declining asset in their advisor base and have started to help advisors establish succession and continuity agreements with the broker-dealer. Similarly, custodians have also built out internal capabilities to capitalize on this trend.

Roll-up firms or consolidators, such as National Financial Partners, Wealth Trust, United Capital, and Focus Financial, are also potential buyers. These companies buy up a bunch of smaller firms and "roll them up" into one large business to monetize the combined entity. This way, consolidators can achieve economies of scale, lower risk by disbursing it across the group, and expand the multiple for the aggregated firm. For the seller, this is a way to diversify its asset while continuing to operate the firm with a high level of independence.

Certified public accounting (CPA) firms or banks may consider purchasing an advisory practice, looking to expand their service offerings and capitalize on greater diversification of revenue, deeper client engagement, and the ability to cross-sell products. However, regulatory restrictions may require partners of the CPA firm to register before receiving compensation generated by the wealth management side of the business. This hurdle is often enough to keep each entity working autonomously, with the key benefit being reciprocal referrals between them. Those who do integrate often find themselves challenged by different cultures and compensation structures, as well as by the difficulty of developing a successful process for managing clients between the firms. At banks, advisors may have to negotiate to stay independent.

Given where the industry was just decades ago, we are on an accelerated path for value realization. This raises the important questions:

- How do advisors build value?
- How do they define the value of their firms?
- What is their exit strategy?

The final chapters explore some of the options for leaving the business and how to determine maximum value for both buyers and sellers.

CHAPTER 32

External Sales

Advisors who have not planned ahead have limited options for extracting value from their businesses. Ideally, we recommend three to five years to adequately prepare for sale to an internal buyer. Firms certainly can and have done so in less time, but the shorter the timeline, the greater the need to get it right the first time. For advisors with a time horizon of less than three years, we recommend finding an external buyer. Notably, this is not an easy process.

Whether transitioning to an internal successor or seeking an outside buyer, many advisors have learned the hard way that finding the right buyer at the right time at the right price is no small task. The more time an advisor gives himself or herself, the more options he or she has and the greater probability of reaching a solution that delivers the desired outcome.

The Mergers and Acquisitions Process

Advisors who may consider selling their firms to an outside party should understand the mergers and acquisitions (M&A) process thoroughly to avoid pitfalls and to help ensure they're making the right decision. Generally, the steps are as follows:

1. *Know what you're looking for.* It's extremely important to know exactly what you want in a buyer. Take some time to write down the characteristics and philosophies your firm represents, and work from that profile as you evaluate candidates. Identify things such as investment and planning philosophy, cultural fit, client service model, client profile, and geographic location. You want to be as sure as possible that the buyer will continue to run the firm in a fashion similar to how you have built and run it.
2. *Identify prospective candidates.* As you develop your buyer profile, think about potential candidates in your local area affiliated with your broker-dealer or members of industry organizations. Selling to a buyer affiliated

with your custodian or broker-dealer may simplify the process. Selling to an industry-organization member ensures alignment of your philosophies and, perhaps, cultural compatibility.

3. *Elicit indications of interest.* Be careful to approach potential acquirers selectively so that you don't compromise your position or client base. You might want to consider engaging a third party, such as a sell-side investment banking firm, to elicit indications of interest so you can remain anonymous. That said, if the advisor has a good relationship with a relationship manager at the broker-dealer or the custodian, they could both discuss possible acquirers that would fit the advisor's criteria.

4. *Evaluate compatibility.* Compatibility is one of the keys to a successful transaction. It's important that both firms, including the advisors, have similar outlooks concerning investments, client engagement, target markets, and so on. Without strong compatibility, the combined firm will lack consistency and will risk client attrition.

5. *Prepare a letter of intent (LOI).* The LOI sets forth basic terms of the transaction, the due diligence review, continued employment, restrictive covenants, the transition expectations, and so on. LOIs are helpful to identify deal breakers and avoid the time and expense of drafting definitive agreements if your main terms aren't in sync with the buyer's.

   Typically, parties prefer nonbinding LOIs, except for a few specific provisions. Some binding provisions may include an exclusivity clause prohibiting you from engaging in parallel discussions with third parties. Another provision may concern the allocation of costs and expenses.

6. *Conduct due diligence.* It's important to be prepared for the due diligence process. Buyers will want to evaluate your business prior to purchase. Have three to five years' worth of business income and balance sheet statements, procedure manuals, branding and positioning statements, client segmentation and benchmarking, and so on, available. This conveys that your firm has a high level of sophistication.

   - *Conduct a valuation.* It's imperative that you have an outside party conduct a valuation assessment of your practice prior to entering into final negotiations. A good valuation will give you a reality check and a strong starting point from which to negotiate.
   - *Final negotiations.* As you enter final negotiations, strive to develop an agreement that is mutually beneficial to both parties. You should negotiate all aspects of the deal, including the buyout price, the deal structure, roles and expectations, and how conflicts will be resolved.

Once you have found a buyer, the due diligence and negotiation process generally require about six months to complete.

M&A Agreements

When you enter into a transaction, you should engage a qualified attorney with experience in the securities industry, as well as in mergers and acquisitions, due to the unique nature of the regulatory issues involved. Following are a few of the core agreements you and your attorney should draft when executing a well-structured transaction that will help ensure your protection.

- *Confidentiality agreement.* Prior to exchanging information, execute the confidentiality agreement, which protects each party's proprietary, confidential information. Neither party can use the information against the other party at a later date.
- *Letter of intent.* The LOI sets out the key terms of a transaction agreed on in principle by the parties. It is usually entered into at the beginning of the transition or before the due diligence phase. The LOI sets forth:
  - What is being acquired
  - Purchase price
  - Escrow
  - Timetable

  As we mentioned earlier, it's helpful to identify deal breakers early on to avoid the time and expense of drafting definitive agreements when there's no agreement on major terms. That's why LOIs are typically nonbinding except for a few specific provisions. These provisions may include:
  - Right to conduct due diligence.
  - Confidentiality restrictions regarding the parties' proprietary information.
  - Privacy restrictions.
  - An exclusivity clause that prohibits the potential seller from engaging in parallel discussions with third parties.
  - Allocation of costs and expenses.

  The LOI should explicitly state that these provisions are binding on the parties and also explicitly state that the remainder of the document is nonbinding.
- *Purchase agreement.* The purchase agreement is a comprehensive document executed between the parties that sets forth the terms and conditions of the purchase. A critical element of this agreement establishes provisions for conflict resolution in case the transaction doesn't go as planned. Such issues include material misrepresentations, significant client attrition, or missed payments.

Both parties must engage a professional when structuring a transaction to help avoid postsale legal action. Advisors should strive to create a mutually beneficial transaction that is fair to all involved. Working with an experienced attorney can help navigate the risks associated with such agreements and protect all parties in case of unforeseen circumstances.

Funding the Deal

Generally speaking, there are three methods for financing the sale of an independent advisory business: cash buyout, installment note, and earn-out (or contingency payments).

Cash Buyouts

Although historical client retention rates for acquisitions are strong, at 85 to 90 percent, the buyer does take a significant risk that these relationships will end. A cash buyout offers no recourse if the firm loses a substantial number of clients. To mitigate this risk, sellers should consider assisting with the transition for a period of time, generally six months to a year, to ensure stability in the client base. This will help the transaction achieve its highest potential.

Cash transactions usually involve a down payment of about 25 to 35 percent, depending on the risks involved and the viability of the deal. This down payment is often contingent on the seller's staying engaged throughout the transition. Cash in hand favors the seller.

Installment Sales or Promissory Notes

An installment sale is a promissory note that requires the buyer to make fixed payments of both principal and interest over time. In an effort to strike a balance between the purchase price and an assurance of payments, sellers may consider discounting the value of the business in exchange for guaranteed payments over time—less risky for the buyer than an all-cash transaction. And "look-back" provisions can adjust the payment stream if there is significant client attrition.

A structured installment transaction allows the buyer to spread out payments over a period of time, thereby creating a better cash flow stream for the business. It also enables the seller to spread out the tax consequences of the payments. Fixed payments work well for both the buyer and the seller, allowing the buyer to stretch payments over longer periods of time (typically five to seven years). The seller enjoys an assured income stream, generally guaranteed absent any provisions for loss of clients or assets. Also, sellers can charge interest on the note. The challenge for the seller is that he or she has to wait for payments for up to seven years.

Earn-Outs

The most common form of financing for a financial advisory practice is an earn-out arrangement, a contingency payment to the seller based on the revenue, profits, or assets under management retained during the length of the deal. Under the earn-out structure, the seller self-finances the deal by holding a note for the balance of the purchase price. The earn-out is most frequently used when the buyer does not agree to fixed installment or promissory note payments, when disagreements make the value of the business difficult to determine, or when sellers believe that the business will have greater value in the near future than at present.

The problem with an earn-out is that the seller assumes a substantial amount of performance risk that the buyer will be able to retain the client relationships over the life of the deal. As a result, sellers usually require a purchase premium as compensation. At the end of the day, the earn-out structure favors the buyer.

Making the Deal Happen

Many transactions are roughly one-third down, one-third promissory note, and one-third earn-out payments. The combination guarantees two-thirds of the transaction and provides a high level of certainty to the seller that there will be appropriate compensation for the business. It also offers the seller upside potential if the buyer is able to increase revenues in the acquired business through the earn-out.

Given the lack of capital available in the marketplace, sellers sometimes have a hard time finding a buyer who has cash in hand to fund the down payment. If you believe that this is the right person to take over your business, you may need to be flexible on the deal terms and structure the transaction in a way that compensates you appropriately but enables the buyer to be cash-flow solvent during the terms of the transaction. Let's look at a couple of examples:

1. Let's say your business is generating $500,000 in revenue and is valued at $1 million. You have found a buyer who is willing to acquire your firm for the one-third down, one-third promissory note, and one-third earn-out. You agree to these terms. The buyer pays you the $333,333 down payment, with the balance spread over the next five years. The seller is required to pay you monthly payments of principal and interest equaling approximately $6,416 on the promissory note you hold for $333,333. In addition, the buyer will pay you quarterly payments of approximately 13 percent of the revenues generated on the business over five years. At the end of five years, all things being equal, you will have received approximately $1,044,000 for your business.

2. What if you find a desirable buyer who doesn't have the cash available for the purchase or feels there is too much risk involved in committing to this size of capital investment? She says she is willing to pay your asking price of $1 million but wants to structure the deal as 50 percent promissory note

and 50 percent earn-out. There is obviously much more risk shifted back to you as the seller. A suitable counteroffer may be to accept the deal structure but increase your purchase price to $1.3 million over four years. The upside for you is a reduced time period and appropriate compensation for the risk you incur in a deal more heavily weighted to earn-out.

As you can see, these two simplistic examples highlight the wide spectrum of variations that can occur in structuring a sale. That's why it's beneficial to have a team of experts—such as investment bankers, attorneys, and certified public accountants—supporting you through a transaction that protects your interests, maximizes your equity, accounts for the impact on others, and helps you realize your goals for transitioning your business.

CHAPTER 33

Internal Succession

In general, advisors can expect to receive more value for their firms if they sell externally than if they transition the business internally. Yet there are qualitative benefits to an internal deal, primarily that advisors can perpetuate the business legacy they have spent their entire career creating—and, to a degree, can stay involved.

Nearly 40 percent of advisors plan to exit the business via formal internal succession, selling shares of ownership to junior advisors and employees over time. This maximizes the equity in the business. The problem is that most advisors don't adequately plan for an internal transition by grooming existing talent to take over the firm. As a rule of thumb, advisors should start planning their transition at least five years before implementing it. This gives the owner enough time to evaluate the employee's ability to manage the business over the long term, integrate the future partner with the existing client base, and mentor the employee to perpetuate the firm's legacy. If the intended successor does not work out, then the advisor has some latitude in locating a new successor so long as the discovery does not happen too late in the succession process, negatively impacting the succession.

Many advisors neglect succession planning because they claimed they want to "die with their boots on." Yet the unfortunate reality is that all advisors will inevitably have to stop practicing at some point, most likely before they pass away. By developing a plan in advance, advisors can retire on their own terms, rather than having it forced on them. They can decide whether they're ready to sell and retire immediately or transition the business gradually, while maintaining a long-term role in the firm. Either way, advisors need an internal succession plan to realize the value they have built in their firms. Failure to create and execute this plan can result in significant unintended consequences:

- Disruption to your client base.
- Dilution of your legacy.

- Vulnerability of your spouse, children, and dependents.
- A compromising of your employees with uncertainty.
- Limited options upon your exit.
- Devaluation of your firm.

The benefit of an internal succession plan is that it allows the advisor to transition the business over time and have a longer runway up to retirement. He can transition the most stressful responsibilities to a junior partner and focus only on the areas of the business that he finds most interesting and enjoyable.

Other advantages of an internal succession plan include:

- Owners can retire on their own terms and in their chosen time period.
- Owners can create high morale among employees.
- Owners can create career paths for key contributors.
- Employee retention and loyalty are higher.
- It's an opportunity to attract new talent.
- Owners can maintain control of the company, while realizing business value over time.

Typical internal succession plans transition ownership over 5 to 10 years. During this time, owners enjoy benefits such as a longer payment stream, capital appreciation of the firm's equity, and potential interest on the note. Moreover, an internal transition may allow the owner to maintain a minority interest in the company for an extended period of time. The ability to stay involved often helps reduce the anxiety many owners face when planning their transitions. It's not an abrupt end. Often, key employees expect to receive a discount on the purchase price of about 10 to 30 percent, due to the sweat equity they have already put into the practice.

Sam was an advisor we worked with who developed a sound transition plan. He had built a thriving business with more than $1 million in annual revenues and a strong growth trajectory that resulted from a strategic alliance with a midsize certified public accounting (CPA) firm. In his late 40s, Sam was beginning to realize that he had enough money to start over and didn't want to spend the next 20 years as a wealth manager. He had other passions he wanted to pursue.

So he decided to put a partnership track in place for junior employees that would enable him to stay engaged, maintain a healthy income, and slowly transition ownership to the next generation at his firm. Sam began to conduct an active search for talent he felt would be well qualified to take over the reins and maintain his legacy. During the next year, he hired a young planner who seemed to fit the bill.

Sam made it a point to be very open and transparent with his new hire. He told her that she would be required to meet quantitative and qualitative performance measures during a five-year period, after which the junior planner could acquire a 10 percent ownership stake in the business. Assuming she met all of the goals Sam set forth, he would discount the value of the firm by 20 percent to compensate her for her work over the five years. It would be the successor's responsibility to come up with the money to buy into the firm.

During the course of the next five years, he tasked the junior planner with developing relationships with his less-than-ideal clients, converting prospects into clients, building out systems and processes, supervising the implementation of technology solutions, and achieving her CFP®. She was also responsible for building a strong rapport with the staff and being involved in human capital decisions.

At the end of the five years, Sam's business had tripled in growth. He had one junior partner and two other employees on a partnership track because he felt it prudent to diversify his management team, business risk, and ownership structure for long-term success. To fund the purchase, his junior partner took out a Small Business Administration (SBA) loan from a community bank with which the firm had a relationship. The junior partner uses her share of firm profits to pay the loan.

Sam stayed on as a majority owner and continues to transition ownership to his junior partners. His goal is to eventually extract enough value from his business so that he can retire early and maintain a minority ownership stake.

Finding a Successor

We frequently talk to advisors who are interested in designing and implementing a succession plan but lack qualified talent to do the job. Identifying a successor is often the biggest challenge.

The first step is to clearly define the skills needed to run the business in the context of your long-term goals and vision for the firm. For example, it requires a different skill set to nurture a business than it does to increase growth or reinvent the firm. The key is to understand what the goals are for the business and put a strategy and a team in place to support these goals.

Other factors to consider when evaluating talent include:

- Providing your successor with sufficient training to support continued business growth.
- Designing a compensation package to reward performance.
- Communicating the roles and responsibilities of your successor to stakeholders.

The next step is to establish an open dialogue with the candidate to determine what he or she really wants. The goals of the successor are often equally as important as those of the owner.

Some possible successor goals include:

- His or her name on the company.
- Increased compensation.
- Staff, clients, and the public viewing the successor as the owner.
- Growth potential.
- Control of the practice over time.
- Consideration for sweat equity.
- Building a sustainable enterprise for the successor.

Conversations with the potential successor may reveal that the person isn't prepared to upgrade his or her skills or consider leadership under any circumstances. The aim is to identify the successor's true passion and see whether it aligns with the goals of the organization.

Executing the Transaction

Along with choosing a successor, advisors need to develop a business succession plan that anticipates to a degree what the firm will become. There are three steps for implementing a goal-based ownership transfer plan.

Step 1

Determine the goals you want to drive and reward within your practice. Formulate a succession strategy that will help your successors achieve your goals for the firm by motivating them. Whether your goal is to sustain a 20 percent revenue growth rate, increase your average relationship size, or grow assets under management (AUM) to $100 million, put a plan in place that allows key employees to participate in achieving these targets. Your employees should be involved during the planning and execution phases of your strategy. Be sure to hold strategy meetings with your team members and have them contribute to the road map for building on the vision you have laid out for them.

In addition, it is important to hold them accountable for achieving the desired results that support your vision and strategy. For example, if part of your strategy is to establish a new service model for your top-tier clients, discuss appearance and implementation of this model with your client service manager. Incorporate this goal into his or her reviews so that there is a higher level of accountability. Or if you want to increase your growth rate by 5 percent, sit down with your staff to determine how the team members can collectively come together to achieve this goal. From there, establish individual goals that support the 5 percent increased growth rate. As a simple framework, advisors can use the SMART goals model: Goals should be Specific, Measurable, Attainable, Relevant, and Time-bound.

You should have incentive goals, a time frame for ownership transition, and a formula for valuing the practice. Once you establish your goals, you need to determine the amount of ownership you will commit to transferring and the time period during which the transfer will occur. The final step is to develop a formula for valuing your practice, in order to have a basis for key employees to purchase ownership shares. Advisors should consider establishing a baseline valuation for the firm. At that time, the owner can back into a valuation formula that can be used to transition and value future ownership shares. For example, say the firm is generating $1 million in revenue and $250,000 in EBITDA (earnings before interest, taxes, depreciation, and amortization). A valuation expert determines that the firm is valued at $1,500,000; then a simple valuation formula could be 1.5× revenue or 6× EBITDA going forward. This formula then becomes the internal valuation method for ownership going forward.

Step 2

Establish qualitative standards for key employees. In addition to the goals defined in Step 1, advisors should include qualitative goals that help ensure the future success of the firm and prepare key employees for ownership. Owners should consider what types of skill sets successors should demonstrate, such as working in and building an effective client-services team that profitably supports the client base. As part of developing the team, the successor will need to show skills in hiring, training, managing, and motivating his team.

As the successor takes on more responsibility, he should be able to show competency in the key areas of business management: strategy development, financial management, marketing, operations, and human resources. As the owner, you may consider establishing a training program that introduces the successor to these key business disciplines.

Other goals may be for successors to obtain a CFP, a CIMA, or other industry designations, or become involved in industry organizations such as the Financial Planning Association (FPA), Investment Management Consultants Association (IMCA), or National Association of Personal Financial Advisors (NAPFA) so that successors stay current with industry trends and regulatory initiatives. By achieving these goals, key employees grow within the firm and take on additional responsibilities. You can also evaluate successors' leadership ability and provide a forum for coaching them to success as managers.

Step 3

Monitor, refine, and reward results. At least annually, advisors should complete performance evaluations for all employees. These evaluations will cover both the SMART goals established in Step 1 and progress made on the qualitative standards described in Step 2. Based on the owner's predetermined formula, achievement of incentive goals provides key employees the opportunity to buy into the practice.

Consider structuring the buy-in as a lump-sum purchase, an installment sale (with owner carrying a promissory note), or as part of a profit-sharing plan. Once the employee has achieved the goals and considerations agreed upon, he or she would have the ability to buy equity in the firm.

Cross-Purchase Agreement

Once advisors have transitioned ownership shares to a junior partner, they should consider establishing a cross-purchase agreement among partners. This is a pact saying that you and your co-owners agree to buy one another's business interests under the terms and conditions set forth in the agreement.

For example, if you are a business owner bound by a cross-purchase buy-sell agreement and you die, become disabled, or retire, the buyers named in the agreement are legally obligated to purchase your interest in the business, and you're legally obligated to sell to them. You can't transfer your share of the business to anyone except the buyer(s) named in the agreement, though there may be allowable transfers to your spouse, a trust, or another owner. Provisions can be included to address a variety of issues, including the departure of the junior partner.

Very often, a buy-sell agreement will combine the entity purchase and cross-purchase options by providing a right of first refusal to either the entity or the other owner first, or a "wait and see" buy-sell agreement. The options are many. Which are appropriate for you and your business will depend on a number of different circumstances. You should consult your attorney for a description of the full range of possibilities.

Although an internal succession plan is certainly not the only option for a succession and is not right for every situation, if executed well, it can create high morale among employees, drive employee retention, reward key contributors, and facilitate ownership transition on terms that align with the goals of the firm and the owner's retirement aspirations.

Notes

Chapter 1   A Look at the Landscape

1. Genworth Wealth Management/Quantuvis Best Practices Study Series, 2010.
2. Pershing Advisor Services, "Mission Impossible II: Strategies to Sustain Growth in Challenging Times," 2009.

Chapter 2   A View into Top-Performing Firms

1. Genworth Wealth Management, Inc./Quantuvis Best Practices Study Series, 2010.
2. Ibid.
3. Ibid.
4. Ibid.

Chapter 6   Living the Vision

1. Jim Collins, *Built to Last: Successful Habits of Visionary Companies.* (New York: HarperCollins, 2002); Simon Sinek, *Start with Why: How Great Leaders Inspire Everyone to Take Action* (New York: Portfolio Trade, 2009).

Chapter 8   Managing Business Performance

1. Mark Tibergien and Rebecca Pomeroy, *Practice Made Perfect: Transforming a Financial Advisory Practice into a Business* (Princeton, NJ: Bloomberg Financial, 2011).
2. Ibid.
3. Genworth Wealth Management/Quantuvis Best Practices Study Series, 2010.
4. 2010 FA Insight Study of Advisory Firms.
5. 2010 Moss Adams/InvestmentNews Financial Performance Study of Advisory Firms.

Chapter 15 Referrals: An Untapped Opportunity

1. Per regulatory and compliance requirements regarding cash and noncash compensation, gifts to clients should not exceed the allotted annual amount.
2. Genworth Wealth Management/Quantuvis Best Practices Study Series, 2010.

Chapter 16 The Referral Management Process

1. Per regulatory and compliance requirements regarding cash and noncash compensation, gifts to clients should not exceed the allotted annual amount.

Chapter 17 Unlocking Client Feedback

1. Advisor Impact, "Economics of Loyalty," December 2010.
2. Ibid.

Chapter 28 Client-Facing Processes

1. Lewis Carbone, *Clues In: How to Keep Customers Coming Back Again and Again* (Upper Saddle River, New Jersey: Pearson Education Inc. publishing as Financial Times Prentice Hall, 2004)

About the Author

Matt Matrisian currently runs Genworth Financial Wealth Management, Inc.'s Practice Management team, where he applies his considerable industry knowledge to partner with advisors to institute practice management initiatives and develop sustainable growth strategies.

Matt began his career in the financial services industry almost 20 years ago, handling regional compliance oversight at one of the largest independent broker-dealers in the country, building and executing an RIA custody platform, and developing an industry-leading succession and practice acquisition offering for independent advisors. He joined Genworth in 2010 and has built a business transition services program, offering Genworth-affiliated advisors the opportunity to develop acquisition strategies, establish practice valuation models, buy/sell side representation, and succession planning support.

Often quoted in such industry publications as *Financial Planning, Investment Advisor, Investment News*, and *On Wall Street* magazine, Matt is both a published author and sought-after speaker. He has made appearances at a variety of industry conferences hosted by the Financial Planning Association (FPA), the Financial Services Institute (FSI), and the National Association of Personal Financial Advisors (NAPFA). He also participates in firm-specific speaking engagements.

Matt earned a bachelor of arts degree in finance from the University of South Florida and an MBA from the University of Florida. He is also a graduate of the Securities Industry Institute, part of the Wharton School of Business at the University of Pennsylvania. Matt is a Registered Corporate Coach with the Worldwide Association of Business Coaches®, and is a member of FSI.

About Genworth Financial Wealth Management, Inc.

Genworth Financial Wealth Management, Inc. (Genworth Wealth Management) helps independent financial advisors build great businesses by providing comprehensive support across every phase of their operation. We offer a sophisticated investment management platform, robust client relationship tools and support, and innovative practice management programs that combine leading-edge industry research with real-world expertise and experience. A wholly owned subsidiary of Genworth Financial, Inc., Genworth Wealth Management helps thousands of advisors meet their clients' wealth management and investment needs. For more information, visit www.genworthwealth.com.

Index